POLITICAL IDEAS IN CONTEMPORARY POLAND

Political Ideas in Contemporary Poland

JAN ZIELONKA

Department of Political Science
University of Leiden
The Netherlands

Avebury
Aldershot · Brookfield USA · Hong Kong · Singapore · Sydney

Published by

Avebury

Gower Publishing Company Limited
Gower House
Croft Road
Aldershot
Hants GU11 3HR
England

Gower Publishing Company
Old Post Road
Brookfield
Vermont 05036
USA

British Library Cataloguing in Publication Data
Zielonka, Jan, 1955-
    Political Ideas in Contemporary Poland
    1. Poland.   Politics
    I. Title
    320.9438

ISBN 0 566 07012 X

Printed and bound in Great Britain by
Kingprint International, Richmond, Surrey

Contents

ACKNOWLEDGEMENTS   vii

'ABBREVIATIONS   ix

INTRODUCTION   1

I.   REVOLUTION OR EVOLUTION   9
     KOR and the Origin of the Civil Society in Poland
     Doctrinal antecedents   11
     Kolakowski and the new reformism   13
     From social reformism to social action   15
     Formation and evolution of KOR   18
     Political impact of KOR   23

II.   THE ETHICS OF EMANCIPATION   35
     The teachings of the Catholic Church in Poland
     The primacy of ethics over politics   38
     Defence of human rights   43
     The ethics of labour relations   48
     Romantic patriotism   53
     The Church in a marxist state   59

III. TOWARDS THE SELF-GOVERNING
      COMMONWEALTH   71
      Solidarity's vision of the state and society
      Anti-statism and the idea of social self-organization   72
      Other features of Solidarity's evolutionism   76
      Doctrinal parallels   79
      Three questions Solidarity did not answer   86

IV.   SOLIDARITY'S STRATEGY OF SOCIAL CHANGE   93
      Strengths and Weaknesses of Nonviolent Action
      Why nonviolence?   94
      Readiness to resist   97
      The objectives of nonviolent action   100
      Solidarity's successes and failures   103
      The significance of governmental violence   107
      Conclusions   109

V.   THE EXPERIMENT WITH COMMUNIST STATISM   119
      The impact of Solidarity on the transformation
      of the communist system in Poland
      Friends of the modern state   122
      The Army versus the Party   129
      Towards corporatism   135
      Law as a new source of legitimacy   140
      Conclusions   148

VI.   POLAND BETWEEN THE SUPERPOWERS   159
      Polish perceptions of international politics
      How to live with the Soviets   162
      The German question   168
      Polish perceptions of the policy of detente   171
      Solidarity and the policy of sanctions   174
      Ways of preserving peace in Europe   177

BIBLIOGRAPHY   189

INDEX   201

Acknowledgements

In the course of writing this book, I have acquired debts to many people and institutions which I wish to acknowledge, though of course, any blame for what follows attaches solely to me.

I am especially indebted to Aleksander Smolar for offering me his incisive criticism on most parts of this book and to Anna van der Meer-Krok-Paszkowska for correcting my English and editing the whole manuscript.

In addition, several friends and colleagues, including Mark Blaug, Ferdinand Feldbrugge, Herman de Lange, Theo Kuipers, Grazyna and Krzysztof Pomian, Wojciech Sadurski, Gene Sharp and Alfred van Staden provided advice and guidance.

Many thanks go also to Marijke Vink and Anne-Marie Krens for typing the manuscript.

There are institutional debts to acknowledge. The Universities of Leiden and Groningen, as well as the Netherlands Institute for Advanced Study, created excellent conditions for conducting my work.

I am particularly grateful to the following publishers and editors for their permission to reprint, usually in revised and enlarged versions, material which first appeared in their pages. Among these are: Alternatives for an earlier version of Chapter One (published in Spring 1984); OstEuropa for an earlier version of Chapter Three (published in German, no 2, 1986) as well as for some material which appeared in Chapter One; Orbis for an earlier version of Chapter Four (published in Spring 1986) . Chapter Five represents a part of the project "Crises in Soviet-Type Systems", directed by Zdenek Mlynar (Study no.12a). A part of this chapter appeared in: F.J.M. Feldbrugge (ed.). The Distinctiveness of Soviet Law, Martinus Nijhoff Publishers, Dordrecht 1987. Chapter Six uses some material which appeared in the article: Jerzy Milewski, Krzysztof Pomian and Jan Zielonka, "Poland: Four Years After", Foreign Affairs, Winter 1985/86.

Finally, and most important, I should like to thank my wife, Mei Lan Zielonka-Goei - herself a student of politics - for her interest, judgement and encouragement.

Abbreviations

Original initials for Polish terms are normally retained in this study. Because of technical limitations, diacritical marks are not printed in Polish consonants.

COMECON Council of Mutual Economic Assistance (CMEA)
CSCE   Conference on Security and Cooperation in Europe
DiP   Doswiadczenie i Przyszlosc (Experience and Future)
END   European Nuclear Disarmament
IKV   Interkerkelijk Vredesberaad (Inter-Church Peace Council, the Netherlands)
KIK   Klub Inteligencji Katolickiej (Catholic Intelligentsia Club)
KOR   Komitet Obrony Robotnikow (Workers' Defence Committee)
KPN   Konfederacja Polski Niepodleglej (Confederation of Independent Poland)
KSS   Komitet Samoobrony Spolecznej (Committee for Social Self-Defence)
MKS   Miedzyzakladowy Komitet Strajkowy (Inter-enterprise Strike Committee)
NATO   North Atlantic Treaty Organization
NEP   New Economic Policy (USSR)
NKVD   People's Commissariat of Internal Affairs (security police in USSR, later KGB)
PPN   Polskie Porozumienie Niepodleglosciowe (Polish Independence Alliance)
PPP   Polska Partia Pracy (Polish Labour Party)
PPS   Polska Partia Socjalistyczna (Polish Socialist Party)
PUWP   Polish United Workers Party (Polish Communist Party)
ROPCiO   Ruch Obrony Praw Czlowieka i Obywatela (Movement for the Defence of Human and Civil Rights)
SKS   Studencki Komitet Solidarnosci (Student Solidarity Committee)
TKK   Tymczasowa Komisja Koordynacyjna (Provisional Coordinating Commission of Solidarity Underground)
SZSP   Socjalistyczny Zwiazek Studentow Polskich (Socialist Union of Polish Students)
TKN   Towarzystwo Kursow Naukowych (Association for Scientific Education)
ZOMO   Zmotoryzowane Odwody Milicji Obywatelskiej (Militia Motorized Reserve)

Introduction

In recent years a number of studies have appeared dealing with the origin and development of the Polish experiment of the 1980's. However, none of these studies have devoted special attention to the evolution of political ideas in Poland. Moreover, only few of these studies have used and explored the original Polish sources, such as the independent press and samizdat published by the political opposition. This book was prepared with the intention of filling this gap.

In principle, American or Western European students should have less difficulty in comprehending the evolution of political ideas in Poland than in other communist states, such as the Soviet Union or China. After all, Poland shares a certain common intellectual heritage with the Western World. For instance, the average educated Pole is usually familiar with European and American history. He has read at school the same classical novels as have his French, German or American counterparts during their youth. Later, in the course of his studies, he has had to master the works of great European political philosophers such as Erasmus, John Locke or de Tocqueville. Due to

Western broadcasting in the Polish language, he is able to follow current international events. And independent publishing houses offer him the books of Karl Popper, Raymond Aron, George Orwell or Hannah Arendt.

However, despite the fact that Poland shares certain cultural, moral and political values with the West it is difficult to analyse Polish ideas by using classical Western terms, definitions, classifications or popular Western images. For instance, one problem which is often debated is that of the political position of Solidarity. Does the Polish trade union express the views and aspirations of the political Left or of the political Right? Even this seemingly simple question is difficult to answer in an unambigious way. On the one hand, Solidarity carries on a struggle with a political system, which is officially based on Marxism and the ideology of socialism. It also positively cultivates religious and national values. Both of these features classify Solidarity, at least on the surface, as being on the Right. On the other hand, however, Solidarity is unequivocally a workers' movement which fights and strives to defend the economic and political interests of that class with which the political Left is traditionally identified.

A simple classification of Solidarity into the political Right or Left is therefore impossible. But that only raises the question: how should we characterize Solidarity in political terms?

The questions of Left or Right seem even more complicated if we refer to other political phenomena in contemporary Poland. Consider, for example, (a) the specific role of the Catholic Church in Poland, ideologically the enemy of Marxism but also the guardian of some of the fundamental values of the Left; (b) the autocratic standpoint of the communist party towards its alleged "masters" - the working class; (c) the difficult history of Polish-Russian relations, but also the traditional ties of many Poles with North America.

Similar problems arise with the classification of the Polish experiment in the present-day mainstreams of social, political and economic systems. The simultaneous support of Solidarity by both American conservatives as well as by West European socialists, and even many communists, underline the difficulties. Conservatives supported Solidarity for its identification with a national and religious tradition. Liberals thought that Solidarity represented the vision of freedom of expression and individualism. Euro-communists considered

Solidarity's struggle as a real implementation of the ideal of "the dictatorship of the proletariat". In the economic field, reforms promoted by Solidarity were warmly welcomed, on the one hand, by supply-side economists on the "radical right", on the other, by neo-Keynesians and post-Keynesians who are generally in favour of intervention and planning.

The backing of so many different, and even opposed, political schools of thought suggests that there is either total confusion about the nature of Solidarity or that Solidarity is in fact a new political phenomenon sui generis.

Solidarity's vision of society and economy thus may evoke a certain amount of confusion, but so does its description of the path to be taken towards that society. The terms which are often used to describe this path - "self-limiting revolution", "pragmatic revolution", etc. - do imply a certain degree of contradiction. Ordinarily, vast social movements which strive toward a fundamental change in existing political and economic relations are accompanied by force and violence. Emotions, rather than pragmatism and cool calculation are the foundation stones for decisions. Terror and superior power are its general characteristics. It is fascinating to see how in Poland it proved possible to combine violent social emotions with the self-discipline of the civilian population. Even under the threat of military police action, the peaceful road of social change was still advocated. The result was a strange paradox: the underground resistance forces of Solidarity declared their intention to conspire against the authorities to force them to come to an agreement, while rejecting all thoughts of overthrowing the regime, rooting out foreign armies, or offering active resistance. Time and again students have found it difficult to comprehend this paradox.

The role of the Roman Catholic Church in Poland has also been frequently debated. So far successive studies have indicated the mass identification of Poles with Christianity. They have pointed to various personal or even institutional links between Solidarity and the Church hierarchy. They have explored the role of the Church in cultivating Polish national culture and historical tradition. They have described the conflict between the Church and the communist authorities in the field of ideology. Nevertheless, some basic questions still await elaboration. For instance, what is the meaning of the moral concepts promoted by the Church, such as truth, dignity, hope or moral order? Are these

3

moral concepts complementary or contradictory to traditional political concepts of freedom, democracy or justice? In what way does the teaching of the Church represent a moral guideline for a mass social movement such as Solidarity? What specific model of nationalism is promoted by the Church in Poland? Can the Church's hierarchy play any political role in bridging the gap between the authorities and society in Poland; and if so, does this require any doctrinal compromises on its part?

The rhetoric and the behaviour of the authorities in Poland also evoke a certain amount of confusion and therefore require further analysis. The Polish crisis manifested itself not only through economic catastrophe, but also through the collapse of ideological political legitimacy and a deep crisis in the communist party itself (the Polish United Worker's Party). In consequence, the military coup d'etat in December 1981 stimulated the development of a new political trend in Poland towards some sort of statism and corporatism. In other words, dictatorship by the party has been replaced by a new version of communist etatism in which the Army and the state bureaucracy now work in tandem. These developments have raised several important questions, such as: does Polish statism represent a departure from the original Leninist-Stalinist model of state and society? What are the roles of the Army and the party within this new etatist model? Under what conditions can various groups and associations join the corporate agreement promoted by the state? What are the new sources of political legitimacy in contemporary Poland?

Solidarity originated in a period of great international tensions. The events in Poland made the situation even more confused, which resulted in reactions from the West being diverse, contradictory and often inexplicable. For instance, those who were consistently in favour of detente asked themselves the question: what if Poland becomes a free country? And gradually, they came to the conclusion that such a development could only increase the arms race because of the fact that the Soviet Union would feel insecure. Above all, the freedom of Poland would encourage similar ambitions in the peoples of other Eastern European countries. This, they claimed, would create even greater tensions in international relations.

Similarly, many groups in the West have more interests at stake in Eastern Europe than just the question of Solidarity. For instance, West

Germany's greatest interest is not in Poland, nor even in the Soviet Union, but in East Germany. The birth of Solidarity has produced circumstances which threaten West Germany's "Ost-politik".

For many years Western bankers have been doing business with representatives from communist regimes, although ideologically speaking they have nothing in common with communism. In consequence, their interest in Poland is not always identical with that of the Polish people, nor for that matter, with the governments of Western Europe or the United States.

Likewise, Solidarity was a great mystery for the other countries in Eastern Europe and awoke fears that similar movements might spread throughout the COMECON World. In this respect the attitude of the Soviet Union was again especially crucial. But can we say, for instance, that the limits of Soviet tolerance toward Poland are clearly defined and can be known in advance? All these international questions deserve analysis.

This book consists of six essays which try to deal with the above-mentioned issues. The first essay presents the ideas promoted by one of the forerunners of Solidarity - the Workers' Defence Committee (KOR). It tries to answer the question of how and why the Polish opposition rejected any thoughts of promoting revolutionary social change and instead sought to transform the existing system through a gradual and peaceful evolution. This essay also describes the origin of the concept of civil society and its application against the aspirations of the state in Poland.

The second essay analyses the teachings of the Roman Catholic Church in Poland. This essay tries to translate the Church's moral arguments into political terms as expressed by the popular movement in Poland. Special attention is paid to the Church's defence of human rights and its ethics of labour relations. The second essay also analyses the Church's association with Polish nationalism. In particular, it tries to answer two basic questions: (a) Does the Church in contemporary Poland support the "open" or "closed" type of nationalism?; and (b) Does it cultivate the "romantic" or "positivistic" tradition of nationalism?

The third essay analyses the doctrinal creed of Solidarity. It points to the fact that the Polish movement gave its support not to the liberal view of social individualism, but, instead to a collectivist vision. However, in contrast to communism and modern social democracy, the

Solidarity programme expresses a sense of a "self-guiding republic" which is to be found within the doctrinal stream of anti-state collectivism, often described as social anarchism, and based on fundamental notions of participation and self-management. The accent lies on decentralization and regionalization. The origins of that vision cannot be found in the works of Karl Marx but rather in the books of Peter Kropotkin and Joseph Proudhon.

Essay four examines the nonviolent strategy of Solidarity. It focuses on why Solidarity has chosen nonviolent forms of struggle and for what objectives; the strengths and weaknesses of Solidarity's particular tactics; those forms of nonviolent action best suited to the union's objectives; the crucial organizational shortcomings of Solidarity's nonviolent struggle; and finally, what Solidarity was able, and what it was unable to accomplish through nonviolence, in particular when it met with governmental violence.

The fifth essay analyses doctrinal and political developments on the part of the authorities in Poland. It points out that the sort of "Polish statism" promoted by the authorities represents something more than a mere justification for the iron fist policy of the government. Indeed, the Polish crisis brought about significant changes in Poland's political system and in consequence, a remarkable departure from the original Leninist-Stalinist model of state and society. For instance, the ideological indifference of the new statism promotes nationalism and a corporate vision of society rather than dictatorship of the proletariat or a leading role of the party. The present Polish rulers are also trying to create a new source of legitimacy based on a system of law, no matter how arbitrarily created. They oppose the group collectivism of Solidarity with the all-national interest which is exclusively embodied by the state.

Essay six analyses Polish perceptions of various international issues. This essay presents the most characteristic features of independent foreign policy thinking in Poland, such as the special concern about Poland's geopolitical position, the preoccupation with the heritage of Yalta, the Eurocentric perception of international politics and the promotion of the idea of the brotherhood of democratic nations. Polish attitudes toward the Soviet Union and Germany are treated separately. Finally, the essay compares Polish and Western concerns about peace and security in Europe.

In principle, all six essays can be treated as separate entities.

They are not only concerned with various aspects of the Polish experiment, but they also try to look at these issues from different theoretical perspectives. For instance, essays one and four were written in the course of my studies on nonviolence while essay five represents a comparative analysis of the Soviet-type system of state, law, and society. Nevertheless, in all six essays the emphasis is put on the ideas encompassed by the Polish experiment, their origin, meaning and political application. It should be said, however, that this book is not another history of Solidarity. Neither does it present all currents of political thinking in contemporary Poland. The historical context in which the presented ideas evolved and took hold is mentioned only briefly (and mainly in the first essay). The selection of subjects dealt with in the six essays reflects only the author's personal views about the importance and originality of various political ideas in contemporary Poland.

This book deals with ideas born before 1985, and there are only few exceptions to this rule. Since that time, Poland has gone through a significant political transformation. New opposition groups have emerged within the country and new programmes, visions, political orientations have gained popularity and influence developments in Poland. Solidarity as an organization and as a symbol of resistance still plays an important political role. Nevertheless, it now operates in a different political and doctrinal environment than was the case in the early 1980's. Since 1987 more and more commentators are writing about a "new opposition" and about new "characteristic ways of thinking" in contemporary Poland. As Abraham Brumberg put it in February 1988: "The scale of political opposition in Poland is now much more modest and its center of gravity has shifted...conservative economic and political doctrines flourish (with Milton Friedman something of a cult figure). So does a resurrected and 'sanitized' version of the teachings of Roman Dmowski, the pre-war leader of the nationalistic and anti-semitic National Democrats".[1] Before 1985 neither conservatist nor nationalist ideas could gain a recognition comparable to that which is apparent in present-day Poland. This explains why these ideas will not be treated separately in this book.

My analysis is based on Polish as well as on Western literature. Polish sources consist of various documents, appeals, political statements as well as scientific and journalistic reports and analyses prepared in Poland and published illegally in Poland or abroad. Polish governmental press and other official sources have also been taken into consideration.

As far as Western literature is concerned it is difficult to present any specific guidelines. Different questions under consideration have involved studies of different sorts of literature. For instance, studies on Solidarity's doctrinal vision of a self-governing commonwealth required reference to various historical currents of political philosophy. Studies on Solidarity's strategy and tactics required analysis of the literature on nonviolence and civilian-based defence. Studies on experiments with the communist version of statism and corporatism required the analysis of various works on marxism and sovietism. Of course, special attention is also devoted to recent works on Poland published in Western Europe and the United States.

I began my studies on the evolution of political ideas at Warsaw University in the late 1970's. In 1982 I left Warsaw University and continued my research at the Dutch universities of Leiden and Groningen.

NOTE

1.   Abraham Brumberg. Poland: The New Opposition. The New York Review of Books. 18 February 1988, p. 24. See also: Bernard Guetta. Otwarcia Wladzy Dziela Opozycje. Kontakt no.12, 1987, pp. 21-25, originally published in: Le Monde, 10 November 1987.

I Revolution or evolution

The independent trade union Solidarity was born spontaneously during workers' strikes in Summer 1980. Nevertheless, it did not emerge in a political vacuum. In the late 1970's Poland witnessed an unprecedented development of various sorts of oppositional and semi-oppositional organizations all over the country. These independent groups emerged in different political and social environments; at universities but also in factories, in Churches but also within the communist establishment. Some of them promoted intellectual and artistic freedoms, others put emphasis on the freedom of conscience and religion. Some of them struggled for the rights of workers, others put emphasis on the question of Poland's national independence. For some organizations economic reforms represented the key to Poland's well-being, while other groups promoted defence of basic civil and human rights in their country. This essay presents one of the most important groups - the Workers' Defence Committee.[1]

KOR was founded in 1976 by a small group of intellectuals. Though it confined itself to the defence of those being persecuted for their part in the workers' protests of June 1976, and did not aspire to be a mass organization (there were only thirty three members in 1980), it rapidly developed into an influential political pressure group. It helped to shape the organization of the emerging opposition movement in Poland and inspired its most important doctrines. The principal demands of KOR, such as the right to form an independent trade union and to go on strike, as well as the general idea of social self-organization, were adopted by the masses agitating in the summer of 1980 and later constituted the basis of Solidarity's programme. Indeed, many KOR leaders were to play a leading role in the establishment and development of that independent trade union.

KOR officially dissolved itself in the middle of 1981. Over the five years that it was in existence it wielded tremendous influence. But while the extent of this influence was unchallenged, there were ambiguous and conflicting interpretations about the actual role of KOR. This engendered much controversy and even hostility toward it, even from opposition organizations, such as the nationalistic Confederation of Independent Poland (KPN). For example, when leading KOR members were detained by the government and strikes were in progress in the summer of 1980, the workers demanded the release of the KOR activists. But they were more ambivalent about KOR itself, and debated fiercely about its position. In fact, Tadeusz Kowalik, an official adviser to the workers during the strike at the Lenin Shipyard in Gdansk, actually argued that KOR members should not be allowed to join the group of advisers helping with the negotiations. According to him, their presence could make the negotiations with the authorities more difficult because of KOR's view that communism is a totalitarian system that is impossible to reform.[2] Likewise, the appointment of many KOR members to important governing and advisory positions in Solidarity did not mean that the union had come out unquestionably in support of KOR. Indeed, during the First National Congress of Solidarity, the draft of a resolution expressing gratitude for KOR's defence of workers' rights generated some controversy, and some Solidarity delegates even went so far as to oppose it.

Was KOR a political organization or was it a social action group? Did KOR only want to help workers or did it aspire also to political power? Did KOR intend to overthrow the communist government of Poland, or did it hope for a gradual transformation of the system? And what about the personal background and aspirations of particular KOR leaders? These are some of the questions still being asked about KOR. I shall not treat all of them in this chapter.[3] Rather, I shall confine my discussion to the doctrinal origins of KOR and the whole social self-defence movement in Poland, programmes developed by KOR, and the political impact of KOR's activities.

DOCTRINAL ANTECEDENTS

Opposition to the communist regime in Poland evolved in two separate directions. The first current was represented by the Catholic intelligentsia, which was linked to the Polish Catholic Church. The second current of opposition was represented by the "secular left". It consisted of "dissident" Marxists and other socialist thinkers who were opposed to the policies of the Polish Communist Party, although many of them were, at least for a time, members of the Party.[4] The former has always believed in the possibility of gradual and non-violent systemic transformation by following the principles of Christianity; the latter, on the other hand, believed in a sort of "true" marxism, which entails, among other things, supporting a revolutionary socialist transformation in Poland and political atheism.

The Catholic intelligentsia promoted moral and philosophical rather than political resistance to communist rule in Poland. It opposed the ideological materialism of the party and called for equal rights for both Catholics and non-believers. It was also the Catholic intelligentisia which cultivated or even glorified Polish national and cultural tradition.[5]

The secular left emphasized the need for political and economic changes. It had a "derisive" attitude towards Polish national tradition. It also tended to ignore the role of Catholicism in the national culture and the function of the Church in Polish society.

Opposition from secular leftish thinkers, many of whom later became members of KOR, intensified during the mid-1960's. At that time it was already evident that the post-Stalinist thaw would not lead to any fundamental changes in the political system in Poland. This naturally evoked critical reactions from contesting circles within the party. One should especially mention the noteworthy "Open letter" to members of the Polish United Workers' Party at Warsaw University written by Jacek Kuron and Karol Modzelewski. The letter described Polish society as exploitative in the Marxist sense, and in true Marxist fashion, concluded that revolution was necessary to bring about social change.

According to Kuron and Modzelewski, the existing system must be overthrown: "revolution is necessary for development ... the revolution that will overthrow the bureaucratic system will be a proletarian revolution".[6]

Another important manifestation of dissent by the secular opposition were two highly critical lectures at Warsaw University deliverd by Professors Leszek Kolakowski and Krzysztof Pomian. Kolakowski and Pomian were especially critical of the government's cultural policy during the last decade. Kolakowski also criticized legal practices in Poland, while Pomian presented his views on the need for the youth movement to be independent.

However, Kuron and Modzelewski were imprisoned. Pomian and Kolakowski were expelled from the party. Those party members who officially protested against these repressive steps were either expelled from the party or left the party of their own accord. Student demonstrations in March 1968 which were at least partially generated by the ideas of the secular left were brutally dispersed by the police.

Thus, the leadership of the party made it clear that it would not tolerate any contest within its rank and file. Even more important was the fact that the secular opposition did not gain any popular support within the country. This was due to at least three basic factors. First, many people viewed the Marxist rhetoric of the secular left with suspicion, and considered the conflict between the secular left intelligentsia and the regime as an external manifestation of some acute intra-communist power struggle. Second, many Poles had difficulty in accepting the secular left's somewhat cynical attitude towards Polish national culture and tradition. Third, the militant atheism and anti-clericalism of the secular opposition could hardly be welcomed by the predominantly Catholic population.

In consequence, the secular opposition found itself repressed by the authorities and isolated within Polish society. The 1968 Warsaw Pact invasion of Czechoslovkia and the crushing of the Prague Spring reforms represented yet another serious blow to those who believed that "communism with a human face" could soon become a reality in Eastern Europe.

The failure of the secular left to influence either the Polish authorities or the general public as such, plus the fall of Dubcek in Czechoslovakia stimulated major doctrinal transformations within the secular left. It also demonstrated the necessity for some sort of alliance between the secular left and Catholic circles in Poland. Such an alliance would have been impossible immediately after the Second World War. At that time, as far as the secular left was concerned, Catholicism was "synonymous with anti-Semitism, fascism, narrow-minded bigotry, fanaticism, and all that was anti-progressive and anti-cultural".[7] It took about thirty years of communist rule and significant developments within the Church to change these perceptions. Indeed, in the 1970's, a majority of secular intellectuals would agree with the sentiments of Antoni Slonimski, a famous Polish poet and a rationalist libertarian, who observed that "before the war, the Church was reactionary and Communism was progressive, today it is the other way around."[8]

Many prominent leftist intellectuals came to recognize the relevance of Christian ethics and sought to integrate those precepts into their political programmes during the 1970's.[9] Jacek Kuron, who had preached revolution and militant atheism in the previous decade, now supported non-violent reforms. He even declared publicly that he had "recently discovered the Bible to be the most universal moral code".[10] Adam Michnik became an advocate of a strong alliance between the (leftist) secular opposition and the Polish Catholic Church, in both the organizational and doctrinal sense. For instance, in his book entitled "The Church and the Left: A Dialogue", Michnik argued:

> "For us - the secular Left - the encounter with Christianity, centering on such values as tolerance, justice, human dignity, and the search for truth, opens the way for encounters free from material interests, and it promises an ideological community in a new dimension, important for the formulation of the direction of our struggle for democratic socialism".[11]

And it was Leszek Kolakowski, a former Marxist and atheist, who provided the philosophical basis of the new Polish reformism, integrating anti-Marxism and Christian ethics.

KOLAKOWSKI AND THE NEW REFORMISM

Kolakowski was strongly opposed to concepts such as the "revolutionary spirit" and even dismissed revolution as a "beautiful illness".[12] He did not believe in the possibility of a "total salvation of mankind", but argued that belief in promises of total liberation would lead inevitably to totalitarianism and, consequently, to the abolition of the democratic and cultural heritage of civilizations. Kolakowski considered Marxism an ideology where the "revolutionary spirit" plays an important role and much of his work criticizes Marxism.[13]

In his seminal article entitled "Tezy o nadziei i beznadziejnosci" (Theses on Hope and Hopelessness),[14] Kolakowski observes that East European communism seems to be a very inflexible system lacking self-regulating devices and capable of change only in the face of "violent catastrophies". According to him, the main function of this system is to protect and perpetuate the monopolistic grip of the ruling apparatus on power. All past and future reforms within its framework are modest and are easily reversed, for they cannot be institutionalized without destroying the whole system. Consequently, the basic aspirations of both the working class and the intelligentsia could hardly be realized within such limits.

Since he opposed the use of violence to effect social change, Kolakowski's findings led him to seek specific contradictions within communism that might allow for gradual change. In this context, conflicts among ruling elites are particularly relevant. From the time of Stalin, the history of communism has shown the system to be incapable of peaceful transfers of power. Rather, a partial paralysis and deterioration of the administrative processes invariably result. Kolakowski argues that it is this feature which allows for the development of some form of resistance movement within the system.

Kolakowski went on to question whether political systems are ever totally inflexible. He pointed out that there are tremendous differences between the political situation in Poland during the period of Stalinist terror, and that which prevailed after 1956. He argued, moreover, that to believe the present form of socialism is so inflexible that it could never absorb changes, but could only be destroyed in one fell swoop, will only serve to justify opportunism. And, in turn, to believe that no reform is possible is to absolve in advance every act of cowardice, passivity, and cooperation with evil. Indeed, not only can the internal contradictions of despotic socialism be resolved, failure to attempt to resolve them will lead to even more difficulties. According to Kolakowski, if silence and fear were to prevail, the system will respond to its own problems by increasing the degree of oppression. Rather than allowing this to happen through lack of resistance, it is important that the people make clear their opposition and exploit weaknesses in the system to achieve a gradual improvement in their situation.

Kolakowski's reformism was additionally supported by an analysis of the geopolitical situation of Poland. According to Kolakowski, the goal of Poland, as of the other nations of the Soviet zone, is not to provoke an armed conflict, but to exert ceaseless pressure aimed at diminishing Polish dependence on the USSR, a dependence which can only be weakened through pressure. In this sphere, too, Kolakowski argued, thinking along the lines of "all or nothing" is futile and the adoption of such a principle means in practice to accept nothing. Dependence and non-sovereignty can exist in different degrees and the differences in the degree of dependence are of enormous significance for the existence of a nation.

Kolakowski believed it is possible to transform communism in a gradual, peaceful manner. His ideas were disseminated at the beginning of the 1970's, and were adopted by the majority of the Polish opposition, in particular by KOR. But Kolakowski did not suggest any ideas about the form an opposition movement should take. The two people who were most involved in efforts to transform the general idea of social evolutionism into a programme of social action were Jacek Kuron and Adam Michnik.

FROM SOCIAL REFORMISM TO SOCIAL ACTION

Like Kolakowski, Jacek Kuron had also come to reject the use of force. In his book "Zasady Ideowe" (Doctrinal Principles), he developed a moral framework which had a strong impact on the social self-defence movement. Kuron envisaged a social utopia, "a vision based on a system of values". It follows from this precept that the means employed to achieve social goals should not violate any moral principle: "If a social movement wishes to realize a social utopia, then it must not use force or compulsion".[15]

Kuron is quite aware, of course, that conflicts are usually resolved with the use of force or compulsion. Indeed, he recognized that liberation movements themselves often resort to such means in order to defend themselves against military aggression, state repression, and the expropriation of citizens' rights in general. To allow for these occasions, Kuron qualified his stricture against violence by maintaining that although "compulsion is always an evil, it is a necessary evil when it constrains another form of compulsion". [16] Such a provision applies to the state as well. While Kuron considers the state as inherently isolated from society, and to have employed its resources to compel and repress people, he acknowledges that at times states do organize some important cooperative endeavours among the people, and that the use of its (repressive) powers could be a "necessary evil" too.

To reduce the occasions for "necessary evil", from either side, Kuron proposed the creation of an independent social action network, or a self-governmental movement. Such an entity should reduce the need for repression by the state because the people would cooperate in an extra-governmental organization. At the same time, it should eliminate the need to forcibly abolish the state as opposition groups would have achieved their aspirations for self-management, which would eventually lead to a reduction of state power. [17] In addition, Kuron believed that self-government should create a federation of independent grassroots units which would engender gradual, peaceful change in the existing system as well as stimulate creativity and efficiency.

Kuron's ideas have been strongly criticized by various opposition thinkers for being unscientific and ahistorical.

Socjusz, for instance, called Kuron's vision "dogmatic anarchism". [18] He went on to accuse Kuron of using a very abstract notion of "compulsion", which refers to all possible forms of resolving conflicts between the individual and social groups. According to others, Kuron's vision presents people as being always of good will, and being ready to cooperate within a framework of self-government, and that it is only the compulsory power of the state which blocks this. Such a view was considered naive. There are substantial grounds for these charges, but here it should be noted that its simplistic nature affords Kuron's study the very important advantage of being much more readily adopted as a political credo than more sophisticated analyses. More serious is the lack of attention paid to the possibility that the independent social network or self-governmental movement itself might be too much of a threat, to the monopolistic aspirations of the state to power. How should the liberation movements react if those wielding state power use it to prevent the development of self-government? The basic issue here, which Kuron has not dealt with, is whether non-violent action can be both morally respectable and still politically effective within a totalitarian system.[19]

Kuron's deficiencies aside, there are important parallels with the work of others like George Lakey and Severyn Bruyn who see self-government and social development as the main purposes of non-violent action against the state authorities. Bruyn, for example, maintains that "radical non-violent action assumes that social norms can point towards the basis of self-development and self-governance", so that those "social norms created by the process of non-violent action should lead directly towards the cultivation of human resources and a reduction in the need for a state".[20] However, Kuron considers non-violent action only as a means towards certain social goals, such as self-government or participation, while other thinkers consider it as an end in itself. Indeed, Kuron seems to be closer to those thinkers who advocate "civilian power" rather than "non-violence".[21]

Adam Michnik, another KOR activist, criticized revolution and violence even more sharply. He believed that revolutionary programmes and conspiracy on the part of opposition groups can only assist a police state in fanning hysteria and facilitating repression. In an article entitled "The New Evolutionism", he argued that "to think of revolution turning out the dictatorship of the party, or to organize attempts towards that end, would be as unrealistic as it would be dangerous".[22] Not surprisingly, Michnik considered the only alternative open to East European dissidents to be an increased struggle for reforms that would extend civil liberties and guarantee human rights. He advocated a social defence movement as the best way to meet the aspirations of Polish society, [23] and argued the Polish opposition to support "progressive and partial changes rather than the violent overthrow of the existing regime".[24]

The theoretical disagreements between various opposition groups in Poland have never dissipated completely. Nevertheless, the critics of KOR were unable to present more realistic alternatives to Kuron's "utopia", and the rapid development of independent grassroots movements resulting in the formation of Solidarity confirmed the viability of KOR's programme to support a peaceful resistance movement of self-organization. In the Polish context, every kind of self-defence activity was simultaneously an example of self-organization and resistance. To be sure, KOR members considered themselves to be in a purely self-defence movement; however, much of its activity was also directed at resisting the monopolistic and repressive aspirations of the communist government. The peaceful nature of this resistance movement contrasts sharply with other resistance movements in Polish history, most recently during the Second World War. Like them, however, it could only have developed and expanded with popular self-organization, requiring various forms of positive input and assistance from society.

For Kolakowski, a resistance movement is possible in a communist country and, indeed, its creation is demanded by human dignity.[25] Michnik would have the opposition in Poland informing society how to proceed, rather than inducing the government to change and improve itself. In his view, the government will change and improve itself only when confronted with pressure from below. And according to Kuron, the creation of a resistance movement aware of its goals and strengths was the only way to constrain a violent social explosion in Poland at the end of the 1970's.[26] From analysing various patterns of resistance in modern Polish history, he concludes that the most effective form of resistance is based on solidarity, and not on corruption, cliques, and the like because they are in conflict with human dignity and morality. Solidarity is crucial because an effective social movement can emerge only when all resistance groups share common goals. Kuron points out that many Polish scientists, artists, and writers have followed independent lines of cultural and scientific creativity despite government persecution. All these resistance groups should be organized into various forms of self-defence and self-organization, and with solidarity, compel the authorities to negotiate with society.[27]

FORMATION AND EVOLUTION OF KOR

KOR was not the first oppositional organization to emerge in Poland in the mid-1970's. In May 1976 a programme of the PPN (The Polish Independence Alliance) was issued. The PPN programme described the crisis of the communist system in Poland and presented twenty-six proposals for making Poland a more sovereign and democratic country. The programme demanded, among other things, a separation of political and economic prerogatives of the state, a strengthening of the private

18

sector in agriculture and services, and a new shape of Polish-Soviet relations based on the principle of equality of the two sovereign countries.

However, the PPN did not call for the creation of any "organizational community" which would work for practical changes in Poland. The PPN limited its efforts to trying to influence the sphere of people's consciousness. It preferred to be a clandestine organization of intellectuals offering theoretical solutions for democratic change rather than itself being a vehicle of such a change.[28] KOR adopted an entirely opposite approach which, in my view, enabled it to play a much greater political role than the one played by the PPN. KOR's concept was to establish a public body which would organize help for persecuted workers. The initial aim of the organization was to provide concrete help for people rather than debating about far-reaching political programmes. The persecution of workers who had taken part in protests against the price rises in June 1976 represented a direct stimulus for creating the organization. As one author put it:

> "It was just one of the remarkable qualities of this organization that its members were willing to suffer government reprisal not in the name of some sweeping political programme or visionary goal but in order to get some money into the hands of the fatherless family or to arrange for favourable testimony in the trial of a worker. Only great goals might seem to warrant great sacrificies, but the KOR workers were ready to make great sacrifices for modest goals".[29]

On June 24th, 1976, an unexpected rise in food prices set off widespread protests. Strike committees were quickly set up - especially in the cities of Ursus, Plock, Grudziac, and Radom - and workers stopped work the following day all over the country.

The most severe riots took place in Radom. A strike in a metal factory had expanded, as workers from other factories joined in, into a demonstration which marched on the Regional Party Committee headquarters. At the building, the crowd gathered and asked to speak to representatives. However, they came across a lavishly stocked buffet which had some food items whose prices had just been raised. The workers' mood turned ugly as they destroyed and burned the interior of the building before resuming their march, smashing shop windows along the way. Motorized detachments of police began their pacification of

Radom soon after. Mass arrests were made, with those being detained often beaten up. About 2,000 people in Radom were arrested, and many made "to run a gauntlet between files of policemen armed with batons".[30]

In Ursus, striking workers tore up the tracks of an important railway line. The militia went into action shortly afterwards to restrain and arrest them. Those arrested were dismissed from their jobs and even evicted from their hostels. Special summary courts were set up and sentenced many workers from Radom and Ursus to prison terms. And in cities such as Lodz, Poznan and Grudziac, strikers were dismissed en masse, even though there had been no riots in those cities. The repression against the striking workers continued, but the intensity of the protests forced the authorities to cancel the increase in prices.

Protests about the treatment of the workers were raised almost immediately. Jacek Kuron and Jerzy Andrzejewski, a famous writer, wrote open letters defending the workers' protests. Thirteen other intellectuals delivered strong appeals expressing solidarity with the "June protests". In addition, there was a spontaneous move a month later by Zbigniew Romaszewski, Antoni Maciarewicz, Wojciech Onyszkiewicz, Bogdan Borusewicz, and other well-known figures to help the workers by collecting money for them and their families.

An "Appeal to Society" was made on September 23rd, 1976, informing the public about the establishment of the Workers' Defence Committee (KOR). The appeal explained that though the "workers' protests against unjustified price increases was the expressed opinion of the majority of society, it had been met with brutal punishment."[31] It described the brutality and terrorism practised by the police, indicated the illegal steps taken by the special summary courts, and condemned the repressive policies of the authorities. Furthermore, the appeal noted that victims of the recent repressions could not rely for help from traditional institutions such as trade unions, which had played "a deplorable role". Instead, society itself would have to assume the role of defending the persecuted. But since, as the authors of the appeal explained, "society can only defend itself against lawlessness through solidarity and mutual aid", the Workers' Defence Committee was created to "initiate various forms of help and assistance". Specifically, the appeal called for financial, medical, and legal help for the workers, and urged that grassroots initiatives be undertaken at shop and plant levels. It also emphasized the importance of keeping the public informed about individual cases of persecution and the extent of repression in general. In sum, the appeal operated on the principle that "where people are being repressed in a country, its society has an obligation to organize itself in order to defend those who are being repressed." [32]

The appeal was signed by twelve intellectuals who represented different professions, ideologies, and political views. Among them were the writer Jerzy Andrzejewski, the well-known poet Stanislaw Baranczak, and the distinguished professor of economics, Edward Lipinski. There was Jacek Kuron, a former militant atheist, and Jan Zieja, a priest. Some of the signatories were in their thirties; others were two or three generations older. Their political viewpoints also differed - some were identified with a left, social-democratic current, while others leaned more towards a Christian-democratic or "patriotic" orientation. But these differences mattered very little as KOR was created as an action group, an organization intended to provide help to persecuted workers rather than to make any political or ideological statement. As Jacek Kuron said, "KOR was far more apolitical than one could imagine".[33] Not surprisingly, KOR's main activities centred around the so-called "Office of Intervention", which dealt with specific cases of persecution.

There were four kinds of activity that were of equal importance to KOR. First, it took a direct part in the successive trials of the workers who had protested in June 1976. KOR members attended the trials and tried to organize a good legal defence for the accused. Second, KOR organized financial support for the persecuted workers and their families. It provided financial assistance to the families of those workers sentenced to prison or dismissed from their jobs because of their participation in the strikes by covering their legal, medical, and educational expenses. A special fund, the "Foundation for Social Self-Defence", was created for these purposes, assisting more than 1,000 persons. Third, KOR organized medical assistance for workers and their families, a necessity in view of police brutality, especially toward the organizers of the workers' protests. And finally, KOR established an independent information network that reported all cases of government persecution and terror. This was of tremendous importance, not only because it ensured the implementation of the three other forms of activity mentioned above, but also because it helped to prevent further repression.

On September 29th, the first KOR Report was published, and this was followed a few days later by the first issue of KOR's Information Bulletin. These publications informed the public about the extent and varieties of government repression, and provided information about the people who were personally involved in executing those policies. At the same time, they also kept the public informed about the initiatives and programmes of KOR and the government's reaction to them.

On November 15th, 1976, KOR asked the Polish Parliament to establish the "Extraordinary Enquiry Commission" to investigate the cases of repression at Radom and Ursus. Prior to this, KOR had given strong support to an appeal from the workers of the Ursus track factory, asking for the reinstatement of those workers dismissed for participating in the strikes of June 25th. As Jacek Kuron explained, "Solidarity is more important for us than political claims".[34] While the Polish authorities did not respond directly to these appeals, or to other KOR demands, there was a noticeable reduction in its pressure on workers. Finally, on February 3rd and July 19th, 1977, the Polish Council of State announced two successive "Amnesty Acts", which resulted in the release of all imprisoned workers. It is reasonable to assume that these acts were in some part an answer to KOR's demands.

Two months after the Amnesty Acts came into force, KOR announced that "the basic goals of the Committee for the Defence of Workers have been fulfilled", and concluded that "its activities should be expanded or replaced by an organization with more general social goals". [35] Accordingly, on September 29th, 1977, the Committee for Social Self-Defence (KSS-KOR) was established. The declaration announcing the creation of this new organization affirmed its continuation of the struggle against the remaining repression directed against those who had taken part in the workers' protests of June 1976. It simultaneously enumerated four additional basic goals of the new Committee.

First, the Committee for Social Self-Defence was committed to fighting all forms of political, ideological, religious, or racial discrimination, and vowed to help victims of such discrimination. Second, the Committee announced that it would fight any illegal behaviour on the part of the authorities; this would include helping the victims of any such illegal official behaviour. Third, the Committee promised to initiate a procedure that would lead to the institutional protection of citizens' rights and freedom. And lastly, the Committee guaranteed its support for every social initiative that would lead to the realization of basic human and citizens' rights. In effect, KSS-KOR had undertaken to fight not only institutionalized violence and individual cases of repression, but also to develop a social self-defence and self-organization network. As Jacek Kuron declared at the time, the "political opposition should immediately begin to organize a network of social movements which would cooperate with the organization and which would express the aspirations of the whole society".[36] Thus the basic goals of the movement had become more general and far-reaching.

POLITICAL IMPACT OF KOR

Among the various different theoretical approaches which have tried to evaluate the political impact of KOR at least three deserve our special attention. One of them was presented by Michael Bernhard.[37] Bernhard tried to fit KOR into categorization of the roles intellectuals can play in politics and on that ground he evaluated the impact which KOR exerted on the whole spectrum of various groups and social classes in Poland.[38] For this he used Christopher Lasch's typology which distinguished three types of roles that intellectuals play in politics.[39] One is the mandarin intellectual who uses his or her knowledge in the service of power. The second type is the revolutionary intellectual, who puts his or her knowledge to use on behalf of a dispossessed social group which will replace the powers that be. Unlike the first two, Lasch's third category, the "rebel, alien, or renegade" has no power ambitions. Often, however, he finds himself in sympathy with the dispossessed and provides a sort of "public accusatory testimony". Bernhard argues that KOR is close to the third type presented by Lasch, namely "alien, rebel, renegade" intellectuals. According to Bernhard, while KOR certainly sympathized with the dispossesed, KOR did not indulge in a pathos of victimization. KOR did indeed chonicle oppression, but this was not merely "bearing witness". KOR also acted to counter injustice. It was this practical activity to counter injustice which, according to Bernhard, permitted intellectuals from KOR to overcome the barriers that traditionally divided Polish society and to reach other social groups and classes, thus making an impact on society as a whole.

Another interesting approach to the political impact of KOR was presented by Jonathan Schell.[40] Schell argues that KOR's success in generating its enormous political impact was due to the adoption of a number of policies that were novel in the closed society of Poland. These were the policies of openness, truthfulness, autonomy of action and trust. For instance, KOR members believed in telling the truth for its own sake, but they also believed that in a society surfeited with lies an organization that kept strictly to the truth would win support and gain strength. "Autonomy" was what KOR wished for Poland as a whole and for every person in the country. "Trust" was for KOR equally relevant in relations between each individual person, as well as in relations between the state and each citizen. In this way, KOR was able to bridge the gap which existed between general political values appealing to a nation or a society as a whole and values appealing to every individual. Schell describes KOR's policies of openness, truthfulness, autonomy of action and trust as policies of "militant decency", which equipped KOR not so much to do battle with the government as to work around it. KOR discovered, says Schell, that merely by fearlessly carrying on the business of daily life it grew powerful.

Finally, we should mention the approach which evaluated the political impact of KOR in institutional terms, by showing KOR's success in encouraging the development of institutions that were independent from the state social institutions, in the field of labour relations, culture, information or education. This approach stresses the importance of the political awakening of a "civil society" within the state, and points out that KOR was the first group in Poland to publicly practice independent organized political activity from below. As Andrew Arato put it:

"the categories of civil society are not extraneous to the Polish events... The participants [in KOR's activities - J.Z.] themselves and their Western collaborators have characterized their struggle in terms of society against the state... As Kuron put it: 'Society organizes itself as a democratic movement and becomes active outside the limits of the institutions of the totalitarian state'. KOR (an acronym for Workers' Defence Committee) is renamed KSS-KOR (Social Self-Defence Committee-KOR) to indicate its support of all initiatives for both interest representation and the defense of civil rights".[41]

The approach which tries to evaluate the political impact of KOR by pointing to its success in generating the institutional framework of a civil society is certainly the most popular one in the existing literature.[42] There exists at least one good reason for the popularity of this approach, namely it can easily be tested by studying the development of independent institutions in Poland in the late 1970's. Let me illustrate this point by several important examples.

In 1977 and 1978, many professional circles developed opposition groups, most of which were either stimulated or supported by KOR. A new magazine, Robotnik (The Worker), began to promote the idea of workers' self-defence. Robotnik was a well-edited magazine dealing with the social and industrial problems of the working class; it particularly encouraged discussions about the role of trade unions. Until then, the official trade unions had neither defended the interests of the working class nor created the opportunity for workers' self-organization. As Robotnik began to reach workers in various large industrial plants, its local supporters, who were linked with KOR, began to organize free trade unions. The first independent trade union was established by Kazimierz Switon in the province of Silesia. A second was established in the Baltic Coast region. There was another group in Gdansk, which even started its own newspaper, Robotnik Wybrzeza (Worker of the Coast), edited by a KOR member, Bogdan Borusewicz. In April 1978, the "Free Trade Unions of the Coast", with less than a dozen affiliates, issued its first declaration from Gdansk, and it was not long before some of its activists - viz., Lech Walesa, Anna Walentynowcz, Bogdan Lis, Andrzej Gwiazda - became very famous.

These early free trade unions concentrated mainly on typical workers' grievances, such as the obligation of miners to work on Sundays, or the twelve-hour working day common in some industries. They defended workers who were fired for political reasons and dealt with problems of wages, employment, conditions of work, and independent workers' representation. In this way, the free trade unions began to challenge the position of the government-supported trade unions, and achieved results after a few years.

In 1979 Robotnik published the "Charter of Workers' Rights" which can be seen as the earliest draft of the demands of August 1980. The charter stated that citizens were deprived of participation in decision-making in areas that concerned them, and that the rights of working people were not respected, particularly "safe and sensible work" and "adequate wages, and rest".[43] According to the Charter, social injustice and inequality were growing in Poland and there were no institutions to defend the interests of working people. In particular, official trade unions did not fulfill the function of defence of workers. Workers were even deprived of their basic rights to defence, that is the right to strike.

After listing a series of grievances, the Charter tried to formulate practical solutions for solving the existing problems. It suggested, among other things, the development of a genuine representation of workers' interests at the plant and shop level, further efforts to freely disseminate information and concrete steps aimed at the improvement of labour and living conditions of the working people.

On August 1st, 1978, the "Temporary Committee for the Self-Defence of Peasants from the Lublin District" was established as a reaction to the government's repression of those peasants who refused to pay to obligatory fee for a new peasant retirement fund. The peasants' first reaction was to call a one-day strike, in which they withheld milk supplies. They also agreed not to negotiate separately with the authorities. This action led to the formation of the Committee, which also took the opportunity to deal with more general questions, such as land taxes, territorial self-government for peasants, and their representation in the National Parliament. Other districts soon followed the Lublin example.

Polish students had established their independent committees a little earlier. In May 1977, the death of Stanislaw Pyjas - a student at the University of Krakow and a supporter of KOR - from head injuries which might have been inflicted by the police caused great consternation in student circles. A "Student Solidarity Committee" (SKS) was established as a result, and its first action was to demand a public inquiry into Pyjas' death and the punishment of those responsible for it. The accompanying statement also announced the Committee's intention to institutionalize students' self-defence against government repression. It invited all students to make public every case of persecution and asked for their solidarity in the struggle against the violation of laws by the Polish authorities.

Institutionalization of the civil society throughout Poland was neccessarily accompanied by the introduction of an independent information network, various publishing activities, and initiatives for self-education. The roles of KOR's Information Bulletin and the worker-oriented magazine Robotnik have already been mentioned. By 1979, there were already more than thirty independent newspapers and magazines in Poland, as well as a few independent publishing houses. For example, over a hundred Polish writers, among them some of the most famous names in Polish literature, contributed to the quarterly Zapis. Self-education was largely promoted by the independent Association of Scientific Education (TKN), and was supplemented by the development of independent libraries.

In spite of the fact that the government did not consider them legal, all these self-defence initiatives were given a lot of publicity. Government repression required much of the work to be carried out secretly, but this neccessity was made easier by the fact that many of these initiatives were channeled or otherwise closely linked to the activities of some officially recognized groups. For instance, many people from the established institutions of the "Clubs of the Catholic Intelligentsia" (KIK), and the Catholic magazines Wiez, Znak, and Tygodnik Powszechny, worked closely with opposition circles. Opposition inside the Communist Party also developed following the events of 1976. Stefan Bratkowski, the well-known journalist and party member, formed a group known as "Future and Experience" (DiP), which became famous following its publication of a series of reports critical of the situation unfolding in Poland. Many authors of the DiP reports were also members of the party. In the universities, the "illegal" Students Solidarity Committee (SKS) cooperated fruitfully with some of the officially recognized "scientific circles", which, although part of the pro-government student organization (SZSP), were also able to develop an independent programme of activity.

When the first massive strikes began in the summer of 1980, KOR quickly set itself up as an information exchange that allowed the people of Poland to learn quickly about all the major strikes and settlements. The first moves during the initial wave of strikes took a classical corporatist form. Separate strike committees were organized in individual factories. Individual demands (mainly local ones for wage increases) were made and individual solutions were reached. At that time, the strikers' solidarity was built on a functional rather than on a class basis.[44]

KOR soon went far beyond acting as the only source of news about the strikes. In early August 1980, KOR declared that it would henceforth not only give out information but also actively contact and link factories to help transform the strikes from scattered local disputes into a self-aware and coordinated movement of national protest. KOR members and supporters also had a direct hand in particular strike actions. For instance, at the Gdansk shipyard, the main strike centre in Poland, KOR activists edited the strike newspaper Solidarnosc. In large part because of KOR's efforts, by the middle of August, a significant change had taken place in the nature of workers' protest in Poland.

First, striking workers began to link economic demands with a number of political ones: freedom of speech and information, independent trade unions, amnesty for political prisoners, etc. Second, workers concluded that negotiations should be conducted at a higher level than that of the industry, and in consequence, separate discussions by various strike committees should be suspended or restricted. This led to the creation of the "Inter-enterprise Strike Committee" (MKS) in Gdansk. The leadership of MKS included leading activists of the "Free Trade Unions of the Coast": Lech Walesa, Bogdan Lis, Andrzej Gwiazda, and others. It was, therefore, not by accident that these new developments followed, to a remarkable extent, original KOR ideas about the form of social protest.

The authorities reacted by increasing their propaganda campaign against KOR and finally by detaining some KOR members. The counter-reaction by workers, however, was immediate and strong. They presented a demand to the government delegations negotiating with strikers at Gdansk and Szczecin that political prisoners be released. It later became one of the provisions of the Gdansk, Szczecin and Jastrzebie Agreements so that on September 1st, all political prisoners in Poland were released.

Those agreements and the creation of the independent trade union Solidarity drastically changed the position of KOR. Many KOR members felt that the goals of KOR from then on could be and should be realized through Solidarity. Indeed, many of them had already joined Solidarity. Jacek Kuron, for instance, was appointed MKS' chief adviser on union organization. Andrzej Celinski, another KOR member, had become the secretary of Solidarity's National Coordinating Committee.

And the most important institution within KOR, the Office of Intervention, was transformed into an organ of Solidarity. Other KOR members joined the Solidarity News Agency and Solidarity Press. Meetings of KOR itself had become less frequent, and KOR members were often acting in various Solidarity branches in their personal capacity rather than as official representatives of KOR.

One of the last independent actions of KOR was the final elaboration of the "Madrid Report on the human rights situation in Poland". In September 1979, KOR had established the Polish Helsinki Watch Committee to monitor the international obligations of Poland resulting from the Helsinki Final Act of the Conference on Security and Cooperation in Europe (CSCE). Its report on the human rights situation in Poland was presented to the CSCE Conference in Madrid in November 1980. *became went into solidarity*

KOR was finally dissolved on September 18th, 1981. As Professor Edward Lipinski announced during the First National Congress of Solidarity, "We concluded that everybody who was associated with the ideas of KOR should today devote his efforts and abilities to Solidarity". Jacek Kuron's summary of the significance of KOR is especially apt:

> "KOR was created to stimulate self-organization. We understood that the idea is for people to organize themselves. This is the revolution - the most peaceful one you can imagine - that will abolish the system where the state monopolizes the organization of people. Suddenly the citizens are doing it themselves. They are able to do it themselves. And from the moment they do it, everything changes".[45]

Kuron's words represent an excellent synthesis of the idea of "civil society" promoted by KOR in Poland.

NOTES

1. Timothy Garton Ash identifies three tendencies within the Polish opposition of the late 1970's: (1) Fundamentalist national opposition, (2) Loyal opposition, and (3) Marxist "revisionism". See: Timothy Garton Ash. The Polish Revolution. Solidarity 1980-82. Jonathan Cape, London 1983, pp. 21-22.

2. Tadeusz Kowalik. Proba Kompromisu. Zeszyty Literackie no.2, Paris 1983, p. 97.

3. Jan Jozef Lipski, a member of KOR, has answered most of these questions in his monograph about KOR. See: Jan Jozef Lipski. KOR, Aneks, London 1983, 434 pp. English edition: Jan Jozef Lipski. KOR, A History of the Workers' Defense Committee in Poland 1976-1981. University of California Press, Berkeley 1985.

4. This group is known under the name "revisionists". In my view, however, the name "revisionists" is highly confusing. It is practically impossible to establish what views are revisionist per se. One is not a revisionist in general, but only in relation to the current party line, which often changes and is not always clear. See e.g., Jakub Karpinski. Count-Down. The Polish Upheavals of 1956, 1968, 1970, 1976, 1980 ... Karz-Cohl Publ., New York 1982, pp. 108-109.

5. See e.g., Krzysztof Pomian. Wymiary Polskiego Konfliktu. 1945-1981. Aneks, London 1985, pp. 81-85. The Catholic intelligentsia was a very large and often anonymous group. Its most active representatives could be found within the parliamentary group Znak (at least until 1976), the Clubs of Catholic Intelligentsia, the Catholic newspaper Tygodnik Powszechny and the Catholic periodicals Znak and Wiez.

6. Jacek Kuron and Karol Modzelewski. An Open Letter to the Party. International Socialist Publications, London 1969, p. 15.

7. Jerzy Zawiejski. Droga Katechumena. Biblioteka Wiezi, Warsaw 1975, p. 35.

8. Quoted by Adam Michnik. The Church and the Left: A Dialogue, in: Frantisek Silnitsky, et al., (eds.) Communism in Eastern Europe. Karz-Cohl Publ., New York 1979, p. 82.

9. This drastic doctrinal switch caused them many problems later. It was often perceived as being unauthentic and made only for tactical political reasons. Doctrinal reasons apart, the change in the secular left's opinion of the Catholic circles was brought about by the attitude of the five Catholic deputies to the Sejm from the Znak. On March 11th, 1968, Znak deputies addressed an interpellation to the prime-minister in which they asked what the government was doing to "restrain the brutal actions of the police and ORMO (the secret police) against the students and to investigate who was responsible for the brutal attacks against the young people". This interpellation evoked crude attacks against Znak by the party authorities.

10. Jacek Kuron. Zasady Ideowe. Instytut Literacki, Paris 1978, p. 51. See also: Jacek Kuron. Chrzescijanie bez Boga, in: Polityka i Odpowiedzialnosc. Aneks, London 1984, pp. 17-36. This article was originally published in 1975 under the pseudonym Maciej Gajka.

11. Adam Michnik. Op.cit...p. 95.

12. See, for example, his article entitled: O duchu rewolucyjnym, in: Czy diabel moze byc zbawiony. Aneks, London 1982, pp. 217-224, or the article: Rewolucja jako piekna choroba, in: Czy diabel moze byc zbawiony. Op.cit...pp. 225-232. It should be mentioned that Kolakowski has undergone a progressive transformation from an orthodox Marxist philosopher in the Stalinist period, to "revisionist" spokesman in the late 1950's, to oppositional theorist by 1970. As a result of governmental repressions in 1968, Kolakowski emigrated to the West, and although he was a member of KOR from its beginnings his role in KOR differed from those members who lived permanently in Poland.

13. See especially: Leszek Kolakowski. The Main Currents of Marxism, Clarendon Press, Oxford 1978, vols. I-III.

14. Leszek Kolakowski. Thesis on Hope and Hopelessness. Survey, Summer 1971, pp. 37-52. One can recognize a resemblance between Kolakowski's arguments and Gene Sharp's choice for the "pluralistic theory" of power and government over the "monolithic" one. See: Gene Sharp. The Politics of Non-Violent Action. Porter Sargent, Boston 1973, pp. 8-10.
Of course, one might discuss the question of power as well as other key issues raised in this essay in a general context of political philosophy. However, this essay was written in the course of my studies on nonviolent popular movements and I basically refer to the literature which exists in this specific field. The next chapter will adopt a broader point of reference.

15. Jacek Kuron. Zasady Ideowe. Op.cit...p. 59.

16. Ibidem, see notes 23, 24, p. 71.

17. Kuron's suggestions are similar to those promoted by radical factions during the French Revolution. For example, Marat, writing in the Ami du Peuple, on June 30th, 1790, warned the "aristocracy of rich men", that instead of taking revenge, the poor could simply leave the rich to themselves, for "...to take your place, we only have to stand with folded arms. Reduced, as you will then become our equals...". Quoted by Gene Sharp. Op.cit...p. 35.

18. Socjusz. Teorie, Wytyczne i Spory. Kultura no. 11, Paris 1979, p. 59. Socjusz was the pseudonym of Zdzislaw Najder, a well-known political oppositionist.

19. Gene Sharp deals with precisely this issue in: Facing Totalitarianism Without War, in: T. Dunn, (ed.). Alternatives to War and Violence: A Search. James Clarke, London 1963, p. 139.

20. Severyn Bruyn. Social Theory of Nonviolent Action, in: S. Bruyn and P.M. Rayman, (eds.). Nonviolent Action and Social Change. Irvington, New York 1979, p. 37.

21. Egbert Jahn. Social and Political Conditions of the Expansion of the Nonviolent Movement, in: G. Geeraerts, (ed.). Possibilities of Civilian Defence in Western Europe. Polemological Center of

the Free University, Brussels 1977, p. 32.

22. Adam Michnik. The New Evolutionism. Survey, Winter 1976, p. 272.

23. Ibidem, p. 274.

24. Ibidem, p. 273.

25. Leszek Kolakowski. Thesis on Hope and Hopelessness. Op.cit...p. 51.

26. Jacek Kuron. The Situation in my Country and the Programme of the Opposition. Labour Focus no.3, London 1979, p. 12. This article orgininally appeared in KOR's Biuletyn Informacyjny in the third issue of 1979, just before the first visit to Poland of Pope John Paul II.

27. Jacek Kuron. Zasady Ideowe. Op.cit...p. 30

28. See e.g., Jerzy Holzer. Solidarnosc 1980-1981. Geneza i Historia. Instytut Literacki, Paris 1984, pp. 66-68.

29. Jonathan Schell in the introduction to Adam Michnik's: Letters from Prison and Other Essays. University of California Press, Berkeley, Los Angeles, London 1985, p. xxvii.

30. Neal Ascherson. The Polish August: the Self-Limiting Revolution. Penguin, Harmondsworth 1981, p. 114.

31. See, for example, Samorzadnosc no.3, Gdansk 1981, pp. 10-11.

32. Ibidem.

33. Jacek Kuron, interview in Samorzadnosc. Op.cit...p. 8.

34. Jacek Kuron. Co robic? Instytut Literacki, Paris 1978, p. 31.

35. Jacek Kuron in: Samorzadnosc. Op.cit...p. 8.

36. Jacek Kuron. Co robic? Op.cit...p. 30.

37. See: Michael Bernhard. The Rebirth of Public Politics in Poland: Workers and Intellectuals in the Democratic Opposition, 1976-1980. Ph.D. thesis at Columbia University, New York 1988, Chapter VI. Unpublished, pp. 14-17.

38. Wojciech Karpinski also paid special attention to the role of intellectuals in Polish politics. See: Polish Intellectuals in Opposition. Problems of Communism, July-August 1987, pp. 44-57.

39. See: Christopher Lasch. A Typology of Intellectuals. Salmagundi no.70-71, 1986, pp. 27-30. Compare also with: Alvin W. Gouldner. The Future of Intellectuals and the Rise of the New Class. The Seabury Press, New York 1979, pp. 1-9 and ff.

40. Jonathan Schell. Introduction to: Adam Michnik. Letters From Prison and Other Essays. Op.cit...pp. xxvii–xxix.

41. Andrew Arato. Civil Society Against the State: Poland 1980–81. Telos, Spring 1981, p. 23.

42. See e.g., Maria Markus. Constitution and Functioning of a Civil Society in Poland, in: Bronislaw Misztal, (ed.). Poland After Solidarity. Social Movements versus the State. Transaction Books, New Brunswick and Oxford 1985, pp. 57–84, or Jan Tomasz Gross. Poland: Society and the State, in: M. Drachkovitch, (ed.). East Central Europe, Yesterday-Today-Tomorrow. Hoover Institution Press, Stanford 1982, pp. 311 and ff.

43. The Charter of Workers' Rights is printed in English in: Jan Jozef Lipski. KOR. Op.cit...pp. 492–500.

44. For a more detailed analysis of the patterns of workers' protests in August 1980 see especially: Jadwiga Staniszkis. Poland's Self-Limiting Revolution. Princeton University Press, Princeton, New Jersey 1984, pp. 40 and ff.

45. Jacek Kuron in Samorzadnosc. Op.cit...p. 8.

II The ethics of emancipation

The Polish experiment is difficult to understand without first comprehending the role of the Catholic Church in Poland. By the same
token it would be difficult to analyse the evolution of political ideas in
Poland without taking into account the teachings of the Catholic Church.

Students of the Polish case have pointed out that Solidarity's
programme officially recognized Christian ethics as a major source of
inspiration.[1] They report that Christ's suffering on the cross became a
symbol of workers' strikes and national manifestations; that specific
churches became strongholds of the underground resistance. They also
argue that the Catholic clergy - the Polish Pope, bishops as well as
ordinary priests - play a crucial role in the process of political
bargaining on a national as well as at the local level.

The link between the Polish experiment and the activity of the
Catholic Church in Poland is therefore well established. Yet, scholars
who try to explore more fully the nature of this link (or relationship)
are faced with enormous problems. Can the Church's activity be defined
in traditional political terms? Does the Church speak with the one voice
of the Pope or with the thousands of voices of local parishes? How

should one interpret the Church's relations with the authorities and the opposition? Can we say that the Church makes any political choices in this respect? Does the Church in Poland pursue national rather than universal objectives or the other way around? These are all difficult questions frequently asked by political commentators in Poland and elsewhere.

An analysis of the Church's teachings in the context of the history of political ideas has to overcome certain specific difficulties. First of all, any application of political criteria to an analysis of the ideas promoted by the Church will give rise to serious doubts and controversy. Of course, the Church's contemporary teachings have certain political implications. Not surprisingly, therefore, some scholars have gone so far as to link the so-called "Church's social doctrine" with political ideology.[2] On the other hand, however, the Church itself insists that its teachings have an exclusively moral character and cannot be identified with any concrete political programme, doctrine or ideology.

This study acknowledges that the Church's approach to social and political phenomena has a predominantly moral character. Nevertheless, it will try to translate the moral creed of the Church into political terms and categories.

This type of approach is encouraged by the representatives of the Church themselves. The Polish Primate, Cardinal Stefan Wyszynski, stated that although "the Church does not issue detailed instructions" it nevertheless "does have its own social philosophy, social doctrine and social psychology. Up to a point, it even has its economic perennis".[3] And a well-known philosopher, Father Jozef Tischner, has argued that the Church speaks about politics because its morals encompass all aspects of social intercourse.[4]

Our analysis will indicate that although the Church does not present any detailed and comprehensive guidelines to contemporary political debates, it nevertheless tries to establish moral dimensions of all major political problems, such as liberty, justice or problems of labour relations. We will study this process and its consequences.

The second major dilemma which has to be faced at the beginning of this essay concerns the understanding of the concept of the Church. In particular, we have to know whose and which ideas are representative of the Church in Poland. After all, students of theology point out that John Paul II uses no less than nine different concepts of the

Church, from the Holy See to the quasi-church of the home confined in an ascetic ideal.[5]

In this context we should ask, for instance, whether the early philosophical writings of Karol Wojtyla are as representative of the Church as are the Encyclicals of John Paul II? Should we limit our analysis to the Pastoral Letters of the Bishop's Episcopate in Poland or should we also study numerous sermons, interviews and public statements of bishops and cardinals? And what about the sermons and publications of some well-known Polish priests who are not at the top of the Church's hierarchy? Should we also consider writings of Catholic laymen? Is it appropriate to study the political rhetoric of members of parliament representing Catholic clubs in the Sejm?

In this study our choice is determined by a need to understand the Church's influence on the evolution of political ideas in Poland rather than by strict rules of canonic law. In principle, we will not refer to works of Catholic laymen.[6] However, various writings and public statements by the Polish clergy will be taken into consideration regardless of whether or not the Church officially recognizes them as being "representative" enough.

To a certain extent our choice is based on the assumption that the writings of priests such as Jozef Tischner or Jerzy Popieluszko can influence political thinking in Poland as much as the bishops' Pastoral Letters do. Or that the sermons delivered by John Paul II during his pilgrimages to Poland are, from our perspective, as important as his official Encyclicals announced by the Vatican.

Finally, we should mention problems which emerge if one tries to look for a theoretical point of reference to the teachings of the Church in Poland. For instance, are we able to find certain parallels between the ideas promoted by the Church and certain major political works in modern history? Can we classify the Church's teachings into major currents of political philosophy, such as conservatism or socialism? Has the Church defined its response to major political or ideological schools of thinking? Can we say that the teachings of the Church in Poland emerge form a specific national tradition?

My studies have been unable to give clear answers to these questions. For instance, it would seem that the Polish Church shares a major conservative belief that political problems are basically religious and moral problems. On the other hand, however, the present Church does not subscribe to many other principles of conservatism, such as that, for instance, which says that freedom and property are closely linked.[7] To go a step further, the Church's teaching is neither entirely collectivist nor purely individualistic. The Church advocates neither statism nor anarchism. The Church conducts various polemics with Marxism, but avoids speaking of socialism versus capitalism in contradictory terms.

In fact the Church has a different historical perspective than do most of the modern schools of political philosophy. For instance, the works of St. Paul, St. Augustine and St. Thomas Aquino are today no less inspiring for the Church than the works of modern heads of the Vatican such as Leo XIII or Jan XXIII.

The specific experiences of various national churches make any comparisons and classifications even more difficult. For instance, so-called "liberation theology" can hardly create a point of reference for our analysis because of the entirely different experience with Marxism in Poland and in Latin American countries. Works of famous political moralists, such as Mahatma Gandhi or Jacques Maritain are also not very helpful in trying to understand the Polish Church which is so deeply rooted in the specific historical traditions of the Polish nation.

In consequence, this study considers the teachings of the Catholic Church as a phenomenon sui generis which can hardly be classified within any of the traditional currents of political philosophy. The teachings of the Church in Poland with its striking national characteristics is considered as a special case within the universal Church. As Jozef Tischner has put it, Polish Christianity did not create a great theology, nevertheless it created something more important- that is a "religious thinking", which finds its expression in literature and painting, which can be felt in a common preception of history, in the entire Polish ethos.[8]

THE PRIMACY OF ETHICS OVER POLITICS

In a study of Solidarity published in 1985 a Polish sociologist, Ireneusz Krzeminski, suggested that the religious idea of social order promoted by the Church is much richer and spiritually more important than traditional Western ideas of political pluralism.[9] According to Krzeminski, the religious idea of social order is based on the principle of dignity of human beings which considers people as "equal moral subjects". People are equal in their "moral condition", they are equal in their dignity, they are equally called to salvation. The contradiction between "equality " and "liberty" no longer exists. Equality before the law and the abolition of all privileges which affect human dignity, these are the metaphysical contents of the idea of a "citizens' society" promoted by the Church.[10]

Krzeminski acknowledges that the "religious idea of social order understood as a moral duty given to all human beings by the Lord" is as yet not fully elaborated. Nevertheless, he refers to serious sociological studies which indicate that the ideas of "human dignity and subjectiveness" are today central for people's understanding of all other political categories, such as democracy, equality or freedom.[11]

An analysis of Solidarity's various statements and documents confirms the fact that many moral concepts promoted by the Church, such as the concept of truth, conscience, hope, dignity, love, dialogue, moral order or moral victory have become an integral part of political rhetoric in contemporary Poland. For instance, Solidarity's official programme stated that the union struggles not only for democracy and a rule of law, but also for truth and human dignity.[12] It even went further and announced that "dignity and respect for human beings" form the basis of the union's existence.[13]

What is the meaning of the moral concepts promoted by the Church? Are these moral concepts complementary or contradictory to traditional political concepts of freedom, democracy or justice? Can we say, as Krzeminski does, that the moral idea of social order promoted by the Church represents a theoretical alternative to the traditional idea of political pluralism? Or should one rather argue that the concepts of truth, dignity, moral order, hope or dialogue have merely an ethical character and can hardly influence political choices? Are the Church's teachings then a rhetorical decoration, at least from a political point of view? Or do they provide a theoretical guideline to cope with various dilemmas of politics? Let us try to answer some of these questions.

At the center of the Church teachings is man and his <u>human dignity</u>.[14] According to the Church man is a free and reasonable being. Thus he or she cannot be tailored to fit some programme or even some philosophy. Man is not just a piece of matter. Man is an image of his God - God made him into his own likeness. This is why a human possesses an exceptional dignity which has to be defended by the Church.

The concept of human dignity defies simple definition and has rather an intuitive nature. As one priest has put it: "human dignity is a value that can be seen and felt but one about which it is difficult to speak.... everyone feels this idea in one's own way, but.... the idea is basically held in common".[15]

Due to the lack of any clear definition we should turn our attention toward the value of dignity by pointing out the context in which it is found. According to the Church, the context of human dignity is human rights. In other words, human dignity expresses itself through the rights afforded to human beings such as the right to hope, the right to worthwhile work or the right to independence.

A man cannot be deprived of his dignity by any ideology or political system. The Church denies moral legitimacy to any economic or political system which tries to limit human dignity. As Cardinal Wyszynski has put it: "Every nation and every government should recognize the primacy of man and should respect human dignity".[16]

According to the Church, human dignity outlines the moral perspectives of human development. It speaks of the need for a social system that would provide the possibility for human development from within. What is external should be based upon what which is internal. By the same token, the idea of human dignity promoted by the Church becomes an idea of "concrete democracy"; democracy which arises from ethics.[17]

The second crucial concept promoted by the Church is the concept of hope. We can distinguish three major dimensions of hope. First of all, the Church considers hope as the source of people's spiritual life. Hope directs people toward the future, through hope the future becomes their spiritual value. Because hope directs people to future values it allows them to overcome today's difficulties. In this context, Polish priests could say that the post-war efforts of the Church in Poland were mainly aimed at preserving and defending the Christian ethic of hope, constantly threatened by the communist authorities.[18]

The second dimension of hope is its human reference. Here hope is closely linked with the concept of trust. For instance, the Church argues that there is always someone in whom one can place one's hope. Or, what does it mean to be a father? It means to become the trustee

40

of someone's hope. When we reflect upon problems of education, we enter the world of hope of a maturing human being. Only those who have hope truly educate and bring up others. According to the Church a person's work is also an expression of a certain hope.

In this way all social interactions are based on the ethics of hope. People's social choices are in fact choices between various hopes. This brings us closer to the Church's understanding of the concept of freedom. Since the essence of people's activity and choices is reduced to hope, freedom can only be realized within hope.[19]

Finally, there is a third dimension to the entrusting of hope, the bond between those who project a comprehensive plan of work in a given society and those who carry it out. Here trust and confidence also exists. Betrayal in this context expresses itself as a crisis of work. Against this background, the Polish crisis of 1980 was frequently described by the Church as a crisis of hope.

Another major concept promoted by the Church is the concept of truth. The Church argues that the right to truth represents a basic right of man. Every man is called to be a witness of the truth. Truth is free and confers freedom. The real freedom of man is based on truth. As one bishop has put it, in the right kind of social order

"every man has the right to speak his mind, no one is forced to hide truth in some sort of underground, no one is denied the necessary means of expressing this truth, and truth is not manipulated in the interest of one particular set of ideas which is foisted upon society to the exclusion of others".[20]

In the Church's view, freedom of a nation is also based on truth- "Every nation lives by the truth about itself".[21]

Many other political categories are also defined by truth. For instance, according to the Church true work is work that truly serves life, and true speech is speech that is consistent with reality; it is speech that grows from an agreement between people and promotes it. Truth is also linked with social dialogue, love, peace and conscience. For instance, let us consider Father Tischner's statement: "Dialogue, by bringing light, unveils the truth".[22] Or Father Popieluszko's sermon:

"Truth is always linked with love, and love costs, for true love is self-sacrificing, truth must also bear a cost. To live in truth is to be at peace with one's conscience. Truth always joins and unites people... the magnitude of truth horrifies and brings to light the lies of little, frightened people....".[23]

The Church is committed to the proclamation and protection of truth. As Cardinal Wojtyla has put it: "the Church in Poland seeks no authority other than to bear witness to the truth about God and about man".[24] Cardinal Wyszynski expressed this idea in a similar way: "The Church, her supranatural power, gives you truth and testifies to truth.... through inner spiritual freedom she inspires in you the desire for all other freedoms".[25]

Finally, there are concepts of social love and solidarity. According to Pope John Paul II (and also to Pope Paul VI) social love is a kind of "civilization of love" toward which all societies should be directed.[26]

In other words, love is one of the most important human values. For instance, in the Church's view love is greater than justice. And social love is greater than social justice. If it is true that justice should prepare the ground for love – then it is even more true that only love can guarantee full justice.

To build a society according to the Church is to be on the side of fraternity and love. A hunger for justice should not lead to a struggle of man against man. It should not lead to egoism and hatred. People must persist in love in order to overcome egoism and hatred. As Cardinal Glemp has put it: "Hatred and passion lead nowhere... forgiveness and love are the only means of gaining things".[27]

Love, then, creates the foundation for social solidarity. Real solidarity is the struggle for a just social order, an order which would be able to absorb all tensions and conflicts. In order to build a world of social peace and justice, solidarity has to cut off the roots of egoism, injustice and hatred which are often promoted by various ideologies and political systems. According to the Church the idea of transforming the world of work into a world of justice is not an utopia. It could be done through love and solidarity.[28] Such an achievement would represent the moral victory advocated by the Church.

Solidarity implies not only a struggle for overcoming class divisions and for social justice. Solidarity implies also an effort to bridge the gap between the ruled and the rulers in specific countries. In Spring 1980, Polish bishops expressed this idea of solidarity in the following words:

"All daughters and sons of the Church and all citizens have to consciously join efforts to overcome the manifold problems in the

42

life of our society. The Church which, by virtue of its tasks and prerogative, does not identify itself with any political community or political system, is both a symbol and a guardian of the transcedent nature of a human being. The political community and the Church are each in its field independent and autonomous. However, those two communities, although on different grounds, serve the individual and social vocation of the same people. Their service for the benefit of all will be more effective the better they develop sound cooperation between them".[29]

So far our study of the basic moral concepts used by the Church to describe social and political developments has not answered all our initial questions. We could remark, nevertheless, that for the Church in Poland political categories have primarily a moral character. Dignity, hope or truth come before freedom, liberty or justice in describing all sorts of relations between individuals and collectives. Or as Jozef Tischner put it during the First National Congress of Solidarity: "Our basic problem is not an economic one; neither is it political. Economics and politics are only derivative problems. Our basic problem is a problem of consciousness".[30] However, we are still unable to grasp the political consequences of the primacy of ethics over politics, advocated by the Church. For instance, what is meant, from a political point of view, by the fact that a man cannot be deprived of his dignity and hope? Or, what does it mean for political decision makers that social justice must be based on social love and solidarity? Our study indicates that the Church presents its moral concepts in a vague and abstract manner. Can such moral concepts thus provide any clear political guideline? We will try to answer these questions by looking at the Church's teaching, first, in the field of human rights and later, in the field of labour relations.

DEFENCE OF HUMAN RIGHTS

According to the Church the rights of man are an essential part of being human, and God, by becoming man, confirmed the dignity of being human. That is why human rights cannot be arbitrarily circumscribed. The Church argues that no one can say: you have these rights because you are a member of such a nation, race, class or party, and you are denied these rights because you do not belong to this nation, race, class or party.

For instance, every man by virtue of being man has a right to social advancement in the framework of a community. And every man has the duty to shape the life of the whole community by promoting justice and love. In particular, the Polish clergy believes that "every man born on Polish soil" is by this very token "a child of the Polish motherland. It is impossible to tell anyone that he or she is a lesser kind of Pole than any other Pole".[31]

Human rights, the rights of the individual and, in their wake, the rights of communities - the Church is just such a body in Poland - are indispensable. They cannot be given in the form of a concession. Man is born with them and seeks to realize them in the course of his life. And if they are not realized or experienced, then man rebels. In fact, the Church believes that it cannot be otherwise, because he is a man. His sense of honour expects this.

According to Cardinal Wojtyla,

"it is certainly in the interests of all authorities everywhere in the world, no less than in Poland or in Cracow, to appreciate the need to respect human rights. The man who feels that he is being deprived in this respect is ready to commit any act. He is prepared to make many sacrifices. He cannot cease being a man, a Pole or a Christian".[32]

The Church argues that it is impossible to resolve these problems by means of oppression. Police and prisons provide no answer either. They only raise the price that will ultimately have to be paid. The solution does not lie with expanding police organizations and state security departments. The Church is convinced that there is only one road to peace and national unity, and this is through "unfettered respect for the rights of man, of the citizen, of the Pole, and the Christian, and to see that their rights are fully respected".[33]

A detailed catalogue of basic human rights to be respected by the authorities was elaborated by Cardinal Wyszynski.[34] First of all every man has the rights to a decent living standard. It is the duty of the public authorities to guarantee that right, and the duty of all citizens to give it their honest support.

Second, man has a right to his moral and cultural values.

Third, man has the right to freedom in searching for truth and in expressing and communicating his opinions, including the right to free artistic expression. (Here, governmental censorship comes especially

44

under fire from the Church.)

Fourth, man has the right to choose the conditions of life which best suit him: to establish a family - where men and women have equal rights and duties - or to choose the priesthood or monastic life.

Fifth, man has a natural right to choose his trade and his profession and to exercise it freely. That means, among other things, that conditions of work must not be injurious to health or morals, nor must they stunt man's natural development. Man also has the right to just wages.

Sixth, man has the right to free association.

Seventh, man has the right to participate in public affairs.

And finally, eighth, every man must be permitted to stand up in defence of his own rights and those of others, in accordance with "true justice".

Cardinal Wyszynski stated that the bishops of Poland have continually claimed all these rights from the authorities. Whenever these rights were violated - and according to Wyszynski this was very often the case - the Church asserted them and demanded that they should be respected.

The modern history of Poland seems to confirm the Cardinal's statement. During the last four decades, the Episcopate of Polish bishops repeatedly criticized the Polish authorities for violating especially the right of conscience and freedom of religious life.[35]

In the 1970's the Church's criticism of violations of human rights and the lack of respect for a wide range of economic and political freedoms intensified. For instance, after the workers' strikes in December 1970 the Polish Episcopate addressed a letter "To all compatriots of our common Motherland" in which the bishops called for the central authorities and the entire state administration to respect basic human rights such as the right to social justice, the right to truth, the right to free cultural activity, and the right of citizens to be treated without abuse, unfair injury, or persecution.[36]

After the workers' protests in Radom, in June 1976, the Polish Episcopate again appealed to the authorities on behalf of the workers. In their letter, the bishop declared that it was a disparagement to the workers to connect their justified protest against excessive price increases on foodstuffs with the acts of violence which had been committed at the time by a few disreputable individuals. The bishops also stated that the prison sentences meted out were too harsh and that it was unjust to dismiss workers because they had demonstrated and had struck to defend themselves against exorbitant price increases which had been the doing of the authorities.[37]

One year later, in the so-called "vows of Jasna Gora", the bishops addressed the issue of recent violations of human rights in Poland in more general terms. They stated:

"The nation has a duty to watch over its greatest treasure which is man - the citizen. The state exists to ensure for its citizens the necessary conditions for subsistence and for life in freedom within the limits of the fundamental human rights which he fulfils".[38]

In June 1978 Cardinal Wojtyla again elaborated on the theme of human rights. He did it in the aftermath of the death of a Cracow student and KOR activist, Stanislaw Pyjas, who was allegedly killed by the police. The death of Pyjas stimulated oppositional activities in the entire country and was met by further police repression. Cardinal Wojtyla spoke on Corpus Christi day in Cracow: "Our prayers for peace and justice in the modern world and in our Polish land are prayers for Mankind and for each and every man. They are prayers for human rights; rights which cannot be tailored to fit a particular system nor a particular doctrine; rights which have to be seen in the truth of man's greatness and man's freedom. And these rights cannot be taken away from him".[39]

A call for the observance of human rights was repeated by Cardinal Wojtyla in 1979, during his first visit to Poland as Pope John Paul II. It was later echoed many times in Polish churches during the difficult period of 1980-1981.

Naturally the Church's criticism of violations of human rights was especially severe after the imposion of martial law. The first Episcopal statement after December 1981 described the situation in which "the entire nation is terrorized by military force".[40] It expressed clear support for Solidarity, which "by defending the rights of the workers is indispensable in returning balance to public life", and criticized the fact that numerous activists of the labour movement had been interned.

Turning to the Church's role under martial law, religious leaders noted that the Church together with the state is jointly responsible for the nation and its mission is to defend human rights and human dignity.

The bishops went on to say that "beginning today the Church must take positive action". This action, which would be based on the principle that "the episcopate will not renounce the rights and achievements of society as a whole - these are irreversible truths" and the conviction that "the nation will not step backward and cannot give up the democratic renewal that has been announced in the country".[41]

In their communiqué issued on 16 September 1982 the Polish bishops went even further and stated that they consider it their moral duty to stand up in defence of those "who have been beaten, injured, or morally harmed during the latest incidents". The Church would betray its mission if it were to assume the role of a guilty bystander and remained indifferent to the complaints of those "suffering and persecuted".[42]

The Bishops' call for respect of human rights and for prayers on behalf of those who were persecuted was echoed in thousands of local parishes all over the country. In particular, the sermons of Father Jerzy Popieluszko of the St. Stanislaw Kostka parish in Warsaw always drew enormous crowds, including visitors from outside Warsaw. Popieluszko's relentless reminders about the victims of the Polish crisis are typified by his homily of 27 November 1983:

> "Let us remember today the innocent deaths of our brothers, the miners from Wujek, the deaths of our brothers from Lublin, Nowa Huta, and other localities; the cruelty of the crime committed on Grzes Przemyk - the leaders of Solidarity and the Worker's Defence Committee who have been imprisoned for two years now without indictment. Let us remember those who have spent long months away from their families because they do not want to compromise their conscience by coming out of hiding on certain conditions. Those who have been fired from work and who are concerned about the material well-being of their families.... the lines of people, ration cards in hand, in front of shops, such a humiliation of human dignity. The paid informers....".[43]

Several months later Father Popieluszko was assassinated by secret police agents.

Students of theology point out that during the pontificat of John Paul II, the Church's teaching has been able to go beyond an abstract and normative way of thinking characteristic for the school of natural law. The Church has been able to do this by turning toward "concrete thinking". In judging existing legal and political systems the Church began first of all to consider the situation of "specific" individuals in these systems. By the same token, it was able to engage in defence of basic human rights of individuals; rights considered in a concrete rather than in an historical and abstract manner.[44] The teachings of the Polish Church in the field of human rights seem to confirm this hypothesis.

In the context of our analysis it should also be noticed that seemingly vague and ambivalent moral concepts promoted by the Church gain a very concrete political meaning when they are linked to the human rights issue. For instance, the Church's general call that man cannot be deprived of his dignity and hope means that he cannot be deprived of his basic human rights such as the right to free association or the right to participate in public affairs. Similarly, the Church's somewhat enigmatic argument that every man is called to be a witness of the truth means that he should enjoy freedom of expressing and communicating his opinions without any external interference.

A study of the Church's teachings in the field of labour relations also indicates that moral concepts promoted by the Church may be given a very specific political meaning.

THE ETHICS OF LABOUR RELATIONS

John Paul II devoted a special papal encyclical to the problem of labour relations. The ideas expressed in the Encyclical Laborem Exercens were also promoted through his numerous sermons delivered all over the world, including Poland.[45]

Philosophical aspects of labour were tackled in the early writings of Karol Wojtyla (especially in his book of 1969 entitled "Osoba i czyn") and also by Father Jozef Tischner (especially in "Etyka Solidarnosci"). Problems of labour relations had also attracted the special attention of Cardinal Wyszynski.

According to the Church, the problems of labour are of a primary ethical character. The most important factor affecting human labour is not, in the last analysis, technology or even economics, but a more fundamental concept: the concept of the dignity of work, this is to say, of the dignity of man. Economics, technology, and the many other specializations and disciplines have their justification for existing within that simple essential concept. If they fail to draw from that concept and are shaped without reference to the dignity of human labour then, the Church argues, they are in error, they are harmful, they are against humankind.

In particular, one should not see the working man as an instrument of production. According to the Church, the working man is a subject, a subject who, in the production process, has priority over capital.

In its indirect criticism of Marxism, the Church argues that the link between work and human existence bears constant witness to the fact that man has not been alienated from work, that he has not been enslaved. On the contrary, it confirms that, as John Paul II puts it, "work has become the ally of his humanity, which helps him to live in truth and freedom, in a freedom built on truth which enables him to lead, in all fullness, a life more worthy of man".[46]

Again, however, the Church does not limit itself to an abstract philosophical analysis of the nature of human work. It also draws attention to the specific rights of working people. The Church does so because it believes that human work has important moral dimensions and therefore should be governed by a sort of "moral order". This moral order requires that certain basic rights of the working people are not violated by the state (or private) employer. This puts the Church into the core of major political debates in contemporary Poland.

In the first instance, the Church argues that workers have the rights to a just wage (understood as an amount of money sufficient for the present maintenance of workers' families as well as for securing their future).[47] It further argues that the degree of justice present in specific socio-economic systems can, in fact, be measured by the degree to which people's work is properly rewarded. The Church devotes similar attention to the problems of working conditions and of social care.

However, it would be unrealistic to expect that problems of wages, of social care or of proper conditions of work could be automatically resolved by application of any specific economic system. After all, in the Church's view, economic systems are created by man and for man, and not the other way around. Therefore, it is extremely important that "all those who contribute to economic life have the possibility of participating freely and actively in the elaboration and control of all decisions which affect their life on all levels".[48] Moreover, the Church argues that a working man should himself "carry defence of truth and a true dignity of his work", and he "should not be stopped in meeting this duty" which in fact serves the collective good of the people.[49]

In this context, the issue of labour unions emerges as the most important one. In the view of the Church, modern unions have evolved from the struggle of the workers - workers in general, but especially the industrial workers - to protect their just rights vis-a-vis the entrepreneurs and the owners of the means of production. Their task is to defend the interests of workers in all sectors in which their rights are concerned. And the Encyclical Laborem Exercens states that organizations of this type are an "indispensable element of social life", especially in modern industralized societies. They are, indeed, the "mouthpiece of the struggle for social justice, for the just rights of working people in accordance with their individual professions".[50]

The Church believes that a union's struggle for social justice and the rights of workers should be based on the principle of solidarity of- and with - working people. The Church praises and encourages such solidarity especially in countries where there is persistent exploitation of working people and in consequence misery or even hunger. In these cases solidarity turns out to be, as one Polish priest puts it, "a communion of working people who strive to free human work, free them from hardships and sufferings caused by other human beings, that is, from hardships that are not inherent in the process of converting raw materials into a product".[51]

In this way, we come to the problem of exploitation and the ways of dealing with it. Not surprisingly, the Church approaches exploitation in moral rather than in economical terms. In its view, the problem concerns not only what happens to the product, but what happens to the human being. Working people can withstand many physical burdens, suffer hunger, and even sacrifice their lives. However, according to the Church, people are not able to bear moral burdens and therefore they rebel. The Church then justifies workers' protests by saying that "to rebel against moral exploitation [of work- J.Z.] is a basic duty of conscience".[52]

The most common form of workers' protest is a strike. The Church recognizes strikes as a legitimate means of workers' protest, and in its view "all workers should enjoy the right to strike".[53] Some Polish

50

priests have gone even further and presented a sort of moral apotheosis of strike action. Here, the works of Father Jozef Tischner are especially illustrative.

Tischner argues that people become aware of the fact that they are objects of "the moral exploitation of work" when they discover that they are working "senselessly".[54] At this point, a common conscience is born. People who want to do something good, become members of something Tischner calls "a spontaneously formed communion of people of good will". They realize, without special education, that something worthwhile is happening; that in growing toward the point of striking they grow, in Tischner's words, "to their full humanity". Participation in such a strike thus becomes a moral act. An act which is, "dictated by the order of the ethics of work".[55]

Tischner not only glorifies the strike. He also creates a new concept of public property which emerges from workers' association with their workplace, currently owned by the state. In his view, during a strike and somehow because of it, a new and particular attitude of the working person to his workplace crystallizes. From then on, the people become the true masters of their workplaces. The title of ownership is then sealed, not by signature, but by the work itself. As Tischner puts it, the workplaces belong to those who have "soaked them with their sweat and blood", those who have "covered them with their concerns.... times of strike then are times that reveal the mystery of work. Work endows possession. A person wants to give and because of that a person starts to have".[56]

According to Tischner, by industrial action the working person confronts authority, upon which the general system of work depends, with a key decision: Either it will govern work sensibly or it will itself become senseless authority, illusory authority, Authority, if it wishes to be true authority, must serve the logic of work. "The essential power of strike" – says the Polish priest – "is not that it opposes someone but that it turns out to be a sensible action in a world that has lost sense".[57] By the same token, a strike became a means of protest against the existence of a "senseless" economic system rather than merely against unjust wages.

Our brief review of the Church's teachings in the field of labour relations again indicates the level of practical political engagement of the modern Church. The Church's concept of social justice based on love and solidarity encourages people to unite in defence of their rights as citizens and workers. This defence may also include strike action conducted against private or state employers.

The Church refuses to speak in terms of class antagonisms. It also does not take the side of any existing socio-economic system.[58] Nevertheless, it is committed to defence of basic human rights and in particular the rights of working people, whenever they are violated. In Poland, the general ethical commitment of the Church was transformed into an outspoken criticism of violation of human rights by the state authorities. This was transformed into support of popular demands of working people expressed during successive strikes and upheavals. Promoted by the Church, terms and slogans such as "workers' solidarity", "senseless work", "dignity of work", "freedom of labour unions", or "the right to strike", etc., had a direct reference to current political debates which took place in Poland in the 1980's.

In consequence, the Church's influence on emancipatory movements in Poland was very substantial and has been recognized by the leaders of Solidarity. At the same time, some students of the Polish experiment believe that the Church's close association with the struggle for human rights and the rights of workers was decisive in keeping alive popular support for the Church as such.[59]

Of course, in the field of political doctrine it is always difficult to grasp the degree of influence on, and association between, theory and practice. Common perceptions of the Church's moral teachings about politics can be, nevertheless, illustrated by one of Lech Walesa's statements: "Solidarity is a communion of the people who do not wish to participate in a lie. This is the simplest ethic of the common working people". Walesa said this in the afterword to the above quoted book of Father Jozef Tischner, which deals with the complicated ethical questions of Christian truth, dignity, solidarity and the rights of working people.

A nonbeliever, Adam Michnik, described the link between the ideas promoted by the Church and the emancipatory movements in Poland in somewhat more concrete terms. In his letter from prison published in 1985 Michnik wrote: "When the bishops criticize hate campaigns, condemn murders, or plead for dialogue instead of repression, they are expressing the aspirations, including political ones, of an overwhelming majority of Poles".[60]

ROMANTIC PATRIOTISM

The Church's association with Polish nationalism has a long tradition. In fact, the issue was debated by several successive generations of Poles and has given rise to a number of controversies.[61] The question of Polish nationalism as such is very complicated and the Church's association with specific historical currents of nationalism has been both praised and severely criticized.[62] Historical controversies could today be reduced to the analysis of two basic dilemmas: (a) Does the Church in contemporary Poland support the so-called "open" or "closed" trend of nationalism?; and (b) Does it cultivate the so-called "romantic" or "positivistic" tradition of nationalism?

Students of nationalism usually point to two fundamental and opposite types of nationalism – one that corresponds to "open" society and one that corresponds to "closed" society.[63]

"Open" nationalism is inclined toward intercourse, and its basis is generally a territorial organization and a political society, constituting a nation of fellow citizens irrespective of race or ethnic descent. "Closed" nationalism stresses the nation's autochtonous character, its common origins (race, blood) and its roots in the ancestoral soil. These determine the "purity" of national character and preserve it from "alien" influences.

"Open" nationalism stresses the free self-determination of the individual, opposes any form of national egoism and promotes the idea of a "brotherhood of free nations".

"Closed" nationalism stresses biological or historical determination, restricts the rights of national and ethnic minorities, subordinates the interests of the individual to the "objective" interests of the nation and believes in some sort of "real politik" which emerges from the "natural egoism" of all nations.

In practice, no nationalism or phase of nationalism is a pure example of strains: it is always a question of emphasis. Nevertheless, students of "national questions" are usually able to classify specific programmes, books or manifestos, within one or the other strain of nationalism. For instance, the works of contemporary Polish writers such as Piotr Wierzbicki, Jozef Wierny or Henryk Korwin have been classified to the "closed" strain of nationalism (directly or indirectly).[64] The same could be said about the pre-war works of Roman Dmowski and his political organization Endecja.[65]

On the other hand, we would argue in this essay that there are solid grounds to suggest that the Church in today's Poland subscribes to the "open" strain of nationalism.[66]

The Church's association with the open strain of nationalism emerges mainly from the fact that its promotion of the right of the Polish nation is closely linked to its support for the rights of all human beings regardless of their religion, race or political opinions. As John Paul II has put it: "The history of a nation deserves a right kind of assessment according to the contribution it has made to the development of man, of human kind, his consciousness, his heart, his conscience".[67]

Father Tischner, in his book about the Polish nation, expressed this idea in a similar way: "The basic issue for a nation, understood as an ethical substance, is man".[68]

According to the Church, Poland is a "commonwealth of the whole nation" and as such "must be protected by all its sons and daughters".[69] This first of all requires the establishment of a dialogue within the Polish nation. Such a dialogue would be aimed at "solving the existing conflicts" and at looking for a "common good" which would be based on respect for all "cultural, ethnic, and religious groups which constitute the nation".[70]

Work for a "common good" in Poland, according to the Polish pope, is work for "peace, for mutual respect and understanding". This work for a "common good" should not be "directed against anybody", but it should be "aimed at renewal in which all people are able to participate".[71]

The Church's concept of national justice requires security of "rights and needs of all members of the nation". Justice does not tolerate unequal treatment of any groups. The state's first duty is to respect "the common good of all citizens - all citizens without exception".[72]

In the field of international relations, the Church has refused to adopt a concept of national egoism; this is yet another argument to classify its teachings in an open strain of nationalism. As John Paul II has put it: "One nation can never develop at the expense of another, at the expense of its subordination, conquest, oppression, at the expense of exploiting it, at the expense of its death".[73]

Moreover, the Church identifies itself with the community of sovereign people and nations rather than merely with the community of nation-states. For instance, during his first visit to Poland the Pope addressed diplomatic representatives from different countries in the following words: "The Apostolic See welcomes joyfully all diplomatic representatives, not only as spokesman of their own governments, regimes and political structures" but also and above all as "representatives of people and nations which through these political structures manifest their sovereignty, their political independence, and the possibility of deciding their destiny autonomously".[74]

The Pope's frequent appeals to "open the frontiers" represent another example of the Church's understanding of the question of nationalism.[75]

In history, a closed strain of nationalism was often associated with romantic, anti-Enlightment Germanophilism and Slavophilism.[76] It is therefore appropriate to ask whether the Church in contemporary Poland cultivates the romantic tradition of nationalism or as we put it, the positivistic one.

The positivistic tradition of nationalism recognizes common territory, state authority and a common system of law as crucial factors in definding the national question, only then followed by cultural and historical factors.

The romantic tradition of nationalism, on the contrary, puts emphasis on a cultural national identity as well as on a common historical heritage of the nation. In romantic tradition, the spiritual condition or mission of the nation is more important than any legal questions. The historical heritage of the nation, a heritage full of sacrifice and heroism, has a greater meaning than geopolitical considerations. The desired victory of the nation has a moral rather than a political character.

The romantic form of nationalism was created and promoted by XIXth century Polish writers, such as Adam Mickiewicz, Juliusz Slowacki or August Cieszkowski.[77] In some cases it developed into a philosophy of messianism which considered the fate of Poland to be the most significant moment in the universal design of history. Poland was the "Christ of the nations: the nation on the rack, all anguish, all spirit, all idea, a pure principle".[78]

Today, it would be wrong to identify the Church's contemporary teachings with extreme forms of messianism. Nevertheless, there are solid grounds to believe that the Church cultivates a romantic rather than positivistic tradition of nationalism.[79]

For the Church in Poland, the nation represents first of all a cultural and spiritual community. As John Paul II has put it:

"Polish culture is a good on which the spiritual life of the Poles rests. It distinguishes us [i.e. the Poles-J.Z.] as a nation. It has been decisive for us throughout the course of history, more decisive even than martial power. Indeed, it is more decisive than boundaries".[80]

According to the Pope, the nation perishes when it is deprived of its spirit; the nation grows when its spirit is cleansed anew. No external forces can destroy this spirit. Poland has remained spiritually independent throughout the ages because it has its own culture, directly associated with the spiritual teachings of the Church.[81]

Jozef Tischner goes even further in his spiritual perception of the nation. According to him, the question of the Fatherland looms over peoples' conscience. He believes that national conscience has a purely intuitive character, it is a question of feeling. This intuitive conscience dominates peoples' minds and souls, it "rules people individually, and at the same time, it rules the entire nation". Tischner argues that a national conscience has a timeless power: "the voice of Polish conscience leads us through the winding course of history". It has also a supernational character: "The voice [of conscience-J.Z.] awakens hopes that match the ordeal and courage that measures up to the courage of our futures". It defines the boundaries of national freedom: "the limits of Polish freedom are outlined by the Polish conscience". Finally, the Polish conscience represents an ethical guideline for the nation: "The voice of Polish conscience.... points unmistakably to those values for which one must fight as well as those that can be disregarded".[82]

In the view of the Church the Polish nation represents a special kind of community, an "outstanding community" as John Paul II has called it.[83] This "special feature" of the Polish nation emerges from its thousand year old association with Christianity as well as from its history full of martyrs and sacrifices. The Church does not glorify national disasters and sufferings of the Polish people throughout history. However, it does argue that the difficult historical fate of the Polish nation has contributed to a national spiritual integrity of the Poles. It has brought them closer to moral victory.

The cult of national suffering and patriotic heroism was especially underlined by Cardinal Wyszynski. In his view, people should love their country not with words but with deeds. The proof of patriotism is a "willingness to give one's life, to shed one's blood".[84] Patriotism is not shown by resounding and endless speeches, declarations and proclamations. One has to sense the dynamics of patriotism by the readiness to give it everything - "our labour, our blood, our very lives".[85]

The sermons of Father Jerzy Popieluszko have also frequently dealt with the question of national sacrifice. For instance, in June 1982 Popieluszko remakably stated: "That which is great and beautiful is born in suffering. Thus, out of the suffering, the pain, the tears and blood of 1970 grew the patriotic awakening of young people, grew Solidarity".[86]

The suffering of the Polish nation was also frequently recalled by the Episcopate of the Polish bishops.[87] Pope John Paul II has also referred to the "historical injustices" which Poland has suffered.

However, the Church's cult of national defeats is not meant to arouse to despair and pessimism. On the contrary, the Church argues that national suffering and defeats will lead Poland to victory. In fact, a victory of the Polish nation would not be possible without pain and defeats. "Victories through defeats - this is a Christian programme of life for human beings and for a nation" - said John Paul II.[88]

Victory advocated by the Church has a moral nature. "We all realize that there is no question of a military victory, as was the case 300 years ago, but of a moral victory" - said the Pope.[89] Nevertheless, a moral victory carries a number of political consequences. It requires the establishment of real moral and social renewal in Poland. Such a moral victory based on a national renewal could simultaneously be a victory of the rulers and the rule. It would be capable of reintegrating and reuniting the entire Polish nation.[90]

The Church also argues that a nation is only fully free when it is able to develop as a community defined by unity of culture and history. In order to function as an actor in history, a nation needs a certain ethical background, a moral course that is to be found in the nation's cultural heritage. This cultural heritage, which contains the essence of morality lies at the root of all kinds of national ties.[91] According to the Church, a nation is a different kind of reality from the state. It differs from the state because "a nation is a communion of souls, it may exist, at least to a certain extent, independently from the territory or without its own state".[92] The task of the state is to work for the good of the nation. A state is truly sovereign if it governs the people and at the same time "serves the people's common good" and if it lets the nation "fulfill its specific destiny, its specific identity".[93] In other words, the state is only really sovereign if it is able to express the sovereignty of its own nation.

The romantic tradition of nationalism is sometimes criticized for its abstract and unrealistic attitude to the national question; an attitude which loses its link with the real, empirical requirements of a national existence, such as, for instance, the requirements of the state's sovereignty of Poland.[94]

The question arises: can this criticism also be applied to the Church's version of romantic nationalism? It seems to me that we can hardly give a positive answer to this question.

The Church indeed cultivates national suffering and patriotic heroism, but it does so in order to keep people's hope alive for a better future and so stimulate them to work for the good of the country. The Church emphasizes the importance of moral rather than political solutions to the Polish crisis, but its call for a moral rebirth of the Polish nation carries concrete practical suggestions in the field of human rights and participatory democracy. The Church speaks about a somewhat enigmatic national spirit and a spiritual destinity of the nation, but at the same time it presents specific conditions for a political renewal in Poland. The Church indeed believes that the nation may exist independently from the state, but this has never resulted in any calls for the abolishment or weakening of the Polish state. The Church has never said anything which could undermine the integrity of the Polish border.

If we go beyond the Church's rhetoric and analyse its actions it is even more difficult to accuse the Church of a lack of realism and romantic deviations. On the contrary and paradoxically, one can argue that the Church's practical actions resemble a positivistic rather than romantic tradition. For instance, in the 1980's the Church created several institutions to support development of a civil society in Poland, including the Primate's Committee on Trade Unions (August 1980), Committees for Help to Internees (December 1981), and the Primate's

Social Council (December 1981). The last of these was responsible for issuing a series of documents for public discussion, including the theses in the "Matter of Social Accord" that suggested a concrete way out of Poland's social and economic difficulties. The Council also formulated the basic framework for the Church's Recovery Programme in aid of private farmers.

Moreover, romantic glorification of Polish historical destiny and of a national spirit of Polish souls did not prevent the Church from doing business with the state authorities and producing a series of "realistic" compromises with the marxist government.

The paradox which emerges from a comparison of the Church's romantic tradition of nationalism expressed in its doctrine and of the practical actions of the Church resembling a positivistic rather than romantic tradition could only be explained against the historical background of post-war developments in Poland. Therefore, in the last section of this essay we will discuss this puzzling question, by pointing to Church's political and ideological relations with the authorities and the opposition in Poland. However, since these relations have already been illustrated by many authors, we will only mention those aspects of these relations which could have some doctrinal relevance.[95]

THE CHURCH IN A MARXIST STATE

After the Second World War the Church had to carry on its mission in a country where the authorities had committed themselves to the promotion of Marxist-Leninist ideology. The Church had to respond to the official materialism of Marxism and this response could not be limited to doctrinal debates. Marxist authorities threatened the very institutional existence of the Church. By the same token doctrinal debates had to be accommodated to the requirements of the Church's institutional development. This did not mean, however, that doctrinal questions were of secondary importance. After all, one of the basic principles of Marxism-Leninism was its militant atheism. Therefore a part of the Church's efforts to secure its institutional existence had to be directed against the materialistic arguments of Marxism.

The Church conducted its struggle against materialism under the slogan of defending human, religious and national hope. The Church's defence of human hope was based on its thesis that a human being represents the most important value. A man is not just a means of production as marxists have claimed. Relations between people have greater value than relations between people and nature. Man cannot be tailored to any abstract collectivist vision based on class antagonism. An individual's conscience should be respected by all social groups, fractions and classes.

The Church's defence of religious hope implied an effort to preserve the rights of individuals' religious beliefs. People cannot be deprived of their spiritual convictions. Believers are not backward blind people as marxists have argued. People should have the right to believe in God and to share their beliefs with others. They should be allowed to conduct their religious practices. Discrimination of religious people should not take place in Poland.

The defence of national hope meant among other things cultivation of pre-marxist national tradition. The Church did not accept the marxist interpretation of Polish history. In particular, it promoted the idea of national independence rather than the marxist idea of international proletarianism. It persisted in recalling the names of famous fighters for Polish national independence, many of whom were committed anti-marxists. It argued that Polish nationalism flourished due to its links with Christianity rather than due to the proletarian revolution.

However, one should see the doctrinal battle between Marxism and Christianity in its proper perspective. Students of philosophy point to many major theoretical controversies between Marxism and the contemporary teachings of the Church.[96] The Church renewed interest in the questions of labour and labour relations, and social liberation only stimulated these controversies. Today, this is especially apparent within the context of political and religious debates in Latin American countries.[97] Nevertheless, in the Polish context theoretical controversy between the marxist and the Christian vision of man and his labour is of academic rather than political significance. After all, the official Marxism-Leninism promoted by the state has been reduced to a few simple principles such as the leading role of the party or the state ownership of major means of production. In other words, Marxism has lost its doctrinal contents. It has become a sort of rhetorical decoration, at least from a doctrinal point of view. (The legitimizing function of Marxism will be dealt with in another essay). In consequence, Polish students of political doctrines have hardly ever resorted to a comparison of marxist and Christian ideas. Rather they have tried to answer the question to what extent the Church's teachings were influenced by political factors existing in a marxist state; factors other than merely communist ideology. In particular, has the institutional survival (or development) of the Church in Poland required doctrinal compromises? Which have priority for the Church - doctrinal or tactical considerations? To what extent are the Church's teachings influenced by developments in Church-State relations?

When in 1945 Cardinal Hlond tried for the first time to specify the Church's attitude toward the new regime, he made it clear that the Church would never compromise its ethical principles with any materialistic ideology.[98] At the same time, Hlond did not identify the Church with any oppositional group and declared the Church's willingness to cooperate with the authorities in, as he put it, "building a system without privileges and injustice".[99]

August Hlond's successors, Cardinals Wyszynski and Glemp have adopted a similar strategy. According to the Polish columnist, Stefan Kisielewski, Glemp and Wyszynski adhered to two basic principles. First, they held the view that communism would remain in Poland for a long time and that the only effective counteraction against sovietization, and its dehumanizing influence on the Polish people, is the existence of religion and of the Church. In order to fulfill their function, religion and the Church must somehow deal and negotiate with the authorities.[100]

Second, the cardinals believed that the Church should not identify with any opposition. It should be a third force, a mediator, which nonetheless loyally adheres to certain general moral principles. For instance, the Church did bless the persecuted, stressing that it sides with those who fight for freedom, but it did not identify with them.

However, political developments in the 1980's presented the Church with almost insoluble dilemmas: How to remain faithful to its doctrinal committments in defending human rights, social peace and justice, without jeopardizing its role as the mediator between the regime and the estranged nation? How to promote truth in an entirely polarized society? How to adhere to doctrinal principles and at the same time promote successive compromises between the parties in conflict? How to promote the idea of liberation of individuals and a whole nation without endangering its own institutional existence which is threatened by the communist regime?

Cardinal Glemp and the bishops again appear to have adopted a sort of dialectical approach. On the one hand, they continued in their outspoken defence of human rights and the rights of the nation. On the other hand, they negotiated with the authorities and kept a distance from certain actions of the opposition. (For instance, Cardinal Glemp's criticism of the TKK call for a general strike in November 1982 is a very good illustration of this policy).

This dialectical approach was crititicized both by the regime and by the opposition. For instance, an oppositional writer, Daniel Warszawski, has stated that the Church's "conciliatory policy" has not brought about the fulfillment of any of society's significant demands, nor even the Church's own, purely religious demands.[101] And another independent writer has asked whether the Church's "policy of appeasement at any price", as he put it, does not only conflict with the basic principle of the Church which is to adopt an unequivocal position but also turns out to be ineffective from a pragmatic point of view.[102]

Controversy around the Church's political behaviour towards the government and the opposition has obviously influenced people's perceptions of the Church's teachings.[103] This essay will not attempt to evaluate these perceptions.[104] Nevertheless, it should be mentioned that the climate of political debate in Poland was often dominated more by controversy about the Church's political strategy than by considerations of the Church's teachings in the field of political ethics.

Many Poles looked to the Church not only for spiritual guidance but also for practical political direction. In the political area the Church resisted attempts to be drawn into a framework of political opposition, while it also resisted being reduced to playing the role of a supporter of the communist regime. In the area of doctrine, however, the Church's position was much less confussing and represented an important source of inspiration for the opposition movement of Solidarity.

NOTES

1. The Programme - "The Self-Governing Commonwealth".

2. See e.g., Marie-Dominique Chenu. La "Doctrine Sociale" de l'Eglise comme Idéologie. Cerf, Paris 1979, especially pp. 87-96.

3. Cardinal Wyszynski. The Deeds of Faith. Harper & Row, New York 1966, p. 73.

4. Jozef Tischner. Polski ksztalt dialogu. Spotkania, Paris 1981, p. 86.

5. George Huntston Williamson. John Paul II's Concepts of Church, State and Society. Journal of Church and State, Autumn 1982, pp. 463-496.

6. I referred briefly to opinions of Catholic laymen in the first essay. For a more extensive elaboration on the post-war evolution of these opinions see: Andrzej Micewski. Wspolrzadzic czy nie klamac? Pax i Znak w Polsce 1945-1976. Libella, Paris 1978, 269 pp.

7. For a list of principles of conservatism see e.g. Russell Kirk. The Conservative Mind. From Burke to Eliot. Gateway Editions, South Bend 1978, pp. 7-10.

8. Jozef Tischner. Op.cit...p. 13.

9. Ireneusz Krzeminski. Solidarnosc - sens ludzkiego doswiadczenia. Aneks no.40, London 1985, pp. 114-115.

10. Ibidem.

11. Alain Tourain, F. Dubet, M. Wieviorka and J. Strzelecki. Analyse d'un mouvement social. Fayard, Paris 1982, pp. 46-48.

12. The Programme - "The Self-Governing Commonwealth".

13. Ibidem.

14. The increasingly pronounced humanistic orientation of the Church's official teachings has already been discernible in numerous statements made by John XXIII and Paul VI. This was confirmed in the resolutions of the Second Vatican Council. Finally, it became the centrepiece of the first encyclical issued by John Paul II under the title "Redemptor Hominis".

15. Jozef Tischner. The Spirit of Solidarity. Harper & Row, New York 1982, pp. 88 and 43.

16. Cardinal Wyszynski. The Deeds of Faith. Op.cit...p. 80.

17. See especially: Jozef Tischner. The Spirit of Solidarity. Op.cit... p. 43.

18. See e.g., John Paul II's sermon to the Polish bishops published in Osservatore Romano no.33, Vatican 1982, p. 6, or Jozef Tischner. Polski ksztalt dialogu. Op.cit...p. 88.

19. Jozef Tischner. Myslenie o etosie spolecznym, Znak no.3, Crakow 1980, p. 291.

20. Cardinal Karol Wojtyla's sermon in December 1977, quoted in: George Blazynski. Pope John Paul II. Dell Publ., New York 1979, p. 135.

21. Cardinal Karol Wojtyla's sermon in June 1978, quoted in: Spotkania no.6, Lublin 1979, p. 238.

22. Jozef Tischner. The Spirit of Solidarity. Op.cit...p. 10.

23. Jerzy Popieluszko quoted in Radio Free Europe Research, Munich, 27 November 1984, p. 2.

24. Cardinal Karol Wojtyla's sermon in June 1977, quoted in: George Blazynski. Op.cit...p. 140.

25. Cardinal Stefan Wyszynski's sermon in April 1964, published in: Cardinal Wyszynski. The Deeds of Faith. Op.cit...p. 77.

26. Pope Paul VI's sermon on 21 January 1976 quoted by John Paul II on 20 June 1983, published in: Znak no.11-12, Crakow 1983, p. 1791. According to the Church, social love has several major dimensions. Human rights represent the first dimension of social love. The second dimension of social love is family. The third – the nation. The world of labour relations should also be based on the principle of love.

27. Cardinal Jozef Glemp's sermon on 10 January 1982, quoted in: Radio Free Europe Research, Munich, 10 February 1982, p. 8.

28. See especially: John Paul II's statement at the International Labour Organization, on 15 June 1982, published in Osservatore Romano no.31-32, Vatican 1982, p. 5.

29. The Communique issued by the 172nd Plenary Conference of the Polish Episcopate, quoted in Radio Free Europe Research, Munich, 10 March 1980, p. 6.

30. Jozef Tischner. The Time of Rooting. A sermon delivered in Gdansk on 27 September 1981, during the First Congress of Solidarity, published in: Jozef Tischner. The Spirit of Solidarity. Op.cit...p. 103.

31. Cardinal Karol Wojtyla's sermon in December 1977, quoted in: George Blazynski. Op.cit...p. 138.

32. Cardinal Karol Wojtyla's sermon on June 1977, quoted in Spotkania no.6, Lublin 1979, pp. 229-230.

33. Ibidem.

34. See Cardinal Wyszynski's sermon on 26 August 1963, published in: Cardinal Wyszynski. The Deeds of Faith. Op.cit...pp. 3-9.

35. See e.g., Listy Pasterskie Episkopatu Polski. 1945-1974. Editions du Dialogue. Paris 1975, e.g. pp. 205-206, or 355-358.

36. Listy Pasterskie Episkopatu Polski. Op.cit...pp. 614-616.

37. The Polish Episcopate's letter to the authorities issued on 16 July 1976, quoted in: Dissent in Poland. Reports and Documents in Translation. Association of Polish Students and Graduates in Exile. London 1978, p. 151. It should be mentioned that in 1976 the Church also appealed to the workers to end the strikes in the interest of Poland's raison d'etat emerging from the Soviet threat. A similar call for an end to the workers' strikes was repeated by Cardinal Wyszynski in the Summer of 1980. According to many observers these facts manifest the Church's inclination to play a mediating role between the government and the opposition in all difficult periods of Polish history. The reasons for this mediating attitude are briefly presented in the end of this essay.

38. A pastoral letter issued on 24 April 1977, quoted in: Dissent in Poland. Reports and Documents in Translation. Op.cit...p. 163.

39. Cardinal Karol Wojtyla's sermon quoted in: George Blazynski. Op.cit...p. 141.

40. As quoted by Radio Free Europe Research, Munich, 19 February 1982, p. 3.

41. Ibidem, p. 4.

42. As quoted by Radio Free Europe Research, Munich, 6 October 1982, p. 11.

43. Jerzy Popieluszko quoted in: Poland Watch no.5, Washington D.C. 1984, pp. 17-18.

44. See Ernst-Wolfgan Böckenförde. Nowy sposob zaangazowania Kosciola. O "teologii politycznej" Jana Pawla II. Znak no.3, Crakow 1985, pp. 6-7.

45. See especially: John Paul II's sermon delivered on 20 June 1983 in Katowice, published in: Znak no.8-9, Crakow 1983, pp. 1788-1791.

46. John Paul's speech at the ILO, published in Osservatore Romano no.31-32, Vatican 1982, p. 4.

47. Here see especially: the Encyclical Laborem Exercens, e.g. published in: Znak no.7-9, Crakow 1982, p. 1153.

48. John Paul II's statement delivered to workers of Sao Paulo, Brazil, on 3 July 1980, quoted in: Znak no.11-12, Crakow 1983, p. 1908.

49. John Paul II's statement delivered at the ILO. Op.cit...p. 5.

50. Laborem Exercens. Op.cit...p. 1155.

51. Jozef Tischner. The Spirit of Solidarity. Op.cit...p. 13.

52. Jozef Tischner. Op.cit...p. 81.

53. Laborem Exercens. Op.cit...p. 1157.

54. Senseless work may have several variants: the most common is wasted work. People work in vain. Either their work is fruitless – the fruits of the work are too small to sustain and develop life – or there is no need for the work being performed.

55. Jozef Tischner. Op.cit...p. 81.

56. Ibidem, p. 82.

57. Ibidem, p. 83.

58. See e.g., Laborem Exercens. Op.cit...pp. 1136-1138.

59. For instance, Jacques Ellul believes that it transformed the so-called "sociological Christians", linked with the Church via merely participation in Christian customs and rites, into "believing Christians", committed to the Church because of certain ideas carried on by the Church. See: Jacques Ellul. Lech Walesa et le role du Christianisme. Esprit, March 1982, pp. 40-47.

60. Adam Michnik. Letter From the Gdansk Prison. The New York Review of Books. 18 July 1985, p. 46.

61. See e.g., Bohdan Cywinski. Rodowody Niepokornych. Editions Spotkania. Paris 1985, pp. 279-301; or Christopher Cvicc. The Church, in: Abracham Brumberg, (ed.). Poland: Genesis of a Revolution. Random House, New York 1983, pp. 92-92.

62. The Church's attitude toward the Jewish minority in Poland is one of the most controversial questions. See e.g. Adam Michnik. The Church, Left, Dialogue: in: Communism in Eastern Europe. Karz-Cohl Publ., New York 1979, pp. 76-78.

63. Hans Kohn in: International Encyclopedia of the Social Sciences. David C. Sills, (ed.). vol.II. The Macmillan Company & The Free Press, New York. 1968, pp. 65-66.

64. See e.g., Bronislaw Wildstein. Jakiej prawicy Polacy nie potrzebuja. Kontakt no.2, Paris 1986, pp. 3-11.

65. See e.g., Jan Jozef Lipski. KOR. Aneks, London 1983, p. 306.

66. In the Polish language, the term "nationalism" has usually pejorative connotations which suggest identification with the "closed" strain of nationalism. To describe positive aspects of a national question (the "open" strain of nationalism) the Poles use the term "patriotism". See: Jakub Karpinski. Slownik. Polska. Komunizm. Opozycja. Polonia, London 1985, p. 152.

67. John Paul II's sermon in Warsaw on 2 June 1979, published in: The Pope in Poland. Radio Free Europe Research, Munich 1979, p. 69.

68. Jozef Tischner. Polska jest Ojczyzna. Dialog, Paris 1985, p. 108.

69. John Paul II's sermon at Cracow Balice Airport, 23 June 1983, published in: Radio Free Europe Research, Munich, 10 June 1983, p. 14.

70. John Paul II's statement in Warsaw, 17 June 1983, published in: Znak no. 11-12. Op.cit...p. 1689.

71. John Paul II's tv address to the Poles on 24 December 1980, published in: Osservatore Romano no.10, Vatican 1980, p. 1.

72. John Paul II's statement delivered in Nairobi, Kenya, 6 May 1980, published in: Osservatore Romano no.6, Vatican 1980, pp. 14-15.

73. John Paul II's sermon in Oswiecim-Brzezinka, 7 June 1979, published in: The Pope in Poland. Op.cit...p. 69.

74. John Paul II's address to the 169th Episcopal Conference of Polish Bishops, Czestochowa, 6 June 1979, published in: The Pope in Poland. Op.cit...p. 78.

75. See e.g., the Pope's sermon in Cracow on 10 June 1979, published in: The Pope in Poland. Op.cit...p. 69.

76. See e.g., Hans Kohn. International Encyclopedia of the Social Sciences. Op.cit...p. 66.

77. See especially: Andrzej Walicki. Philosophy and Romantic Nationalism: the Case of Poland. Clarendon Press, Oxford 1982.

78. J.L. Talmon. Political Messianism. The Romantic Phase. Secker & Warburg, London 1960, p. 268. See also: Andrzej Walicki. Filozofia a Mesjanizm. PIW, Warsaw 1970, especially pp. 46-52.

79. This was argued already in the 1970's. See e.g. Andrzej Micewski. Tradycje historyczne a nasladownictwo. Res Publica no.3, London 1979, pp. 49-51.

80. John Paul II's sermon in Gniezno, 3 June 1979, published in: The Pope in Poland. Op.cit...p. 73.

81. See e.g,. John Paul II's sermon in Jasna Gora, 19 June 1983, published in: Znak no.11-12, Crakow 1983, pp. 1745-1770.

82. Jozef Tischner. The Spirit of Solidarity. Op.cit...p. 87 as well as Jozef Tischner. Polska jest ojczyzna. Op.cit...pp. 107-113.

83. See e.g., John Paul II's sermon in Warsaw, 16-17 June 1983, published in: Znak no.11-12, Op.cit...p. 1677 or his sermon in Warsaw on 2 June 1979, published in: The Pope in Poland. Op.cit...p. 73.

84. Cardinal Wyszynski. The Deeds of Faith. Op.cit...p. 92.

85. Ibidem, p. 75.

86. Radio Free Europe Research, Munich, 27 November 1984, p. 1.

87. See especially: the bishops' letter to "German brothers", 18 November 1965, published in: Listy Pasterskie Episkopatu Polski. Op.cit...pp. 833-834.

88. John Paul II's sermon in Warsaw, 16-17 June 1983, published in: Znak no.11-12. Op.cit...p. 1704.

89. Ibidem, p. 1705.

90. See e.g., Polish bishops' Pastoral Letter of 29 August 1982, quoted in: Radio Free Europe Research, Munich, 30 June 1983, p. 6.

91. See: Bogdan Szajkowski. The Catholic Church in Defense of Civil Society in Poland, in: Bronislaw Misztal, (ed.). Poland After Solidarity. Op.cit...p. 75.

92. S. Jarocki. Katolicka Nauka Spoleczna. Sociêtê d'Editions Internationales, Paris 1966, p. 387.

93. John Paul II's sermon in Jasna Gora, 19 June 1983, in: Znak no.11-12. Op.cit...p. 1745.

94. See e.g., Andrzej Walicki. Tradycje polskiego patriotyzmu. Aneks no.40, London 1985, p. 63.

95. For a detailed analysis of this problem see especially: Krzysztof Pomian. Religione e politica in Polonia, in: G.Ruggieri, (ed.). Una nuova pace constatiniana. Casale, Monferrato 1985, pp. 114-168 or Krzysztof Pomian. Religion et politique en Pologne. Vingtiême Siêcle. Avril-Juin 1986, pp. 83-101, or Bogdan Szajkowski. Next to God.... Poland: Politics and Religion in Contemporary Poland. Frances Pinter, London 1983.

96. See e.g., Jozef Tischner. Polski ksztalt dialogu. Op.cit...pp. 87-103.

97. See e.g., Michael Novak. Will it Liberate? Questions About Liberation Theology. Paulist Press, New York 1986, 311 pp., or Daniel H. Levine. Churches and Politics in Latin America. Sage, London 1979, 288 pp.

98. Cardinal August Hlond's sermon in Poznan, 28 October 1945, published in: Listy Pasterskie Episkopatu Polski. Op.cit...pp. 11-15.

99. Ibidem, p. 15.

100. Stefan Kisielewski quoted by Maya Litynski. The Church: Between State and Society. Poland Watch no.5, Washington D.C. 1984, p. 22.

101. Daniel Warszawski. Cena koncesji. KOS no.50, Warsaw 1984, p. 4.

102. An anonymous article published in Tygodnik Wojenny, Warsaw 1984, p. 3.

103. For instance, Lech Walesa and many other leaders of Solidarity repeatedly expressed their understanding, if not full support for the Church's actions vis-à-vis the government and the opposition. See e.g. Lech Walesa. De weg van de hoop. Autobiografie. Spectrum, Utrecht 1987, pp. 157-159 or pp. 297-303. Walesa's autobiography was first published in French by Fayard, Paris 1987.

104. A detailed evaluation of this problem would require sociological analyses based on concrete empirical data which are so far not available.

III Towards the self-governing commonwealth

In this essay we will analyse Solidarity's vision of state and society. In normative terms this vision expressed deep-rooted, anti-state sentiments and promoted grassroot self-organization of citizens. It cultivated a view about the autonomy and dignity of the individual as well as a natural human rights concept. It opposed the politicization of public life and carried ethical rather than political messages. It expressed doubts about the revolutionary pattern of change and promoted gradualism as well as evolutionism. It was against any sort of terror or use of force and adhered strictly to the principles of nonviolence.

In institutional terms, this vision stimulated the creation of grassroot social organization among various social classes and professions. This was to be achieved through the development of a system of self-management and local self-government. The far reaching vision of a "self-governing commonwealth" became the original expression of a new way of organization for the Polish nation.

In the first two essays we identified two major doctrinal sources of Solidarity's vision of state and society. There could be no doubt that the concept of social self-organization promoted by the KOR in the late

1970's was crucial in shaping the Polish protest movement of Summer 1980. This idea inspired the programme of the independent trade union and influenced the pattern of popular resistance against the repression of martial law.

The teaching of the Catholic Church in Poland represented another major source of doctrinal inspiration for Solidarity activists. Students of Polish history point to many other different groups and political orientations which also influenced the doctrinal creed of Solidarity, such as the ROPCiO (Movement for the Defence of Civil and Citizen's Rights), the Clubs of Catholic Intelligentsia, the DiP (Experience and Future), Young Poland and many others.

In this essay, the important question of the political and social roots of Solidarity doctrine will not be elaborated any further. (They have already been discussed elsewhere.)[1] Below we will concentrate on Solidarity's doctrine, regardless of its historical and political context. We will notice, however, that all major features of this doctrine, such as anti-statism, self-organization or nonviolence, were already present in works of independent authors in the 1970's. After August 1980 these ideas were echoed and further developed in works and public statements of Solidarity activists and their supporters. The programme of Solidarity adopted in the Autumn of 1981 represents the official endorsement of the union's doctrinal creed. The study of Solidarity's documents after December 1981 indicates that this doctrinal creed was neither greatly modified nor abandoned due to repression under martial law.

In this essay we will not only point to major elements of Solidarity's vision of state and society. Parallels between Solidarity's doctrine and various historical currents in political philosophy will also be looked at. Finally, there will be a brief discussion of some dilemmas which emerge from Solidarity's doctrinal creed.

ANTI-STATISM AND THE IDEA OF SOCIAL SELF-ORGANIZATION

The idea of social self-organization represents one of the most important elements of Solidarity's doctrine. Already in the 1970's the main weakness of all historical dissent within the communist bloc, was that nearly all forms of protest were addressed to the ruling totalitarian elite in the respective communist states. According to Michnik this should be reversed. Opposition should tell society how to

72

act rather than try to persuade the government to improve itself. "As far as the government is concerned it can have no clearer counsel than that provided by the social pressure from below" - said Michnik.[2]

Michnik's views were supported by Jacek Kuron, who said that "the expropriation of the citizen from organization", and in consequence, "a social atomization and decomposition of social links" constitutes the main attribute of all sorts of totalitarianism.[3] |According to Kuron, then, all efforts towards democracy should be based on social self-organization and lead to the creation of self-government independent from the state. |

| Successful implementation of this idea in the late 1970's led to the creation of independent trade unions and various social and professional associations in Poland./ It stimulated grassroot cultural, educational and press activity which operated beyond direct governmental supervision.) Having emerged in this way Solidarity adopted social self-organization as its principle idea. |"We are aiming at strong reforms of the structure of the state and at the establishment of independent institutions in every area of social life" - said the first official programme of Solidarity which was entitled "The Self-Governing Commonwealth".[4]

ʃThe programme emphasized the special importance of all grassroot organizations and their initiatives. It made it clear that Solidarity was particularly interested in the idea of workers' self-management. Enterprises were to be ruled by workers' councils elected in a democratic way. These workers' councils would elect the directors of firms and would play a crucial role in the industrial decision-making process.ʃ

|This idea of socialization of the whole system of management and production was followed by proposals to introduce a system of territorial and local self-government. The new territorial self-governing bodies would be legally, organizationally and financially self-reliant, thus being the authentic voice of local communities.|

In fact, the intention was for the self-governing system to be introduced into nearly every area of social life. In 1981 there was especially much public discussion concerning a self-governing organization for science, education and culture. "We have to stop the central and bureaucratic management of Polish science... universities should become independent, self-governing communities" - argued Maciej Ilowiecki for instance.[5]

The independent trade union Solidarity was to be the main

guardian and stimulator of all these inititiatives. Moreover, some newly created organizations committed themselves in particular to promotion of the idea of social self-organization in the form of self-management and self-government. These were the "Clubs of the Self-Governing Commonwealth" (led by KOR members), and the Polish Labour Party (led by the network of Solidarity organizations in leading factories, the "Siec"). For instance, the 1981 provisional constitution of the PPP (the Polish Labour Party) said explicitly:

"the new socio-economic system of Poland should be based on self-government, that is on the self-organization of society into various collectives, groups and unions which independently can realize their own goals. The sum of all these activities creates the contents of the activity of the whole society".[6]

In this light Solidarity's inititiatives aimed at the improvement of the system of parliamentary democracy in Poland (e.g. the proposal to establish a second chamber in the Sejm, the so-called socio-economic chamber) were apparently of secondary importance, at least from a doctrinal point of view. In fact, Solidarity activists rarely pointed at the difference (if not contradiction) between their vision of self-governing republic (commonwealth) and traditional systems of parliamentary democracy.[7]

The introduction of military rule in December 1981 opened a new dramatic chapter in the realization of the concept of social self-organization. In 1982 the first comprehensive programme of Solidarity's underground leadership (the TKK) confirmed that the aim of the union was still the same, namely: "building a self-governing society".[8] However, under the new circumstances it would be carried on through underground activity which "would reduce people's feeling of loneliness, teach them collective action and strengthen their conviction that only through self-organization and grassroot inititiative can they achieve their goals".

According to the programme, the underground decentralized movement should in the first instance:
(a) organize various sorts of aid and self-assistance;
(b) organize an independent teaching and self-educational network;
(c) promote independent teaching and self-educational activities;
(d) organize actions manifesting the existence of popular social resistance;
(e) promote various sorts of independent economic activity through

the system of cooperatives and production workshops.[9]

According to Zbigniew Bujak, one of the authors of this programme, individual groups and social circles must build a mechanism of resistance against the monopolistic activities of the government in various spheres of life. Through the existence of a mass organization like Solidarity, and through the activities of independent peasants', craftsmen's, and students' unions, this resistance might become so widespread as to create the possibility of evolving an independent structure of social life.[10] "Such a movement" - said another Solidarity leader, Wiktor Kulerski - "should lead to a situation where the authorities control empty shops but not the market, workers' employment but not their livelihood, state-owned mass media but not the circulation of information, printing houses but not publishing, the post and telephones but not communication, the schools but not education".[11] Kulerski believes that this kind of social independence could in due time lead to a situation where the rulers would control only the police and a handful of sworn collaborators.

These voices from the underground lead us to the next feature of Solidarity's doctrine, namely, anti-statism. "We are united in our protest against the state which treats citizens like its property" - stated Solidarity's programme "The Self-Governing Commonwealth". In 1981 Solidarity delegates to the First National Congress of the Union expressed their conviction that the state should serve man and not dominate him, state organizations should serve society and should not be identified with a single political party, the state should work for the common good of the whole nation, etc.[12]

Anti-state sentiments had been promoted by KOR's leaders as early as in the 1970's, and were primarily concerned with the communist form of state domination. This, however, implied some more general choices. For instance, Jacek Kuron openly declared that the state is always isolated from society and uses its power of compulsion against society. In his view, dreams of abolishing the state arose from social radicalism and represented efforts to apply the principle of the Gospel to the whole area of human life.[13]

In their 1981 declaration "the Clubs of the Self-Governing Commonwealth" echoed all these anti-state feelings and set out the limits for possible state intervention in public life. The declaration claimed that the state may interfere in society only in order to realize

75

basic social goals but all its activity should be under public control. "State power should be limited as far as possible by society which in turn should be organized into workers' self-management, various associations and its federations" - the declaration stated.[14] State property should be seen as public property directed by local self-government and various associations.

Anti-state sentiments were also shared by many other groups within Solidarity. For instance, during the Congress of Polish Culture, in December 1981, Andrzej Kijowski, a famous writer, said: "What Polish writers can say about their success during the last 35 years, is that the sole receiver of their creation was the state machine... it is time to replace this state receiver by a social one".[15] And several months earlier Wojciech Sadurski, a Solidarity activist at Warsaw University, argued in the governmental weekly that all sorts of statism are incompatible with self-government:

> "slogans advocating a steady growth of the state, ultimately leading to... a dying away of this state, or slogans about the re-transformation of the state into the popular self-government are primitive verbal tricks... the reality is that the more self-governing the regulation, the more limited are the functions of the state apparatus".[16]

The above arguments were especially relevant after the ·introduction of military rule in Poland. The authorities began to promote a communist version of statism. The role of the Party and its ideology was reduced. The old doctrinal vision of the dictatorship of the proletariat was softened. The state, supported by the Army was supposed to play the new role of absolute arbiter within society.[17] Not surprisingly then, in 1983 the underground Solidarity leaders declared that "breaking the state monopoly" was to be the first task of their resistance struggle.[18]

OTHER FEATURES OF SOLIDARITY'S EVOLUTIONISM

The next important feature of Solidarity's doctrine was its particular concern about the autonomy and dignity of the individual. According to Solidarity's programme of 1981, "Dignity and respect for human beings" form the basis of the union's existence.[19]

Solidarity activists argued that while state totalitarism restricts the autonomy of individuals, the system based on self-government paves the way for spontaneous and voluntary association of the individuals in various economic, cultural or educational collectives. Social self-organization in the form of self-management and self-government permits breaking what Adam Michnik called "the psychology of slaves" in societies ruled by autocratic regimes.[20] It allows individuals to regain their freedom of action and autonomy.

Under no circumstances can man be deprived of his natural rights. Jan Jozef Lipski used to quote the Polish Primate, Cardinal Stefan Wyszynski, who insisted that even a drunkard lying unconscious under the fence cannot be deprived of his civil and human rights; because he is a man.[21]

(According to Solidarity advocates, the communist state tried to deprive people of their personal dignity, and workers of the dignity of their work.) This system denied the people their basic human and economic rights. It tried to impose the arbitrary power of the state and the party apparatus over the aspirations and beliefs of all members of society. "We started our struggle" - says Solidarity's programme of 1981 - "for justice, democracy, truth, rule of law, human dignity, freedom of opinion, reparation of Poland and not only for bread, butter and sausage ... power of some groups over others cannot be accepted... and therefore we aim at building a self-governing Poland".[22]

These principles were re-stated by the underground leadership after the military takeover. In 1983 the TKK committed itself to a struggle for "the simplest and most basic human, social and national rights, and for the right to truth, dignity and hope".[23]

This belief in the autonomy and dignity of the individuals is closely associated with strong ethical elements in Solidarity's doctrine. Solidarity described itself as the "moral movement for national regeneration". [24] As Jadwiga Staniszkis, a Warsaw sociologist, has put it, the Union accepted moral values as a rationale for its operation; it had the character of a "moral crusade".[25] In 1981 Solidarity's programme explained that under Polish systemic conditions, economic protest would simultaneously be a social one, and a social protest would at the same time be a moral one.[26]

Moral arguments were important within the political opposition in Poland already in the 1970's. Jan Jozef Lipski reported that the original idea of KOR's founders was to appeal to ethical values rather than to political attitudes.[27] Of course, KOR members were aware that people acting against totalitarianism would be considered by the communist authorities as political activists. (Since the communist authorities aspire to the control of all areas of social life, it follows that all sorts of public activity is political by definition.) However, KOR's aim was to overcome people's fear and stimulate social solidarity. Consequently, KOR chose the area of ethics as its field of battle with the system.[28] It committed itself to help those persecuted by the system. In this light, Jacek Kuron could say that "KOR was far more apolitical than one might imagine",[29] and that Solidarity should carry out a moral revolution rather than a political one.[30]

It was these moral arguments which influenced Solidarity's attitude towards the means of social change.[31] Solidarity always opted for evolutionary rather than revolutionary means of social transformation and it disassociated itself from all acts of violence.

According to Adam Michnik, the dilemma of the Left in the nineteenth century - reform or revolution - is not a dilemma for the Polish opposition. To consider the possibility of revolution overthrowing the dictatorship of the Party, or to organize attempts towards that end, would be as unrealistic as it would be dangerous.[32]

Leszek Kolakowski has described revolution as a "beautiful illness" and argues that belief in total liberation will always lead towards the introduction of totalitarian revolutionary power and, consequently, to the abolition of the democratic and cultural heritage of a civilization.[33]

"The poverty of revolution consists of its reluctance to anticipate any event" - said Leszek Nowak, Solidarity activist at Poznan University.[34]

Solidarity therefore advocates a movement which presses for evolutionary changes in the system, even though its members often described the social changes caused by workers' protest as being revolutionary. Lech Walesa, in his Nobel Prize speech expressed this conviction clearly enough. "My deepest hope is that Poland will regain its historical chance for a peaceful evolution" - he said.[35] And the underground Solidarity leaders stated that their programme is based on the assumption that "far reaching economic, political and social reforms are needed" in Poland and that the situation "makes it necessary for these reforms to be introduced gradually".[36]

Solidarity's refusal to resort to violence constitutes the last doctrinal element which will be elaborated in this essay. In the 1970's it was KOR who promoted the slogan "instead of putting the Party's committees into the fire, organize your own committees".[37] As Jan Jozef Lipski put it: "The iron principle of KOR was its refusal to use compulsion... KOR members were also aware that hatred is self-destructive and should thus be denied".[38] In fact, KOR considered the creation of an independent opposition movement as the way to avoid violent social explosion in Poland.[39]

The form of protest chosen in Summer 1980, the occupational strike, was clearly aimed at avoiding violence. Later, Solidarity leaders repeatedly disassociated themselves from the use of violence.[40]

Solidarity's commitment to nonviolence became even more apparent when union activists were met with violence after December 1981. Time and again various statements by Solidarity leaders advocated nonviolent forms of resistance and condemned the use of violence. According to Lech Walesa, the lesson learned from the experience of the post-war social upheavals in Poland was that Solidarity would be able to resist violence only when it did not use violence itself.[41] Zbigniew Bujak expressed this idea in a similar way:

"the basic principle of Solidarity, and still valid [June 1982 - J.Z.]. is the use of exclusively peaceful means in its activity. Contrary to the slanders against Solidarity, the union never made any preparations to use force and does not wish to use force. We are against any acts of violence, street battles, hit-squads, acts of terror, armed organizations ...".[42]

The strongest weapon of Solidarity's resistance strategy was supposed to be a peaceful general strike, unlimited if necessary.[43] A direct violent confrontation with the authorities has always been ruled out by Solidarity strategists on moral, tactical and doctrinal grounds.[44]

DOCTRINAL PARALLELS

When a Western observer looks for parallels between the ideas promoted by Solidarity and the views of the men he can call its "precursors", he will certainly direct his attention to trends in social philosophy, such as those presented by Robert Nozick in his book "Anarchy, State and Utopia".[45] This trend strongly advocates a minimal state limited to the narrow functions of protection against force, theft, fraud, enforcement of contracts, and so on. Nozick argues that a more extensive state will violate the right of people not to be forced to do certain things, and is thus unjustified. In my opinion, however, it is a mistake to identify Solidarity's doctrine with the ideas which are promoted by Nozick.[46] Nozick's arguments, i.e. that a "minimal state is inspiring as well as right", emerge from a purely individualistic approach, while Solidarity's anti-state arguments have rather a collectivist nature.[47] It would therefore be better to include Solidarity into the trend which Rodney Backer recently called "the anti-state collectivism".[48] This is not only because these new Polish ideas are more comparable to Peter Kropotkin's idea of "mutual aid" than to Max Stirner's idea of a "union of egoists" (as is indicated even by the name of the movement - Solidarity). It is mainly because Solidarity, although calling for the replacement of the authoritarian state by certain forms of nongovernmental cooperation between individuals, considered these forms as collectivist by nature.

Here we recognize the ideas of David Owen, Charles Fourier and Pierre Proudhon. All three writers, as do Solidarity activists, put special emphasis on cooperation and association rather than competition and individual egoism. All three writers were opposed to the idea of omnipotent power of the state and promoted grassroot cooperation of voluntary collectives which could lead to the creation of the sort of self-governing commonwealth promoted by Solidarity. All three writers rejected revolutionary violence and emphasized the importance of moral rather than political values; something which is also characteristic for Solidarity's way of thinking.

Proudhon, for instance, argued against "revolutionary action as a means of social reform", because that would simply be "an appeal to force, to arbitrariness, in brief, a contradiction".[49] In Proudhon's view, it is possible to achieve a peaceful transformation of society by creating of a network of independent craftsmen and peasants, and of associations of workers.

The writing of another anti-state collectivist, Peter Kropotkin, and especially his vision of local communes and the idea of "mutual agreement" between the members of a society, also resemble Solidarity's doctrine. Kropotkin argued, as do many Solidarity activists, that in the place of the separate institutions of the state, there could be a form of direct, occasional politics, communal self-management in small units which in the early phases of transformation would emerge through a mixture of encroaching control and independent alternative organization. Kropotkin believed that society, unlike government, is a natural phenomenon. And in a spirit similar to the one present within Solidarity, Kropotkin stated that people should establish voluntary collaboration and exert "moral pressure" on the government. "To sweep away that collaboration and to trust to the genius of party dictators is" – according to Kropotkin – "to destroy all the independent nuclei, such as trade unions and the local distributive cooperative organizations, turning them into the bureaucratic organs of the party".[50]

Leo Tolstoy should also be mentioned when we look for historical parallels to Solidarity's doctrine. In fact, Tolstoy and Kropotkin held many views in common. As Thornton Anderson observed, they both shared inordinate confidence in men and their cooperation, but perhaps too little in men who held power. They wanted to build their societies from the bottom, from the individual and the commune, and not from the top with a revolutionary government. They were vehemently opposed to coercion, exploitation, and inequality in both the political and the economic realms. Finally, both Tolstoy and Kropotkin had a sensitive social conscience and high moral ideas, they were strongly individualistic, yet they subordinated individualism to the solidarity of the group.[51] All these features of Kropotkin and Tolstoi were manifested in Solidarity's way of thinking.

The works of Tolstoy are also relevant because of his strong emphasis on nonviolence as a means of social change. In Tolstoi's view, "attempts to abolish violence by violence neither have in the past nor, evidently, can in the future emancipate people from violence nor, consequently, from slavery".[52]

Tolstoy, in common with Thoreau, Gandhi and Michnik, Bujak or Walesa, argued that gradual reforms depend upon individual withdrawal of support from existing governments. Rejection of violence and the acceptance of brotherhood and of productive labour represent, according to Tolstoy, key elements of the required new social order.

Solidarity's doctrine also resembles the ideas promoted by another influential group of anti-state collectivists, namely the nineteenth century syndicalists. For instance, French delegates to the First International in the 1860's promoted the view that social change should be achieved through economic or industrial action rather than through any political revolution. They put special emphasis on the revolutionary trade union, both as an organ of struggle and as a foundation on which the future free society might be constructed. These French syndicalists also accepted the idea of a general strike as a weapon which, on the one hand, allows for fundamental social change and, on the other hand, does not compromise the pacifist ideal by using violent means.

In the area of industrial relations we can also see the parallel between Solidarity's concept of self-mangement and the British theory of guild socialism. G.D.H. Cole and other guild socialists argued that the control of each industry should be left to democratically organized, decentralized guilds, while the state should merely own the property that the guilds will use.[53]

Guild socialists, like the leaders of Solidarity, promoted the idea of a pluralistic rather than monistic sovereign nation and argued that associations do not derive their life from the state. They both further maintained that human personality is likely to develop most freely in a society where voluntary associations are encouraged and direct state administration is peripheral. In their view, if socialism were to be domocratic, it must devolve as much authority as possible on nonstate or local government groups. According to both guild socialists and Solidarity members, this would limit the tendency for centralized state bureaucracy to dominate and control industry for its own ends and would also curtail the rigidity of thinking and action characteristic for all central bureaucracies.[54]

Followers of guild socialism in the early XXth century, Harol Lasky and Sidney and Beatrice Webb, proposed that the national legislative body be split into two - a social-economic parliament and a political parliament. A similar idea was voiced by Solidarity in 1981.

It is also characteristic that in going beyond these original socialist roots we can more easily find some parallels to the thoughts of conservative collectivists, like D.H. Lawrence or G.K. Chesterton than to the pure individualistic trends of liberals or neoliberals (such as von Mises, Hayek or Friedman). Chesterton, for instance, considered the state and its government, at best as a necessary evil which rested on force, and which corrupted rather than cured. Chesterton was probably not hostile to the state to the extent that many socialist anti-state collectivists were, but like them he was attracted to something other than the state. He believed in popular instincts and in public collective action as their most accurate expression. In his view, the crowd expresses the quality of the nation in a direct way, cutting through the compromises, distortion and clear "speakeasy" of conventional politics.[55] This way of thinking was clearly present within Solidarity.

An anti-state collectivist family of this kind, divided and diverse as it is, shares a common approach to the basic social questions. For instance, all these doctrinal trends emphasize the special role of social and economic relations as the principal field in which organization is necessary. Some distrust all cooperation beyond the barest minimum necessary for an ascetic lifestyle while others envisage an extensive network of interconnecting mutual aid institutions. But they all share the view that economic and social relations should dominate political ones. Some have called themselves apolitical or even anti-political.

All these trends share a naturalistic view of society. They believe that man is naturally social and that he naturally has all the attributes which enable him to live in freedom and in social harmony. Their emphasis on the natural origin of societies leads them to reject not only Rousseau's idea of a social contract, but also the authoritarian communism of Marx with its emphasis on dictatorship of the proletariat to impose equality by external force.

All of these trends contain deeply moralistic elements. They see progress not in terms of a steady increase in material wealth and complexity of living, but rather in terms of the moralization of society.

Peter Kropotkin recognizes two main doctrinal currents.[56] The first tendency, based on "mutual aid", is exemplified in tribal customs, village communities, medieval guilds, where all institutions are developed and worked out, not by legislation, but by the creative spirit of the masses. The second is the authoritarian current beginning with magi, shamans, wizards, rain-makers, oracles and priests and continuing to include the records of laws and the "chiefs of military bands". Solidarity is easily seen as belonging to the first current.

Although these parallels sound very convincing, they, nevertheless, were not clearly recognized by Solidarity itself. Members of KOR and other groups within Solidarity traced their doctrinal ancestry almost exclusively to the Polish historical background. Moreover, when we study relevant official documents, the picture is rather confusing. Solidarity recognized its ancestry only in a general way, pointing to Christian ethics, a national Polish tradition as well as to the industrial and democratic traditions of working people.[57]

The "Clubs for Independence" (KSN - established on 24 September 1981) identified themselves with the national-democratic right-wing tradition led in the first decades of this century by Roman Dmowski.[58] The Polish Labour Party, on the contrary, identified itself with the left-wing pre-war tradition represented especially by the Polish Socialist Party, PPS.[59]

The Clubs of the Self-Governing Commonwealth acknowledged four men as their doctrinal fathers - Jozef Pilsudski, Wincenty Witos, Ignacy Daszynski and Edward Abramowski.[60] Since these four men had always been considered as one another's political and doctrinal enemies, the statement of the Clubs led to a certain amount of confusion.

This lack of clarity emerges primarily from the specific Polish context of any historical, as well as of the current doctrinal, debates which always had to simultaneously address two crucial issues. Namely: (a) a socio-economic model of the state and society; and (b) a model of national independence. As Antoni Maciarewicz explained, the discussion inside KOR was about the "attitude towards the tradition of Polish independence, the tradition of socialism and marxism in Poland, the origins of Polish communism and its development".[61] A similar situation existed in Solidarity itself. And in this context, contradictions and debates arose from questions of tactics and methods of action rather than from basic ideological problems.[62]

However, despite all these difficulties it is easy to indicate the particular popularity of some theories among the Solidarity rank and file. And, although it would be difficult (if not wrong) to identify Solidarity's ancestry with any single doctrinal historical current, we can safely point to the remarkable popularity of the theory of Edward Abramowski.

Edward Abramowski (1868-1918), a well known Polish social-anarchist who was also involved in the struggle for Polish national independence, is a typical representative of the above discussed anti-state collectivism.[63] Abramowski's criticism of "bureaucratic revolutions" (carried out by, for instance, Lenin's "professional revolutionaries"), his attack on all sorts of statism and his promotion of various sorts of grassroot social self-organization, greatly influenced Solidarity members.

"After 35 years of state socialism in Poland the answer to many contemporary questions can be found in Abramowski's ideas" - declared Jacek Kuron.[64] Kuron in particular identifies himself with Abramowski's view about the unity of moral, ideological and socio-economic transformations of society.

Adam Michnik, referring to differences between the opinions of Rosa Luxemburg and Abramowski, pointed to Abramowski's practical negation of the state and his appeal to create social organizations independent from the state.[65] Michnik emphasized Abramowski's reluctance to accept ideologies based on hatred and compulsion. He praised Abramowski's criticism of movements which aspired to political power within the state. According to Abramowski, such ideologies can merely bring to power new elites which nevertheless rule by the old methods. Political parties and military organizations are old institutions used in a struggle for domination within the state apparatus. Various sorts of cooperatives and voluntary associations of producers can represent an alternative for this unfortunate syndrome in a world dominated by the political state. These are the ideas which are the basis of Abramowski's vision of the "cooperative republic". Solidarity activists were undoubtedly inspired by this interesting theory.

Solidarity's interpretation of doctrinal currents other than social anarchism is also characteristic. Roman Dmowski and his party "Endecja" are strongly criticized by Adam Michnik for spreading national jingoism. However, Michnik compliments Dmowski for his appeal to create institutions independent of Russia, and for stimulating the development of the Polish national consciousness.[66]

Jozef Pilsudski is praised by Michnik for his efforts to abolish the "psychology of slaves" among the Poles. However, Michnik complains that Pilsudski wanted to achieve these goals by action from the top rather than from the bottom of Polish society. According to Michnik, Pilsudski's vision of the sovereignity of the state deprives the people of their sovereignity.[67]

Michnik criticizes the XIXth century Catholic Church in Poland for its association with feudalism and for its aspirations to build a "clerical state". At the same time, Michnik supports those Catholic writings which cultivated the ethical strength of society and kept alive Polish cultural and spiritual independence at a time when Poland was partitioned by foreign powers.[68]

We may suppose that Edward Abramowski's school of social anarchism would agree with Michnik's interpretation of these various doctrinal currents.

THREE QUESTIONS SOLIDARITY DID NOT ANSWER

It is certainly too early for a critical analysis of the various aspects of Solidarity's doctrinal vision. However, three major dilemmas emerging from this doctrine should be briefly mentioned.

First, Solidarity rarely specified the relationship between the system of self-government/self-management and the activity of an independent trade union. The intention at the beginning was that Solidarity would play a role similar to that of traditional Western trade unions - a role based on opposition to the employer (in the Polish case a state employer) and collective bargaining. One of the reasons for this policy was that Solidarity did not want to take responsibility for a system that it could not sufficiently influence.[69] Later, however, Solidarity changed its attitude and began to promote a comprehensive programme of industrial self-management.[70] This implied taking over responsibility for the industrial decision-making process. From then on, the relationship between, e.g. shop and plant trade union units and the relevant shop and plant workers' councils was very sensitive. Specialists in industrial relations point out, for instance, the difficulties in combining a system of workers' control with a system of workers' participation.[71] Solidarity would hardly be able to avoid these difficulties, despite its general appeal that the newborn popular trade union play a decisive role in creating the system of self-management.[72]

Second, Solidarity did not specify the relationship between its vision of a self-governing commonwealth and two major competitive visions of future scenarios for possible democratization in Poland, namely, the system of state corporatism (emerging from the corporate agreement between the Party, the Church and Solidarity), and the system of parliamentary democracy.[73] It was necessary for both these models to be considered by Solidarity in spite of any doctrinal preferences. The former, because the geopolitical position of Poland required some sort of communist rule in the country. The latter, because it represented the only historically tested model of democratization. Any sort of compromise between the doctrinal vision of anti-statism and the above-mentioned geopolitical and pragmatic requirements would raise serious dilemmas and controversies.

Third, Solidarity's own attitude towards the means of social change also raises questions and dilemmas. The basic weakness of various historical forms of anti-state collectivism is their inability to combine their ultimate aim - a decentralized, grassroot-based organization of society - with a strategy to achieve this goal. History has shown that in order to abolish unjust, centralized, totaliarian systems it is probably necessary to use the centralized, even dictatorial power of a revolutionary movement. However, this usually leads to the establishment of a revolutionary dictatorship following on measures of force, which is the reverse of the anti-state collectivist vision. Gradual reforms have usually been possible in countries with relatively limited oppression and few social contradictions. But this was neither the case in 1789 in France, nor in 1917 in Russia; it was also apparently not the case in 1981 in Poland.

However, even if one believes (as I do) that the gradual nonviolent means of social change is the best form of struggle in contemporary Poland, there remain certain problems with some specific methods of struggle declared by Solidarity. Essay four discusses these problems in detail. Therefore here only one of the most illustrative issues will be pointed out. Namely Solidarity's idea of the "unlimited general strike", considered as a means of forcing the authorities to a compromise. As Aleksander Smolar rightly pointed out, the idea of the unlimited general strike has to be confronted with two major questions.[74] First, it would be very difficult for Solidarity to organize such a popular strike action and it would certainly require extreme emotional determination on the part of the whole nation. Under Polish geopolitical circumstances this might be counter-productive either in the case of the ultimate success of the strike action, or in the case of its failure. The former could imply a Soviet invasion, the latter could imply a total collapse of social self-confidence.

Second, there is a certain danger that despite a general strike the authorities would refuse to negotiate with Solidarity anyway, (as often happens in Western Europe). Strikes cannot last indefinitely. They will either collapse or be transformed into direct violent confrontation with the authorities. Both scenarios run contrary to Solidarity's objectives.[75]

NOTES

1. In this respect see especially: Jerzy Holzer. Solidarnosc 1980-1981. Instytut Literacki, Paris 1984, as well as Jakub Karpinski. Countdown. The Polish Upheavals of 1956, 1968, 1970, 1976, 1980... Karz-Cohl Publ., New York 1982.

2. Adam Michnik. The New Evolutionism. Survey, Winter 1976, p. 272.

3. Jacek Kuron. W Strone Demokracji, in: Jacek Kuron. Polityka i Odpowiedzialnosc. Aneks, London 1984, p. 51.

4. This programme was adopted by the First National Congress of Solidarity in October 1981. In some cases we can meet a translation of the title of this programme "The Self-Governing Republic" instead of "the Self-Governing Commonwealth".

5. Maciej Ilowiecki in Polityka no.13, Warsaw 1981, p. 7.

6. Komunikat nr.13 Sieci Organizacji Zakladowych NSZZ Solidarnosc Wiodacych Zakladow Pracy, Bydgoszcz, 22 November 1981.

7. Jacek Kuron, for instance, openly admitted that these two systems are contradictory to a remarkable extent and indicated that his sympathy is on the side of the system of self-government. However, in the conclusion Kuron stated that the aim of the opposition is to build a system of "parliamentary democracy through the movement of self-management and self-government". See: Jacek Kuron. Notatki o Samorzadzie, in: Jacek Kuron. Polityka i. Odpowiedzialnosc. Op.cit...p. 60.

8. "The Underground Society". A statement on the programme of the Temporary Coordinating Commission of NSZZ Solidarnosc, July 1982.

9. Ibidem.

10. Zbigniew Bujak. Positional Warfare. Survey, Summer 1982, especially pp. 11-14.

11. Wiktor Kulerski. The Third Possibility. Survey, Summer 1982, p. 158.

12. The Programme - "The Self-Governing Commonwealth".

13. Jacek Kuron. Zasady Ideowe. Instytut Literacki, Paris 1978, p. 71.

14. The Programme declaration of the "Clubs of Self-Governing Commonwealth. Freedom-Justice-Independence" issued in Warsaw on 22 November 1981.

15. Andrzej Kijowski. Literatura i Kryzys. Kultura no.6, Paris 1982, p. 3.

16. Wojciech Sadurski in Polityka no.38, Warsaw 1981, pp. 1 and ff.

17. I will describe this phenomenon in the fifth essay of this book.

18. "Solidarity Today". A Statement on the Programme of the Temporary Coordinating Commission of NSZZ Solidarnosc, 22 January 1983.

19. The Programme - "The Self-governing Commonwealth".

20. Adam Michnik. O Oporze. Krytyka no.13-14, London 1983, pp. 10-11.

21. Jan Jozef Lipski. KOR. Aneks, London 1983, p. 26.

22. The Programme - "The Self-Governing Commonwealth".

23. The Programme - "Solidarity Today".

24. The Programme - "The Self-Governing Commonwealth".

25. Jadwiga Staniszkis. Polish Peaceful Revolution. Op.cit...p. 185 and Poland's Self-Limiting Revolution. Princeton University Press, Princeton, New Jersey 1984, p. 140.

26. The Programme - "The Self-Governing Commonwealth".

27. Jan Jozef Lipski. KOR. Op.cit...p. 42.

28. Ibidem.

29. Jacek Kuron in: Samorzadnosc, no.3, Gdansk 1981, p. 8.

30. Jacek Kuron. Nie do druku, in: Jacek Kuron. Polityka i Odpowiedzialnosc. Op.cit...p. 184.

31. For instance, Jacek Kuron made it clear that the means of social change cannot contradict moral principles. See: Jacek Kuron. Zasady Ideowe. Op.cit...p. 46.

32. Adam Michnik. The New Evolutionism. Op.cit...p. 272.

33. Leszek Kolakowski. Rewolucja jako piekna choroba, in: Leszek Kolakowski. Czy diabel moze byc zbawiony i 27 innych kazan. Aneks, London 1982, pp. 225 and ff.

34. Leszek Nowak. Ani Rewolucja ani Ewolucja. Dialog, Frankfurt/Main 1984, p. 131.

35. Lech Walesa's Nobel Peace Prize Speech, printed e.g. in: Solidarnosc. Biuletyn informacyjny no.78, Paris 1983, p. 5.

36. The Programme - "Solidarity Today".

37. Aniela Steinbergowa quoted in: Solidarnosc. Biuletyn Informacyjny no.61, Paris 1983, p. 5.

38. Jan Jozef Lipski in: Samorzadnosc no. 3, Gdansk 1981, pp. 10-11.

39. Jacek Kuron. The Situation in the Country and the Programme of the Oppostition. Labour Focus no.3, London 1979, p. 12.

40. See e.g., the interview with Solidarity leaders in: Polityka no.44, Warsaw 1980, pp. 1 and ff.

41. Lech Walesa. Nobel Peace Prize Speech. Op.cit...p. 4, see also: Wiktor Kulerski quoted in: KOS no.37, Warsaw 1983, p. 3.

42. Zbigniew Bujak. Positional Warfare. Survey. Op.cit...p. 89.

43. See e.g., The Programme - "Solidarity Today".

44. For a more detailed analysis of this problem, see: the fourth essay of this book.

45. Robert Nozick. Anarchy, State and Utopia. Oxford University Press, Oxford 1974, pp. ix and ff.

46. See: Zdzislaw Rurarz, in: D.C. Lavoie, (ed.). Solidarnosc z wolnoscia. Cato Institute, Washington D.C. 1984, pp. 2-5.

47. Collectivism of Solidarity was based on doctrinal as well as on tactical arguments. According to many writers in the Polish geopolitical situation individualism was "out of the question".

48. Rodney Backer. The Modern British Politics. Methuen Co., London 1979, pp. 4-5 and ff. Baker distinguishes between individualism, pro-state collectivism and anti-state collectivism.

49. See especially: Alan Ritter. The Political Thought of Pierre-Joseph Proudhon. Princeton University Press, Princeton 1969, pp. 10 and ff.

50. Quoted in: George Woodcock. Anarchism. A History of Libertarian Ideas and Movements. Penguin, Harmondsworth 1979, p. 205.

51. Thornton Anderson. Russian Political Thought. Cornell University Press, Ithaca, New York 1967, p. 247.

52. Leo Tolstoy. The Slavery of Our Times. Maldon, Essex 1900, p. 148.

53. See especially: G.D.H. Cole. Guild Socialism. L. Parson, London 1920, and Guild Socialism Restated. Friedrich A. Stokes, New York 1921.

54. See: Muford Q. Sibley. Political Ideas and Ideologies. Harper & Row, New York, Eranston, London 1970, p. 526.

55. See: Rodney Backer. Op.cit...pp. 84-87.

56. Peter Kropotkin. Modern Science and Anarchism. Freedom Press, London 1912.

57. The Programme - "The Self-Governing Commonwealth". One should recognize the influence of Catholic doctrine on Solidarity. However, in this chapter I basically do not deal with this question

and refer the reader to e.g. Jozef Tischner. Polski Ksztalt Dialogu. Editions Spotkania, Paris 1981, 198 pp.

58. See: Jerzy Holzer. Solidarnosc. Op.cit...p. 298.

59. See: the PPP Provisional Programme quoted under note no. 6.

60. The Programme Declaration of the "Clubs of Self-Governing Commonwealth". Josef Pilsudski, principal actor in the liberation of Poland in 1918, became the nation's first military commander-in-chief and seized full dictatorial powers in 1926. Wincenty Witos (1874-1945), leader of the Peasant Party (PSL). Ignacy Daszynski, (1866-1936), leader of the Polish Socialist Party (PPS).

61. Antoni Maciarewicz in: Samorzadnosc no.3, Gdansk 1981, p. 9.

62. Ibidem.

63. See especially: Edward Abramowski. Pisma popularno-naukowe i propagandowe. Ksiazka i Wiedza, Warsaw 1979 as well as Bohdan Cywinski. Mysl polityczna Edwarda Abramowskiego, in: Tworcy polskiej mysli politycznej. Ossolineum, Wroclaw 1978, pp. 29-106. It should be mentioned that in 1980 Bohdan Cywinski became a close personal adviser to Lech Walesa.

64. Jacek Kuron. Do redakcji Krytyki, in: Jacek Kuron. Polityka i Odpowiedzialnosc. Op.cit...p. 38.

65. Adam Michnik. Rozmowa w Cytadeli, in: Adam Michnik. Szanse Polskiej Demokracji. Aneks, London 1984, p. 241.

66. As far as the ideas of "Endecja" are concerned see especially: Barbara Torunczyk, (ed.). Narodowa Demokracja. Antologia mysli politycznej Przegladu Wszechpolskiego (1895-1905). Aneks, London 1983.

67. Adam Michnik. Rozmowa w Cytadeli. Op.cit...p. 240.

68. Adam Michnik. Op.cit...p. 247

69. "The government wants us to take responsibility for efficiency of production" - said Bogdan Borusewicz, a leader of Solidarity in the weekly Polityka in the Autumn of 1980 - "We think that it would lead us to the situation of the old trade unions - forcing workers to work". And Lech Walesa had added: "We do not want to be bureaucrats, but activists - examiners. We would like to do our jobs and examine". See: Polityka no.44, Warsaw 1980, pp. 1 and ff. During one of the first Solidarity debates about the creation of the system of self-management (18 March 1981) Professor Bronislaw Geremek, a top adviser to Lech Walesa, still argued against self-management. According to Geremek, Solidarity cannot take responsibility for management before major economic reforms are introduced. See: AS (Solidarity Press Agency Bulletin) no.9, Warsaw 1981, p. 305.

70. There were doctrinal as well as economic reasons for this. Ruled by the Party, the economy was falling down dramatically. One should also recognize tactical arguments advocating self-management. Introduction of the new system of self-management was supposed to curtail the powers of the Communist Party at the shop and plant industrial level.

71. See e.g., H. Clegg. The Changing System of Industrial Relations in Great Britain. Blackwell, Oxford 1979, pp. 444 and ff.

72. See e.g., Jacek Kuron. Czym jest Solidarnosc, in: Jacek Kuron. Polityka i Odpowiedzialnosc. Op.cit...p. 174.

73. I devote particular attention to this problem in the fifth essay of this book.

74. Aleksander Smolar. Miedzy ugoda a powstaniem. Aneks no.28, London 1982, p. 16.

75. In theory, there is a third option, namely that a general strike is accompanied by various other forms of nonviolent action. Such a coordinated strategy of nonviolent struggle could, according to some Western observers, represent a sufficient weapon of political pressure on the authorities. As I already mentioned above, Solidarity leaders devoted particular attention to development of nonviolent means of struggle. So far, however, we can hardly say that they elaborated a comprehensive strategy of nonviolent sanctions (as e.g. advocated by Gene Sharp). Compare: Gene Sharp. The Politics of Nonviolent Action. Porter Sarquent, Boston 1973, pp. 257 and ff. I will return to this question in the next essay.

IV Solidarity's strategy of social change

Within Solidarity, as within many other modern emancipatory movements, discussions about the means of social struggle have often been deeper and more intense than discussions about the ends of such struggle. This chapter will therefore try to approach the question of means in Solidarity's doctrine more specifically than the previous chapter. I will analyse Solidarity's ideas about the ways of creating a Self-Governing Commonwealth, both in terms of strategy and tactics. This amounts, in the first place, to a study of "nonviolence" as a means of social change proclaimed by Solidarity's activists.

I will focus in particular on why Solidarity has chosen nonviolent forms of struggle and for what objectives; the strength and weakness of Solidarity's particular strategies and tactics; those forms of nonviolent action best suited to the union's objectives, the crucial organizational shortcomings of Solidarity's nonviolent struggle; and finally, what Solidarity was able – and what it was unable – to accomplish through nonviolence, in particular when met with governmental violence.

Under scrutiny here are the developments between 1980-85. In this period, Poland passed through three different stages of nonviolent action: (a) the mass strikes of Summer 1980 which led to the creation of the independent trade union Solidarity; (b) a period of legal activity of Solidarity, September 1980 - December 1981; and (c) the resistance against military repression since December 1981. Certain developments prior to 1980 will be considered, especially in tracing the origins of Solidarity's programme of action.

The popular application of nonviolent actions - strikes, demonstrations, political noncooperation, and various symbolic actions - constitutes a powerful weapon of struggle for political democracy and the national independence of many modern emancipatory movements.[1] And in fact the nonviolent resistance of Solidarity resembles the other great movements of nonviolence led and inspired by H. David Thoreau, Mahatma Gandhi, or Martin Luther King. It is therefore useful to analyse the Polish resistance in a certain comparative context. Moreover, the analysis of the Polish struggle could also be useful in testing the relevance and usefulness of particular modern theories of nonviolence.[2]

Of course, since Solidairty's struggle is conducted under specific socio-political circumstances, one should be very careful in basing any absolute conclusions on this particular case.[3] On the other hand, Solidarity is one of the most spectacular historical examples of nonviolent action; it requires special attention and encourages comparative observations.

WHY NONVIOLENCE?

Students of Poland notice that Solidarity does not identify itself directly with nonviolence. While shunning violence and advocating nonviolent means of social struggle Solidarity has hardly acknowledged its adherence to the theory and practice of nonviolence. Two essential reasons pertain here: a) there is no defined historical tradition of nonviolence in Poland; and b) there is a lack of serious theoretical analysis exploring the potential of nonviolent struggle.

Violence abounds in modern Polish history, and the Polish people have always given widespread support to armed resistance, especially where it countered military invasion by a foreign power. One could even say that armed resistance was, in a way, cultivated by Polish culture and tradition. For instance, although during World War II there were many examples of civil disobedience and of successful application of various nonviolent actions by the Poles, the armed opposition to the Nazis enjoyed the greatest esteem and the support of the Polish population.[4] The postwar history of social upheavals is also discouraging from the perspective of nonviolence. The upheavals of 1956, 1968, 1970 and 1976 all created various forms of violence.[5]

Second, deep theoretical considerations about nonviolence have never developed in Poland and we can indicate only a few examples of direct identification with the tradition of nonviolence. At the beginning of 1970's, the Catholic monthly Wiez published a number of translations which described the nonviolent resistance led by Mahatma Gandhi, Martin Luther King, and Brazilian trade unionists. Some years later, in 1977, a group of people who began a hunger strike in protest against the arrest of the nine KOR members identified their action with the tradition of Gandhi, King, and hunger strikes in Spanish churches.[6] Recognition of nonviolence was more apparent after the military take-over of December 1981. Lech Walesa on several occasions referred to Gandhi and other advocates of nonviolence. There also emerged within the country small groups called "without violence" which identified themselves directly with a tradition of nonviolent movements. And two underground publishing companies issued translations of works of Gene Sharp and Jean-Marie Muller on the politics of nonviolent action.[7]

However, these initiatives never developed into a theoretical framework of nonviolence, nor did they create a movement that, as a matter of principle, identified itself with a tradition of nonviolence.

The Polish case does not dramatically differ from other historical cases of nonviolent action. Both Gandhi's India and Thoreau's America have rich traditions of violence. And a nation without a modern tradition of violence, e.g., Czechoslovakia, does not necessarily develop a specific tradition of nonviolence.[8]

Gandhi's theoretical concept of nonviolence was not a blueprint handed to the masses before they entered into the struggle for liberation. In particular, Gandhi's famous concept of satyagraha evolved gradually, together with the development of the Indian resistance. The entire potential of Gandhi's tradition was carefully studied and fully comprehended only after his death.

This lack of a clear (and exclusive) tradition of nonviolence as well as a lack of any comprehensive theoretical framework of nonviolent action in societies practicing nonviolence suggests that there are many different social, ideological as well as tactical factors at the root of nonviolent resistance. In other words, we can hardly say that people choose nonviolent forms of struggle solely because of the existence of a particular theory and tradition of nonviolence.[9] Studies of the Polish resistance indicate three basic factors lying behind the nonviolent option of Solidarity: tactical, doctrinal, ethical.

In the first instance, Solidarity's leaders shared the opinion that violent resistance would dramatically increase the number of victims instead of bringing the union closer to its objectives. In this context it seemed especially likely that any successful violent resistance would unavoidably cause a Soviet invasion.[10] Here, the parallels between Solidarity's concept of resistance and Gene Sharp's theory about the nonviolent control of political power are especially apparent.[11]

Second, Solidarity's struggle is aimed at the creation of a political system based on self-government and grassroot participation.[12] Such a system can hardly be achieved through violent revolutionary means. In other words, from the doctrinal point of view Solidarity could not use a means of struggle that would contradict its social goals. Gandhi too, was faced with similar doctrinal dilemmas. His belief in the decentralization of industrial and political life based on populism and grassroot participation has much in common with the principles of Solidarity's doctrine. Works of famous social anarchists, such as Kropotkin, Tolstoy, or Ruskin, equally influenced Indian and Polish movements.[13] Linkage between nonviolence and decentralized forms of communal life is also strongly advocated by some contemporary writers, such as for instance Severyn Bruyn and George Lakey.[14]

Third, Solidarity's option for nonviolence rested on a strong ethical base.[15] Solidarity's moral arguments for nonviolence are here closely associated with the Christian concept of social love and justice. This concept was especially promoted by Pope John Paul II and echoed in thousands of local parishes across Poland.[16] The official Catholic doctrine does not make nonviolence mandatory and allows for violence in cases of self-defence. (Even Gandhi ethical rejection of violence is not absolute.)[17] However, the nonviolent position is taken seriously by many Catholics, despite the fact that one could argue that this has not a long and honoured position in the Christian tradition.[18]

The basic question for students of nonviolence is why people involve themselves in a struggle in the first place?[19] The two recognized schools of advocates of nonviolence do not present a satisfactory answer to this crucial question.[20] The so-called instrumentalists (Ebert, Roberts, Sharp, and others) use one of the basic concepts of functionalism, viz. the concept of the functional equivalent as a starting point of research. This concept with its socio-technical character puts strong emphasis upon strategy, on the organization, education and training of the population. Instrumentalists either assume that the will to conduct a struggle already exists within a given group (so it should be provided with the most efficient methods of resistance), or they claim that the public could be convinced to enter the struggle through the system of general public education. (When the people comprehend all the advantages of nonviolent forms of struggle they will be eager to engage themselves in it and endure its inconveniences.)

Instrumentalists are basically interested in how to organize nonviolent action. What is the degree of training which the population has to undergo? What is the structure of command and communication in implementing a particular nonviolent action? The general criterion for implementing nonviolent action into practice is efficiency.

The so-called structuralists (Galtung, Jahn, Lakey and others) criticize instrumentalists for (a) their abstractness with regard to practical experiments in nonviolent action; (b) their tendency to extract a method of struggle from the concrete historical liberation movements where it arose; and (c) presentation of nonviolent action as an instructional model in some distant future. Structuralists claim that people readily engage in struggle only under specific historical conditions and with specific ideological motivation. In other words, nonviolent action is conceived as a fundamental component of a larger democratization strategy directed towards the reduction of so-called structural violence existing at all levels of society. This strategy is usually identified with classless socialism or anti-militarism.

A lack of satisfactory answers to the question of readiness also has roots in methodological problems. On the one hand, instrumentalists are unable to indicate a correlation between the level of educational/ organizational preparation and the readiness to resist.[21] On the other hand, structuralists would be hard put to indicate any specific influence wielded by particular ideologies or doctrines on people's readiness to engage in nonviolent action.

My own studies on Poland were unable to overcome the above-mentioned methodological problems, but the Polish case seems to confirm the opinion that people's readiness to resist is not a direct function of application of certain socio-technical methods. For instance, the educational and organizational efforts of Solidarity to stimulate people's readiness to resist have gradually intensified since Spring 1982 and yet the average number of people participating in nonviolent actions has decreased.[22] Wladyslaw Frasyniuk, a leader of Solidarity, described the union's defeat in December 1981:

"In our region we have issued several instructions on how to act in case of martial law. In November 1981 we also distributed a special letter in which we suggested the creation of supplementary secret commissions of the union, the development of a special communications network, the hiding of union equipment, etc. However, all these directives did not have any visible practical effect. In short, I would not overestimate all these preparatory actions... People also knew what they are struggling for; protest actions were conducted not only by workers, but also by their fathers and grandfathers, all those who have realized what could be lost. Technical (organization) factors had a minor significance. First of all, people were not prepared spiritually...".[23]

At this point the instrumentalists would probably cite a number of organizational shortcomings in Solidarity's work. However, in the face of one of the most efficient and widespread nonviolent movements in modern history, this remark would sound like armchair pacifism (Katheder-Pazifismus). Instrumentalists should then acknowledge that there is no guarantee that any other given society would be better able to achieve organizational efficiency when faced with internal or foreign aggression than were the organizers of Solidarity. However criticism of the instrumental approach does not necessarily mean that the Polish example supports the approach of the structuralists.

There are two basic reasons why the opinions of the structuralists are irrelevant in explaining the readiness of the Polish people to resist. Structuralists rightly note that the readiness to resist depends on certain socioeconomic interests of the people. Unfortunately, they usually identify this interest with a stereotype model of social development based on the belief in proletarian revolution and anti-militarism. (The "curious" article of Johan Galtung entitled "Poland, August-September 1980. Is a Socialist Revolution Under State Capitalism Possible?" is a case in point.)[24]

In the 1950's and 1960's leaders of the Polish opposition shared a very similar approach to the question of social development and revolution.[25] It was already mentioned in the first essay that, for instance, in 1965 Jacek Kuron and Karol Modzelewski (later leading advisers to Solidarity) in their "open letter" to the Communist Party described Polish society in terms of class exploitation and drew conclusions concerning the revolutionary method towards social change.[26] However, these revolutionary appeals did not get any popular support in Poland. Consequently Kuron, Modzelewski and other leaders of the Polish opposition lost their enthusiasm for any revolutionary political transformation. In the 1970's they created a new vision of social change that apparently influenced and mobilized the masses of Solidarity. This vision expressed belief in gradual evolutionary reforms, based on grassroots participation.[27] Students of Solidarity's doctrine can easily point to major differences between this doctrine and a programme of socialist revolution advocated by Jahn or Galtung.[28]

The second argument against the structuralist approach relates to the first. The failure of the intellectual upheaval in 1968 convinced the leaders of the Polish opposition that they should advocate defence of basic human rights rather than promote any specific ideology or doctrinal vision of social transformation. In other words, the readiness to resist was supposed to be based not mainly and exclusively on political and economic slogans but on the defence of actual persons. Newly-created free trade unions and defence committees (of students, peasants) were supposed to organize such a social self-defence, and practical actions in defence of actual persons or professional goups were of primary concern from then on. Only then were political programmes created.

This new approach gained a remarkable degree of support from the workers. The famous strike at the Lenin Shipyard in Gdansk on August 14th, 1980, was organized because the management of the shipyard had fired Anna Walentynowicz, a woman admired by the workers in the yard for her battles with the authorities. The strike did not succeed because of any specific programme or ideology.[29]

The demand to release the imprisoned activists of Solidarity was also the principal demand after the imposition of martial law. Far-reaching political demands then followed. Mass support of successive actions in protest against the murder of pro-Solidarity priest, Jerzy Popieluszko, also illustrate this point.

In this situation one might say that the defence of actual persons and a spontaneous human reaction towards injustice constituted a major source of readiness to resist in Poland. This is hardly acknowledged by the structuralist approach towards nonviolence.

THE OBJECTIVES OF NONVIOLENT ACTION

Success or failure of nonviolent action must be measured by the objectives of this action. Literature on nonviolence used to mention many different objectives of nonviolent action, such as total liberation of a country, defence of the population's life-style, denying objectives to the attackers, revolutionary change in the sociopolitical system of the country, and abolishment of the rule of usurpers.

If the objectives of Solidarity's nonviolent actions are consistent with a total liberation, then Solidarity failed to achieve its goal. From that point of view the nonviolent resistance of, for instance, the Czechoslovak population in 1968 was a total failure as well. However, neither the Poles in the 1980's nor the Czechs in the 1960's defined the objectives of their struggle in terms of a total liberation. As far as Poland is concerned, the twenty-one demands formulated by the strikers in the Lenin Shipyard best illustrate the objectives of the strike action. Most of these demands were very pragmatic and were expressed in a specific and concrete manner. The main demands were to establish new independent trade unions with the right to strike and the release of political prisoners (even indicating some names). Economic and welfare demands were formulated in an even more concrete way, e.g., to ensure paid leave of four weeks for those studying for a doctor's degree, or to issue food coupons for the bedridden. Some demands were symbolic and aimed at meeting specific cultural values, e.g., that the government would ensure the regular transmission of Sunday mass on the radio, or that statues and monuments would be erected to commemorate the victims of the workers' protest in December 1970. Remarkably, strikers neither asked for the abolishment of the leading role of the Communist Party nor for the withdrawal from Poland of Soviet troops.

After the creation of Solidarity, the objectives of the struggle were equally unequivocal: for instance, to release Mr. Narozniak (first Solidarity employee detained by the police), to register the union, to investigate the Bydgoszcz affair (the beating of Solidarity activists) and punish those who were guilty.

Even when Solidarity made some far-reaching political proposals, e.g., to introduce the self-management system, it always tried to make the issues of its struggle (bargaining) as concrete as possible. In the case of the self-management system it was the issue of who elects the management of the enterprise - the enterprise self-management or the government.

After the imposition of martial law in 1982, Solidarity continued to make pragmatic, specific demands: (a) to lift matial law; (b) to release political prisoners; (c) to re-legalize Solidarity; (d) to specify the conditions for the national agreement; and (e) to adopt a policy of economic reforms.[30] Such a programme calls to mind that the objectives of the Czechoslovak resistance in 1968 were also very limited, concrete and clear. Students of the Czechoslovak case usually mention four basic objectives of the nonviolent resistance: (a) return of the internal party and state leaders; (b) departure of foreign troops; (c) renewal of full state sovereignty; (d) continuation of the post-January policies of the Communist Party of Czechoslovakia.[31]

A distinction between long-term and short-term objectives of nonviolent action always exists. In fact, Solidarity kept repeating that its struggle is in the end aimed at building a Self-Governing Commonwealth. However, that final far-reaching goal of the nonviolent struggle does not minimize the fact that its real objectives are in practice (or even must be) very limited.[32]

The aims of Solidarity's nonviolent actions could also be expressed in terms of "denying objectives to the attackers" or of "defence of the population's life-style".[33] And a full implementation of Solidarity's objectives would lead to a "change of socio-political system of the country". Nevertheless, the remarkable degree of self-limitation of the objectives of the nonviolent struggle in Poland (and for that matter also in Czechoslovakia) should be taken very seriously, particularly because important strategic arguments prompted Solidarity to limit its objectives.

Solidarity's strategy is often described as a strategy of self-limitation which meant that the union was ready to compromise its political and ethical aspirations with the requirements of struggle conducted under specific sociopolitical circumstances. In practical terms, that first implied a certain accommodation to the Soviet-type system and a belief in a possible agreement with the Polish communist rulers, (as already mentioned in the doctrinal and pragmatic sources of this strategy).[34]

The strategy of self-limitation was clearly adopted during the strikes of summer 1980, and despite governmental repressions it was continued after December 1981. The leader of the underground Solidarity, Zbigniew Bujak, sharply criticized mass actions aimed at overthrowing the authorities.[35] Bujak suggested a decidedly decentralized movement, adopting different methods of action. As was already indicated in an earlier essay, Bujak argued that individual groups and social circles must build a mechanism of resistance against the monopolistic activities of the government. This should be done through the existence of a mass organization like Solidarity and through the activities of independent peasants, craftsmen, students and various cultural and educational associations. One day this resistance might become so widespread as to create the possibility of an independent structure of social life.[36]

According to this strategy, Solidarity does not intend to lead the union towards any ultimate defeat of the communist authorities. The union conducts its struggle in order to press the authorities to compromise with Polish society.

French philosopher André Glucksman named this strategy - "a strategy of dizziness". Glucksman said:

"The Poles do not want to be stronger, but they want to be more clever. They do not believe in the miracle of Austerlitz, but they believe that they can avoid the blood of Waterloo. They play gently, balancing one defeat against another...".[37]

Solidarity's strategy deals with specific sociopolitical circumstances, and is therefore quite unique, even though it is based on ideas similar to Gandhi's. For instance, students of Gandhi emphasize that Gandhi's practical, social, economic, and political programmes "evolved out of the interplay between the existing situation (real) and the principles of satyargracha (ideal)".[38] They recall Gandhi's advice that individuals who live in keeping with an ideal society do not go far enough. Although Gandhi's ideal system was decidely decentralized (as in the case of Solidarity), he realized the limits of reformed and new institutions; progressive social organization could not insure equality and justice. When asked whether the ideal state would have government, Gandhi replied: "Euclid's line is one without breadth, but no one so far has been able to draw it and never will".[39] This conviction implied, among other things, that the aim of the struggle was not to defeat the adversary, to destroy, conquer or humiliate him. The adversary rather has to be "convinced of a common conception of justice and conflict solution on a level of equality".[40]

Certain parallels between the ideas of Gandhi and those of Solidarity's leaders (not fully comprehended by the latter) may arise because in both cases ideas (social philosophy) were emerging in the context of political struggle. Neither Gandhi nor Michnik, Bujak nor Walesa were social philosophers. They were first and primarily social activists. Nevertheless, they all tried to project their individual ethical codes into the social sphere of action.

SOLIDARITY'S SUCCESSES AND FAILURES

Literature on nonviolence advocates the application of a wide range of various forms of nonviolent action (the so-called nonviolent sanctions). So far, however, the argument is based mainly on uncritical historical description of the application of various sanctions. Students of nonviolence usually refer to an historic case of strike, boycott, hunger-strike, street marches, embargoes, or the creation of alternative social institutions. This literature provides important documentation that explores the potential of nonviolent actions. Nevertheless, it does not indicate which sanctions are appropriate to particular circumstances and objectives. Such application could only be suggested after an extensive analysis of unsuccessful rather than successful application of various sanctions; through a critical examination of long and short term implications of these sanctions (in terms of costs and benefits); and through a careful analysis of the complex relationship: sanction-strategy-objectives of the nonviolent resister. Most important to comprehend is that "success" in organizing a particular form of nonviolent action (a street march or strike with a mass participation) does not always mean

103

that this form of action meets its goals and objectives (e.g., the release of political prisoners, increase of wages).[41]

The Polish struggle indicates that some sanctions could actually be counterproductive in meeting the objectives of the nonviolent struggle, and that application of other sanctions might prove insufficient in meeting these objectives. Moreover, a change of sociopolitical circumstances influences the outcome of applying particular forms of actions to a great extent.

In the Summer of 1980, Polish workers successfully applied the occupational form of strike, the sit-in, that proved to have important advantages.[42] First, it protected the workers against police violence on the streets. In this respect the lessons learned from previous upheavals in 1956, 1970 and 1976 were not forgotten. At that time people went into the streets to expres their discontent and clashed with the police. As experience showed, the police were able to organize various sorts of provocation in public places, and a large mass of people could not easily be controlled by its leaders. On the other hand, the occupational strike could hold strikers together. It permitted them to provide democratic discussion, to select their leaders, to formulate demands, and to maintain morale and discipline. Valuable factory equipment became the workers' "hostages". The walls and fences surrounding factories were a natural protection against open attack and police provocation.

These apparent advantages of the sit-in as well as a number of other factors (e.g., the disintegration of the party apparatus, sympathy with the strikers on the part of the official establishment, the limited nature of the workers' demands, the apparent lack of a Soviet will to interfere militarily), brought about the success of strike action in August and September 1980.

Not surprisingly then, the sit-in remained a major weapon after September 1980. Solidarity's activists simply continued calling strikes in cases of conflicts with the authorities. These strikes were well organized and proved to be very successful. It very soon became apparent that the authorities hardly ever made any concessions unless they were faced with a threat of strike action. In other words, every conflict with the authorities implied Solidarity's threat or use of strike action. This had a number of negative consequences.

Since strikes were applied in most cases of conflict, it was difficult to distinguish which conflicts were the most crucial for

Solidarity. No matter whether the particular conflict was caused by an important political issue (such as the court registration of Solidarity) or by secondary local issues (for instance, conflict over the appointment of a rector of the high school in Radom), Solidarity activists always used (or were forced to use) their strongest weapon - strike action. The permanent strike readiness caused a general weakness and apathy among Solidarity's rank and file. A use of the strike weapon by local Solidarity organizations usually implied the involvement of the whole union in local, rather specific, conflicts. Repetitive strike actions added some credibility to government claims which accused Solidarity of stimulating anarchy and civil war in Poland. In consequence, in the Spring of 1981, Solidarity's national leaders made a number of efforts aimed at reduction of this "strike fever". Some alternative nonviolent actions were applied at that time, for instance, street marches (e.g., a hunger march in Lodz), or the blockade of street traffic (as in Warsaw in August 1981). Nevertheless, these alternative forms of nonviolent action appeared to be much less effective in meeting the union's objectives than were the strikes.

Immediately after the imposition of martial law, on December 1981, strikes broke out in most of the large plants across the country. However, motorized riot police units (ZOMO), with the assistance of the military, launched attacks on the strikers. In most cases tanks destroyed factory walls and fences, and the ZOMO forces attacked workers with gas, water, and guns. Police forces were, in some cases, supported by parachute attacks. Moreover, most Solidarity leaders had been arrested, communication within the country was thoroughly disrupted, and the strikers were confronted by specially trained police units. In consequence, the resisting factories collapsed one by one. Only in the coal-mining district of Silesia, where miners could seal off shafts of particular mines, were the strikes able to continue. There, however, the ZOMO used heavy guns and live ammunition, which resulted in several deaths in the Wujek mine.

This violent defeat of strikes on December 1981 did not totally discourage Solidarity's use of the strike weapon from 1982-85. Several strikes, usually symbolic (lasting fifteen minutes) were called by the underground leadership of Solidarity. However, none of these actions brought about a spectacular success. The failure of a general strike in November 1982 was the most disappointing experience for the union.

Solidarity activists indicated three major reasons for this failure of their successive strike actions: a) the governmental policy of violence and intimidation (in cases of strikes major enterprises were usually surrounded by police and army units, the organizers of the strikes were arrested and severely punished); b) organizational shortcomings of Solidarity actions, basically caused by legal restrictions and repression (lack of sufficient information and communication, wrong timing, lack of coordination); c) a general apathy of the population caused, among other factors, by the defeat of December 1981 and a preoccupation with everyday economic problems.[43]

In the same critical manner, Solidarity activists reviewed the application of the other major forms of nonviolent action, namely street marches and demonstrations. A number of successful mass demonstrations were organized after December 1981. However, these actions proved to be costly and ineffective. Marches and demonstrations engendered brutal attacks by the police, further detentions, dismissals from employment, and other reprisals. At the same time, they apparently did not significantly influence the policy of the Polish government. Not suprisingly then, the idea of organizing further marches and demonstrations came under fire within Solidarity.[44]

Such criticism did not lead to a complete abandonment of strikes and street demonstrations. In particular, Solidarity's underground leadership still insisted that "the prospect of a general strike is inevitable".[45] Nevertheless, other forms of nonviolent action were given priority from then on. Solidarity put a great emphasis on various forms of economic self-help and mutual assistance. Various forms of defence of the rights of workers were given special attention. This was done through the continuation of trade union activity, especially at the shop and plant level.[46] Solidarity advocated boycotts of a number of governmental initiatives. Here, a boycott of the official trade unions as well as a boycott of the elections to the local councils in June 1984 and to the Sejm in October 1985 appeared to be especially successful.[47] Solidarity advocated development of various sorts of independent (non-state) activities in education, science and culture. Special attention was devoted to the creation of Solidarity's independent information network. Today, we can say that Solidarity proved to be particularly successful in creating these various sorts of alternative institutions within the entire country.[48] Finally, Solidarity advocated that various symbolic actions be carried out.[49]

Successful application of the above-mentioned forms of nonviolent action permitted Solidarity to meet some of the crucial objectives of its struggle. For instance, the authorities were unable to curtail Solidarity's independent activity, especially in the field of culture and information. In other words, although Solidarity was unable to convince the government that it should ease censorship, the union was, nevertheless, able to print books and newspapers clandestinely without censorship.

At the same time, however, that application of the above-mentioned forms of nonviolent actions did not meet some crucial objectives of Solidarity's resistance. For instance, Solidarity was unable to press the authorities to initiate economic reforms. The economy remains a "private domain" of the state authorities, which makes it impossible to raise the standard of living. Solidarity also failed to regain legal recognition of its trade union activity (even at the shop and plant level).

Whether the successful application of strike actions, for example, could be decisive in meeting these objectives today is unknown. Nevertheless, it appears certain that forms of action currently applied by Solidarity are so far unable to meet some crucial objectives of the struggle even if applied quite succesfully (as in the case of the boycott of the elections or in the field of information and communication).

THE SIGNIFICANCE OF GOVERNMENTAL VIOLENCE

Literature on nonviolence pays little attention to the position and strength of the opponent of nonviolent resisters. In most cases, these are foreign or domestic authorities (usurpers) who use violence to defeat the nonviolent action. This neglect of the authorities (domestic or foreign) against whom the nonviolent action is carried on emerges partly from the theory of political power which lies at the basis of nonviolent philosophy. As Gene Sharp expressed it, nonviolent action is based on the view that "government depends on people, that power is pluralistic, and that political power is fragile because it depends on many groups for reinforcement of its power sources".[50]

In this context, the attitude and activity of the "people" who are eventually ready to engage in nonviolent action is more crucial for the success than are the attitude and activity of the authorities. In other words, advocates of nonviolence associate themselves with Jean Jacques Rousseau's conviction that "the strongest is never strong enough to be always master, unless he transforms his strength into right, and obedience into duty."[51]

For this author the "pluralistic theory of power" is more convincing than the "monolithic theory" which assumes that the power of a government is a relatively fixed quantum. Nevertheless, that government's power depends on people does not yet contradict the statement that success of certain nonviolent actions depends on the strength and integrity of the government (foreign aggressor) at certain times and under certain circumstances. It is an empirical fact that some well-organized popular nonviolent actions failed because they had to face a well-organized violent reaction of the authorities. On the other hand, some hastily organized nonviolent actions achieved spectacular successes due to a weak self-defence by disintegrated authorities. In practice, this problem can be reduced to the ability of the authorities to use organized violence on a mass scale against the nonviolent resisters. True, this ability largely depends on people's cooperation which could always be withdrawn. Nevertheless, it also depends on such factors as the government's ability to maintain internal discipline and on the decisiveness of its apparatus. A disintegrated apparatus of coercion uses violence in a chaotic and disorganized way and, by the same token, makes it relatively easier for the nonviolent resister to endure the inconveniences of the struggle. This was, for instance, the case with the Duma authorities in Russia in 1917 or with Reza Pahlavi's authorities in Iran in 1979. In fact, this was also the case with the Polish authorities in the Summer of 1980.

However, in Bolshevik Russia, as in Khomeini's Iran or for that matter in Jaruzelski's Poland, the internal mobilization of the apparatus of coercion (new or old) did occur after a certain time. This facilitated the use of organized violence on a mass scale and obviously increased the difficulties of nonviolent resistance. The organized machine of terror was able to eliminate nonviolent resistance entirely in the cases of Russia and Iran. However, in Poland the nonviolent opposition was able to survive and maintain organizational structures. This created a chance that in case of the next eventual disintegration of the apparatus of coercion, Solidarity would be able to meet its more advanced objectives.

At this point, it is important to emphasize that the coercive abilities of the government define the effectiveness (action with such and such participation, organizational qualifications and experiences) of any given nonviolent action to a great extent.

As far as the Polish case is concerned, the coercive abilities of Jaruzelski's government made it impossible for Solidarity to achieve a number of its original objectives, expressed in the twenty-one demands of the summer of 1980. Solidarity has never abandoned these objectives, but since December 1981, its struggle has been chiefly one of survival. The outcome of this struggle for survival is remarkable and might bring about certain advantages in future. By now, however, the coercive abilities of the Polish authorities make it impossible for Solidarity to achieve much more than what has been described here.

Finally, foreign aid for one participant in the conflict means an aggregation of the power of this party. There is no need to stress the influence that any significant aggregation of power might have for the final outcome of the conflict. That the Polish government succeeded in getting significant political support from its natural ally, the Soviet Union, undermined the efficacy of Solidarity's struggle to a great extent. The Soviet Union is obviously the most powerful international factor in Eastern Europe and its support had tremendous impact. In practice, Soviet support for Jaruzelski's government could neither be balanced by Western support for Solidarity nor by a similar simultaneous anti-government nonviolent action within the Soviet Union itself.

In consequence, Solidarity's strategy always had to consider the coercive abilities of both the Polish and Soviet authorities.[52]

CONCLUSIONS

The analysis of the Polish resistance shows that nonviolent actions forced the disintegrated Polish authorities to agree to a compromise based on a programme of limited demands presented by the strikers in Summer 1980. After the military takeover in December 1981, the nonviolent actions secured the organizational survival of Solidarity and helped it to develop independently of state activities, especially in the field of culture and information. Therefore, the Polish case represents the most effective application of nonviolent action in the history of communism. At the same time, however, nonviolence has been unable to meet Solidarity's limited objectives such as freedom for trade unions, a certain pattern of economic reforms, freedom for all political prisoners, and official abandonment of censorship.

Solidarity was able to deny the authorities certain objectives. Nevertheless, its nonviolent actions were unable to deny the authorities the major power privileges. They were even unable to force them to grant significant political and economic concessions. It goes without saying that Solidarity was unable to liberate Poland totally from the communist yoke, although this was never a direct aim of Solidarity's struggle.

It is pointless to criticize Solidarity for failing to meet its basic objectives. After all, Solidarity's nonviolent resistance achieved much more than has any emancipatory movement in Eastern Europe during the last decades. It is, however, useful to confront some theoretical expectations concerning nonviolence with the Polish experiences.[53]

NOTES

1. According to Gene Sharp, nonviolent action is a "technique used to control, combat and destroy the opponent's power by nonviolent means of wielding power," See: Gene Sharp. The Politics of Nonviolent Action. Porter Sargent, Boston 1973, p. 4.
   The literature on nonviolence is characterized by an abundance of terminology. Similar nonviolent actions had been termed: nonviolent defence (or offence), nonviolent resistance, defence by civil resistance, unarmed resistance, nonmilitary defence or resistance, social defence or self-defence, etc. Since this essay does not pretend to create any universal operational model of studying nonviolence, the question of the definition of basic terms is not crucial. For instance, this flexible terminological approach is adopted by the Swedish Commission on Resistance. See: Bulletin of Peace Proposals no. 1, Oslo 1985, pp. 26-31. The opposite view is expressed, among others, in Hakan Wiberg. The Conditions of Nonviolent Action, in: Gustaaf Geeraerts, (ed.), Possibilities of Civilian Defence in Western Europe. Polemological Centre of the Free University of Brussels, Brussels 1977, p. 103 and ff.
   Nevertheless, terminological flexibility does not eliminate all the problems that emerge when we try to apply different terms to the Polish case. For instance, the term "nonviolent" is even difficult to translate into Polish. The Polish opposition usually used the term "social self-defence", which was introduced by KOR, a well-known forerunner of Solidarity. This terminological difference does not exclusively express semantic objections, it also includes those of doctrine (although not always clearly defined due to the lack of

tradition and theory of nonviolence). However, terminological problems could be reduced if we consider that a) the Polish social self-defence movement strictly observes the principle of nonviolence which is sufficient to approach it by using Sharp's term of "nonviolent action"; b) the "defence" (self-defence) is usually defined as a "collective attempt to preserve or achieve a form of life and social structure when that form of life and social structure is threatened from without or within". See: Johan Galtung. Peace, War and Defence, vol.2. Christian Ejlers, Copenhagen 1976, p. 379. Social defence is defined by Galtung in similar terms as "defence of what one might call life-style". See: Johan Galtung. Two Concepts of Defence. Bulletin of Peace Proposals no. 4, Oslo 1978, p. 329.

Poland's form of life and social structure is threatened not only from within (the dictatorship of the Party) but also from without (the power and influence of the Soviet Union and the ruling regimes of other countries of the Warsaw Pact). However, it is sometimes impossible to make a clear distinction between these two sorts of threats. In fact, the literature on nonviolence does not make a great distinction between reistance against a foreign aggressor and domestic usurpers who are supported by foreign powers. The Polish events of December 13, 1981 appear to confirm this opinion. See e.g. Leszek Kolakowski. Ja bede lagodniejszym katem. Aneks, no.27, London 1982, pp. 2-4.

2. There exists a rich tradition of approaching problems of violence and nonviolence within the context of theories on social revolutions, with their emphasis on studies of the social bases of power, obedience and revolt. (In fact, beginning with writings of Aristotle and ending with works of Hannah Arendt, Barrington Moore or Theda Skocpol.) In principle, however, I do not refer to these theories in this essay and try to present my argument within the context of modern peace research.

3. Herman de Lange indicated serious dangers in drawing general and universal conclusions from specific cases of nonviolent action. See: Herman de Lange. Gebruik en misbruik van historische "case-studies", in: Met/Zonder Geweld. Schotanus, Utrecht 1972, pp. 14-26.

4. Polish historical tradition of nonviolent actions is presented in: Krzysztof Pomian. L'espoir s'effrite; Alternatives. Non-violence, Paris/Montrond, hiver 1984, pp. 31-32.

5. There were two basic reasons for this. The workers' protests were spontaneous so that rebellion ensued. In other words, the lack of organization and tactics was responsible for the violence. Second, the authorities themselves refused to negotiate and opted for violence. The experiences of 1968 give an even clearer example of governmental provocation. See especially: Wojciech Modzelewski. Nonviolence and the Strike Movements in Poland. Journal of Peace Research no. 2, Oslo 1982, pp. 107-109.

6. Biuletyn Informacyjny KOR. May, Warsaw 1977, p. 3. Initiatives of the kind mentioned above have certainly influenced Solidarity. For instance, Tadeusz Mazowiecki, who in the 1970's was the editor of the Catholic monthly Wiez, became a principal adviser of Lech

111

Walesa. In 1981 he also edited Solidarity's major weekly - Solidarnosc. Many of those who began a hunger strike in 1977 constituted the leadership of Solidarity three years later.

7. Jean-Marie Muller. Strategia politycznego dzialania bez stosowania przemocy. Wydawnictwo Krag, Warsaw 1984, and Gene Sharp. Walka bez uzycia przemocy. Wydawnictwo Ad Sum, Gdansk 1984.

8. The nonviolent popular resistance against the Soviet invasion of 1968 is frequently elaborated in the literature on nonviolence. See especially A. Roberts and P. Windsor. Czechoslovakia 1968, Repression and Resistance. Chatto and Windus, London 1969.

9. This is not fully comprehended by some orthodox advocates of nonviolence, but is acknowledged by, for instance, the Swedish Commission on Resistance. See: Bulletin of Peace Proposals no.1, 1985, pp. 26-31. The case of civilian defence is also studied by governments of other European countries, such as Norway, Germany or the Netherlands. So far, however, the Swedish Report on complementary forms of defence prepared by the Commission on Resistance is the most educational. As far as other studies are concerned see: Hylke Tromp. The Dutch Research Project on Civilian Defence, 1974-1978: An Inquiry Into Alternative Security and Nonviolent Conflict Resolution. Bulletin of Peace Proposals, no.4, 1978, pp. 301 and ff., or M. Stinnes. Theoretical Perspectives in: Civilian Defense. An Issue in West German Peace Research, in: Gustaaf Geeraerts (ed.), Possibilities of Civilian Defence in Western Europe. Op.cit...pp. 77 and ff.

10. Opposition to violence as a means of social struggle emerges from the whole concept of resistance to the communist domination in Poland, which was created by KOR and later inherited by Solidarity. See especially: Leszek Kolakowski. Hope and Hopelessness. Survey, Summer, 1971, pp. 37 and ff., as well as Jacek Kuron. Co robic? Instytut Literacki, Paris 1978, pp. 31 and ff.

11. Gene Sharp. The Politics of Nonviolent Action. Op cit...pp. 10-36.

12. See especially: The programme "The Self-Governing Commonwealth" adopted by the First National Congress of Solidarity, in October 1981. The TKK's (the Temporary Coordinating Commission of Solidarity) statement was issued on July 1982. See also: Timothy Garton Ash. Poland: The Uses of Adversity. The New York Review of Books, June 27, 1985, pp. 5-10.

13. See e.g., Bjorn Hettne. The Vitality of Gandhian Tradition. Journal of Peace Research no.3, Oslo 1976, pp. 230-233. Compare also with: Bohdan Cywinski. Mysl polityczna Edwarda Abramowskiego, in: Tworcy polskiej mysli politycznej. Ossolineum, Wroclaw 1978, pp. 29-106, and Adam Michnik, Rozmowa w Cytadeli, in: Adam Michnik. Szanse polskiej demokracji. Aneks, London 1984, pp. 241 and ff.

14. Severyn T. Bruyn. Social Theory of Nonviolent Action, in: S.T. Bruyn and P.M. Rayman, (eds.), Nonviolent Action and Social Change. Irvington, New York 1979, p. 29, and George Lakey. Strategy for a Living Revolution. W.H. Freeman and Co., San Francisco 1973, p. 47.

15. See e.g., Seweryn Blumsztajn. Renoncer à la violence. Alternatives. Non-violence, Paris/Monstrond, hiver 1984, pp. 60-62.

16. See especially: Solidarnosc. Biuletyn Informacyjny no.65, Paris 1983, pp. 11-12.

17. See e.g. Giuliano Pontara. The Rejection of Violence in Gandhian Ethics of Conflict Resolution, Journal of Peace Research no.2, Oslo 1965, pp. 207-208.

18. See: Kjell Skjelsbaek. The Challenge before Churches. Bulletin of Peace Proposals no.3, Oslo 1984, p. 200, or Bruce Russett. Ethical Dilemmas of Nuclear Deterrence. International Security no.4, Cambridge Mass. 1984, pp. 36-54.

19. Students of history of social revolutions devote their special attention to this question. See e.g., Barrington Moore. Injustice. The Social Bases of Obedience and Revolt. Macmillan, London 1979, pp. 81-110. However, these studies are not under consideration in this article.

20. The distinction between the instrumentalists and structuralists is made by Gustaaf Geeraerts, in: Gustaaf Geeraerts. Two Approaches to Civilian Defense. Bulletin of Peace Proposals, no.4, Oslo 1978, pp. 31 and ff.

21. For instance, the question arises whether the readiness to resist can, in the sense of an independent variable, be related to personality studies. See: Johan Niezing. Rethinking Utopia. Some Sceptical Remarks on the Methodology of Civilian Based Defence Research. Bulletin of Peace Proposals no.4, Oslo 1982, p. 331.

22. Conduct of the boycott of the elections to the local councils in June 1984 is the remarkable exception here. See: The Uncensored Poland. News Bulletin no.9, London 1984, pp. 9-13 (concerning preparations), and the TKK statement concerning the results of the elections, published in: Solidarnosc News no.28, Brussels 1984, p.2.

23. Wladyslaw Frasyniuk quoted in M. Lopinski, M. Moskit and J. Wilk. Konspira. Rzecz o podziemnej Solidarnisci. Spotkania, Paris 1985. pp. 70-71.

24. Journal of Peace Research no.4, Oslo 1980, pp. 281 and ff.

25. See especially: Seweryn Blumsztajn. Je Rentre Au Pays. Calman-Lévy, Paris 1985, pp. 34 and ff.

26. Johan Galtung in the above-quoted article presents nearly an identical analysis of Polish society to this of Kuron and Modzelewski in the 1960's. See: Jacek Kuron and Karol

Modzelewski, An Open Letter to the Party. International Socialist Publications, London 1969, especially page 15.

27. See especially Leszek Kolakowski. Hope and Hopelessness. Survey, Summer 1971, pp. 48 and vff

28. See especially Egbert Jahn. Social and Political Conditions for the Expansion of the Nonviolent Movement, in: Gustaf Geeraerts, (ed.), Possibilities of Civilian Defence in Western Europe. Op.cit...pp. 20-33.

29. A failure to organize a strike action several days earlier supports this thesis. See: Neal Ascherson. Polish August. Penguin, Harmondsworth 1981, p. 146.

30. The TKK statement of July 9, 1982 entitled "Five Times - Yes", in: Solidarnosc. Biuletyn Informacyjny no.29, Paris 1982, p. 2. The terms "national agreement" or "economic reforms" can hardly be understood without further explanation. In fact, we could observe within Solidarity the evolution of opinions concerning the exact meaning of these slogans. See e.g., P. Spiski (ed.), Od trzynastego do trzynastego. Polonia, London, 1983, pp. 126-127, and 166-167.

31. See e.g.: Fred H. Eidlin. Capitulation, Resistance and the Framework of Normalization: the August 1968 Invasion of Czechoslovakia and the Czechoslovak Response. Journal of Peace Research no.4, Oslo 1981, p. 324.

32. For instance, the Report of the Swedish Commission on Resistance states that the aim of nonviolent civilian defence would always be a "total liberation". At the same time, however, the Report states that the purposes of non-military resistance are only to "demonstrate the absolute will of our people to retain or regain freedom, to strengthen national solidarity and unity, to protect the interests and well-being of the Swedish people, and to uphold Swedish ideological and social views and to keep alien influence on our society to a minimum...". See: Complementary Forms of Defence. Report of the Swedish Commission on Resistance. Bulletin of Peace Proposals no.1, Oslo 1985, pp.21-23. In other words, the nonviolent resistance can "contribute towards the aim of Liberation", but itself is not supposed to bring about a total liberation.

33. The same could be said about the aims of the Czechoslovak resistance of 1968.

34. See e.g.: Leszek Nowak. Neither Revolution nor Evolution. Dialog, Frankfurt/Main 1984, pp. 131 and ff., or Leszek Kolakowski. Rewolucja jako piekna choroba. Aneks, London 1982, pp. 225-233. See also: Adam Michnik, The New Evolutionism. Survey, Winter 1976, p. 272.

35. Zbigniew Bujak. Positional Warfare. Survey, Summer 1982, p. 155. The opposite argument is presented by Jacek Kuron. Theses on Solving Insoluble Problem. Survey, Summer 1982, p. 153.

36. See also: Wiktor Kulerski, The Third Possibility. Survey, Summer 1982, p. 158.

37. André Glucksman. Miedzy czerwienia a biela. Aneks no.32, London 1983, p. 8.

38. D.J. Toscano. Gandhi's Decentralist Vision: A Perspective on Nonviolent Economies, in: S.T. Bruyn and P.M. Rayman. Nonviolent Actions and Social Change. Op.cit...p. 75.

39. M.K. Gandhi. Selected Works. Vol.VI. Navajiran Trust, Ahmedabad 1968, p. 437.

40. Egbert Jahn. Prospects and Impasses of the New Peace Movements. Bulletin of Peace Proposals no.1, Oslo 1984, p. 51.

41. Students of nonviolence often use "successful" in a very confusing way. In this chapter I use "successful action" when I want to say that the action itself was well organized and got popular support. For instance, a street march was successful if many people went to the streets at a certain time. When I want to say that the action met its objectives then I use "effective" or "efficient".

42. The potential of strike action was frequently elaborated in the literature on nonviolence. See e.g.: Gene Sharp. The Politics of Nonviolent Action. Op.cit...pp. 268-280. However, the most illustrative and rich material about strikes may be found in the relevant literature on industrial action. See e.g.: E.T. Hiller. The Strike: A Study in Collective Action. University of Chicago Press, Chicago 1928, or J. Barbash. Labor Unions in Action: A Study of the Mainsprings of Unionism. Harper and Bros, New York 1948.

43. See especially the statement of the Regional Solidarity Commission, issued on November 1982, and published in: Solidarnosc. Biuletyn Informacyjny no.44, Paris 1982, as well as the statement of the TKK, also from November 1982, published in: Solidarnosc. Biuletyn Informacyjny no.46, Paris 1982.

44. See for example, a relevant discussion published in: Solidarnosc. Biuletyn Informacyjny no.23, Paris 1982, pp. 2-7, or no.28, Paris 1982, pp. 2-10. See also: M. Lopinski, M. Moskit, and M. Wilk. Konspira. Rzecz o podziemnej Solidarnosci. Op.cit...pp. 68-78, 114-136.

45. Solidarity's programme entitled "Solidarity Today", issued in January 1983. The programme also made it clear that preparatory actions to a general strike do not preclude a "programme of a gradual transformation of the system. A general strike is merely a means of toppling the present dictatorship and creating the necessary conditions for democratic reform".

46. Bogdan Lis. Trade Union in 1984. English version published in August 1984 by the Coordinating Office Abroad of NSZZ Solidarnosc, Brussels 1984, p. 9.

47. See e.g., Solidarnosc. Biuletyn Informacyjny no.45, Paris 1982, p. 12, Solidarnosc News no.28, Brussels 1984, p. 2 or Kontakt no.12, Paris 1985, pp. 30-34.

48. For instance, in 1984 one independent observer noted:
    Hundreds of underground periodicals are being published more or less regularly, scores of new titles are added annually to the already rich library of underground book publishing, some of them in quantities which would seem respectable even to Western commercial publishers. Living-room theatre, underground cabaret, unofficial art exhibitions are flourishing. Tens of thousand of Poles attend unofficial adult education classes... participation in the underground frequently taps professional skills that the state does not call upon. A group of historians is making ready for publication - out of the country and underground, of course - a vast history of Poland during the last forty years. The participants in such activities risk severe reprisals ranging from dismissal from their jobs to long terms of imprisonment under appalling conditions. Even so, their numbers appear to be growing. See: Aryeh Neier. The Poles Suprising New Phase. The International Herald Tribune, May 11, 1984.

49. One can multiply the examples of these sorts of symbolic actions successfully applied by Solidarity's supporters all over the country. In this respect see especially: Solidarnosc. Biuletyn Informacyjny no.87, Paris 1984, pp. 10-12.

50. Gene Sharp. The Politics of Nonviolent Actions. Op.cit...p. 8.

51. Jean Jacques Rousseau. The Social Contract, in: The Social Contract and Discourses. E.P. Dutton, New York 1920, p. 8.

52. Recent studies by Alex Schmid indicated that nonviolence did not bring about any significant results in four cases of resistance against Soviet military interventions, namely in Lithuania (1944-52), East Germany (1953), Hungary (1956) and Czechoslovakia (1968). See Alex Schmid (ed.), Social Defence and Soviet Military Power: An Inquiry into Relevance of an Alternative Defence concept. C.O.M.T., Leiden 1985, pp. 389-398 and 431-432.

53. First of all, students of nonviolence should comprehend that people choose nonviolent means of struggle because of various social ideological, and tactical factors. People do not choose nonviolent forms of struggle because of the mere existence of the theory and tradition of nonviolence.
    Second, people's readiness to resist is not a direct function of the application of certain socio-technical methods but depends instead on various socioeconomic interests of the people. However, these interests can hardly be identified with a stereotype model of social development based on the belief in proletarian revolution and anti-militarism.
    Third, students of nonviolence should abandon any simplistic thoughts concerning the complex relationship between nonviolent action, nonviolent strategy, and objectives of nonviolent action. One can always make a distinction between long-term and short-term objectives of nonviolent action. However, the Polish case

demonstrates that the real objectives of nonviolent resistance are very limited in practice.

Fourth, it is important to comprehend that "success" in organizing a particular form of nonviolent action (e.g., a street march or strike with a mass participation) does not always mean that this form of action met its goals and objectives (e.g., the release of political prisoners, increase of wages).

Fifth, it is important to link studies on nonviolence with studies on political violence. Students of nonviolence should not ignore the fact that the ability and willingness of foreign or domestic authorities to apply violence against nonviolent resistance determines the outcome of the struggle to a great extent.

V The experiment with communist statism

In this essay I will analyse doctrinal and political developments on the part of the authorities in Poland. I will focus on why Polish communist leaders reacted to the socio-political crisis by promoting a sort of doctrinal statism and corporatism; on the role of the state within the traditional communist system and in present-day Poland; on the relations between the Army and the Party, the elements of corporatist structure; and on sources of political legitimacy.

In particular, I will try to answer the question whether all new political developments in Poland represent a remarkable departure from the original Leninist–Stalinist model of state and society?

The position (activities) of the Polish authorities in the 1980's presented students of comparative communism with a certain dilemma. The military coup d'etat in December 1981 stimulated the development of a new political trend in Poland which I call statism. What does the new Polish statism amount to? First of all, it amounts to an apparent reduction in the role of the Communist Party and to a considerable strengthening of the organs of the state. In other words, Polish statism promotes the dictatorship of the state and the Army rather than the dictatorship of the Party. Second, the new statism amounts to a sort of ideological indifference. Polish statism promotes nationalism and a corporate vision of society and at the same time tries to minimize the actual role of the proletariat. |Third, the new statism amounts to an effort to create a new source of legitimacy based on a system of law, no matter how arbitrarily created. Under the new statism the present Polish rulers are trying to set up the rational state and promote the idea of a non-rational society. They oppose the group collectivism of Solidarity against the all-national interest which is exclusively embodied by the state.|

The rulers claim that the state is the only institution which is able to protect individual rights from the dictatorship of trade unions and workers' councils. They believe that only the state can play the role of objective and even indifferent arbiter, a necessary role for resolving Polish conflicts. It is also the state which can protect the national sovereignty of the Poles.

The onmipotent position of the state is a basic principle of the communist system, or at least it has been since Stalin formulated his theory on the special role of the state in the development of communism. According to Stalin: "the withering away of the state will not come about through weakening the state's power, but rather through its maximum strengthening".[1] However, Stalin's theory did not imply any significant reduction in the leading role of the Party, neither ideological indifference nor the establishment of direct military dictatorship. Even at the time when the compulsory power of the state was widely used against millions of Soviet citizens, communist propaganda tried to avoid promotion of any form of doctrinal statism. "Anti-state activity" was punished because it questioned the social substance of the state (i.e., dictatorship of the proletariat, the leading role of the Party, or the rule of comrade Stalin) rather than the formal structure of the state. But such things are no longer the concern of contemporary Polish rulers.

To a certain extent, the new vision of Polish statism is a governmental tactic, expressed through propaganda. Modern Polish history can produce many examples of such policies. "Internationalist socialism" was a favourite slogan under the Stalinist rule of Boleslaw Bierut. His successor, Wladyslaw Gomulka spoke of "Polish socialism", and later, Edward Gierek's policy was often identified with a managerial socialism. General Jaruzelski's statist socialism provides the authorities with three important arguments.[2]

First of all, the authorities claim that the statist coup d'etat neutralized two dangerous extremes. On the one side - the anti-Soviet current represented by Solidarity and, on the other side - the orthodox communist current represented by the dogmatic wing of the Party. Victory of the non-ideological state-oriented group was a victory for the political centre. It represents a realistic choice between complete sovietization of Poland and the naive vision of absolute independence for Poland.

Second, the statist coup d'etat eliminated the moralistic approach to politics and made it possible to apply criteria of rationality. Solidarity's struggle for absolute dignity and nobility, truth and moral virtue opposed pragmatism and rationality. It caused fanaticism and blindness, it cultivated a crusading spirit, which consequently made any compromise impossible.

Three, the statist coup d'etat constrained the collectivist aspirations of Solidarity which, in principle, had been over-optimistic. Solidarity aimed at the introduction of self-management and self-government in all areas of public life without considering the economic and social consequences of such an experiment. Moreover, Solidarity's collectivism implied tyranny of the majority, it eliminated individual initiative and promoted group demagogy. Statism puts an end to the messianic aspirations of the spontaneous Polish movement. It represents a careful and pragmatic policy which promotes efficiency rather than utopian egalitarianism.

The lack of substance and the rhetoric of the above arguments has been pointed out by many writers in the clandestine press as well as by some official columnists. Daniel Passent observed, for instance, that the statist rhetoric confuses the state with the authorities. In consequence, Polish statism means only the infallibility and inviolability of the present government.[3] Maciej Kiersnowski has indicated that the rationality of the state is identified with the rationality of its leaders. But such identification can hardly be called rational.[4] Krystyna Piotrowska-Hochweld has complained that the official argumentation considers society as being unrealistic per se, and as being short-sighted and unable to define long-term social goals. In practice, this implies that only the central government is in a position to "discover and formulate the national interest".[5] Wojciech Lamentowicz argues that "totalitarian, all-national state-promoting realism" represents conservatist dogmatism and facilitates manipulation of and repressions against any authentic social activity.[6]

However, Polish statism represents something more than mere justification of the iron fist policy of the government. Indeed, the crisis brought about a significant change in Poland's political system and in consequence, a remarkable departure from the original Leninist-Stalinist model. This departure from the original Leninist-Stalinist model does not necessarily imply a total change in the very nature of the communist system. One could imagine various ways of executing political and economic power within the Soviet block. Nevertheless, any evolution in this respect requires careful and detailed study.[7]

The most significant of these changes concern the role of the major political forces, namely the Party and the Army. These changing roles have stimulated a reappraisal of the role and function of the state itself. We begin, however, with reviewing the evolution of communist ideas concerning the role of the state and its major institutions in the development of sovietism. This historical review will indicate to what extent the rhetoric of Polish statism differs from the official Soviet doctrine.

FRIENDS OF THE MODERN STATE

There is little doubt that the original ideas of Karl Marx opposed the ideology of statism. First of all, in his long critique of Hegel, Marx especially attacked the idea that the state was, in its origin and value, quite independent of the empirical individuals who composed it.[8] This implied negation of Hegel's thesis that the state acts as a brake on and arbiter in the anarchical war of all against all in civil society. The Hegelian dichotomy of civil society and state is seen by Marx as the very negation of democracy. Marx sees the essence of democracy as the organic unity of the two.[9] Genuinely free man needs to be rescued from two kinds of despotism - the abstract, purely political state, and domination by money, the one conditioning the other.[10]

Secondly, Marx saw the state as an instrument of class rule, to be understood not in any abstract philosophical or legal sense, but as a means to achieve domination. In this context two conclusions follow which are of great importance to Marx's doctrine: (a) the disappearance of the state in a classless society, and (b) the necessity to destroy the existing state machine by a revolution.

The first conclusion is evident. The state is not eternal, but a transient feature of civilization which will disappear with class divisions. Once class division has been abolished there will no longer be a need for an institution whose function is to maintain it and oppress the exploited class.

As far as the second conclusion is concerned, abolition of the bourgeois state is a step towards the abolition of the state in general, but during the period when the victorious working class is still fighting the exploiters, it must possess its own means of coercion - this is the dictatorship of the proletariat. (Marx said nothing about party rule.)[11]

Lenin did not significantly develop the marxist theory of the state. However, from his book entitled "State and Revolution" one may derive basic recommendations which can by no means be identified with statism:[12] (a) A true proletarian revolution must completely smash the old bourgeois state; neither armed forces nor administrative agencies can be taken over by the proletariat; (b) while the proletarian dictatorship would use force to suppress the last remnants of bourgeois resistance, it will need "no special machinery for repression". Instead, the armed people themselves will deal with their own security; (c) the administration of the new proletarian state (or "half-state", as Lenin called it) will be carried out not by highly paid administrators possessed of special knowledge, but by ordinary citizens receiving workers wages; (d) the proletarian dictatorship will be highly centralized in order to smash the last remnants of a bourgeois regime and to operate a vast integrated economic mechanism.

Even more importantly, Lenin created a basis for a special role for the Party, whose correct theoretical consciousness is supposed to "embody proletarian consciousness", and therefore is destined to realize the dictatorship of the proletariat.[13] In fact, however, dictatorship by the Party was seen in terms of the Party's practical role during the Revolution and afterwards, rather than of Lenin's theoretical considerations.

Nevertheless, as far as the Soviet state is concerned the actual situation remained rather unclear in the early 1920's, and in consequence, Sidney and Beatrice Webb were able to present an utopian anti-state self-governmental vision of the Soviet system.[14] Such ambiguity was soon resolved through experience of the development of the Soviet system as well as by the new theoretical works of Stalin.

The role of the state enjoyed a period of rapid growth, especially after completion of the governmental structure in the form of the USSR Constitution of 1923. Party members, however, were not at all certain how important the Party would become. Party officials had rushed to occupy governmental positions in the belief that the governmental structure would now become more important than the Party.[15] Party and governmental organs merged, not in a formal structured way, but through their overlapping personnel, and their day-to-day deliberations. The responsibilities of the Party and the state's assemblies, presidiums, and councils "intermeshed and became ill-defined".[16]

The state ruled by the Party started to dominate all areas of social life and the system drifted towards totalitarianism where nearly all social ties were replaced by state-imposed organization and where consequently, all groups and all individuals were supposed to work only for goals which were both the goals of the state, and defined as such by the state.

The well-known main stages for this development were: (a) elimination of basic forms of representative democracy - parliament, elections, political parties, uncontrolled press, etc.; (b) introduction of so-called "war communism" through, i.e., abrogation of free trade, universal rationing, compulsory labour, etc. After a short term experiment with the New Economic Policy basic features of "war communism" became a permanent element of Soviet policy; (c) destruction of the working class as a political force through, i.e., elimination of all free trade unions or suppression of democracy in the Party itself; (d) coercive collectivization which gave the state the full power to control economic life and destroyed the independence of peasants, craftsmen, and private farmers; (e) great political purges in which millions of potential "enemies" of the system were exterminated.[17]

Stalin himself claimed that the state's repressive and non-repressive functions grew together with the development of socialism. Moreover, the socialist state had still to suppress domestic and foreign enemies (according to Stalin the class struggle was not automatically reduced by the development of socialism). On the other hand, development of socialism required a growth of the state's functions as organizer of the socialist economy, as well as of its functions as educator and promoter of culture.

In consequence, Stalin said that the withering away of the state will not come about through weakening its power, but rather through its maximum strengthening.[18]

Stalin set up the grandiose position of the state which has never been significantly changed since the death of its master. However, the theory and practice of Stalinism cannot be identified with the philosophy of Hegel, nor with any political doctrine of statism.[19] Stalinism neither recognized the Hegelian division between the independent state and "the empirical individuals who composed it" nor did it glorify the "purely political state", which "acts as a brake on and an arbiter in the anarchical society". On the contrary, Stalinism embodied Marxist ideas by the efficient abolition of the distinction between the civil society and the state, and it abrogated all mediating devices that prevented individuals from achieving perfect identity with the "whole". This was achieved through "suppression and elimination of the civil society".[20]

This process has been carried out mainly through the Communist Party. Stalinism crystallized and strengthened the dictatorship of the Party. It is not true that during the period of Stalin, Soviet society was ruled by the police. As Leszek Kolakowski points out: "Stalin governed the country, and the Party itself, with the police machine, yet he governed as party leader, not as police chief. The Party - which for a quarter of a century was identified with Stalin - has never lost its all-embracing sway".[21]

This statement does not under-estimate the role of Stalin's security police - NKVD. In the first place, Khrushchev's claims that the state would certainly wither away, and in fact was already then starting to wither, were directed against the vast and competitive power of the NKVD. The Party should keep society and the economy together until at last it would merge with the remnants of the former state structure and a number of non-governmental organizations into some kind of all-embracing public organization. Khrushchev claimed that the state was temporary and bound to phases of history. In his view, it had now entered the stage of being the "state of all the people", no longer a repressive force except to a few incorrigibles at home and potential enemies abroad, but an expression of voluntary social coordination.[22] In practice, transferral of the state's power to the non-governmental organizations meant exclusively the strengthening of Party control over the state. As Khrushchev expressed it: "the Party has stronger foundations than the state organs. It arose and exists not as a result of the duties of a law-maker: Its development was evoked by circumstances stemming from the political concepts of the people... from principles of a moral nature."[23]

Softened by Khrushchev, Stalinism has continued to the present day. It was not modified by either Leonid Brezhnev or Yuri Andropov. Brezhnev's concept of "developed" or "mature" socialism underlined the role of the so-called "public organizations". The concept assumed that a better level of education and the accummulation of political experience among the population at large have created the possibility of much greater public involvement in political life. Thus, in the concept of "developed socialism" there is room for a broadening and deepening of both the socialist state and socialist democracy.[24] According to official Soviet sources, "the state of the whole people" became "the newest and highest stage in the development of the socialist state", due to "deep changes that have taken place in the social and political life of Soviet society", which "provided the conditions for the transformation of the state of the dictatorship of the proletariat into the state of the whole people".[25]

This approach could have opened the gates for some sort of statism, but it did not. The role of the Party remained unchanged, although it now became "the Party of the whole people".[26]

Since the late 1940's the Soviet system has existed in all East European countries, including Poland.[27] However, some elements of this system were never fully introduced into Poland. Attempts to introduce such elements as collectivization of land were not successful in the 1950's, and the whole sector of the "second economy" was never completely crushed, and even began to grow during the 1970's. The ideological influence of Christianity was never eliminated due to the strong position of the Catholic Church. Several non-governmental organizations were able to preserve some sort of independence, and since the mid-seventies activities in open opposition to the Party have grown very strong.

Despite all this, the basic principles of the Soviet system

dominated Polish political life: the leading role of the Party, the special role of its ideology, the system of law which constitutes the arbitrary power of the authorities over the individual, the oligarchical system of political leadership, the dominant position of the public economy, systematic police control, total control over all means of mass-communication, etc. All these elements of the Soviet system were present in communist Poland until the emergence of Solidarity. As far as the theory of state is concerned, Poland endured all stages of the Soviet evolution with no significant modifications - from the Stalinist-type of one-person autocracy to "the state of the whole people".[28]

Nevertheless, already by the end of the 1970's, the successive crises in Poland stimulated the evolution of the official communist approach to the question of state. The existence and importance of the Polish "islands of separateness" (the Church, the democratic opposition, the universities, the family, etc.), had a tremendous influence on this process. Finally, the last and most serious crisis of 1980 accelerated and sanctioned the new policy of a Polish ruling elite.[29]

The first attack was noticeably directed against the theory of the withering away of the state. Jerzy Smialowski, in his curious but remarkable book described this theory as one which is "inadequate", "ideologically disfunctional", "non-actual", "useless", and which in consequence "plays neither cognitive nor revolutionary functions".[30] In order to support his thesis, Smialowski apotheosized the "non-dogmatic and progressive" works of Stalin and Vyshinsky.

However, neither Smialowski nor other Polish friends of the modern state used Stalin's major arguments which arose from the perception of the class struggle and a historical need for the dictatorship of the proletariat. On the contrary, they argued that the class struggle had disappeared but that the state remained untouched. Moreover, the state which was "liberated from the huge class ballast" could now fully perform all-national, universal functions. It could become the real "state of the whole people".

According to a major ideologist of the present Polish regime, Kazimierz Kozniewski, the state became an "all-national, class-ambivalent institution". The state became the "superior institution" which has a "transcedental value".[31] The state and its authorities play a role of the "natural super-arbiter" in society. The state is like "red and green lights which stay on the cross-roads of people's fates and

127

activities".[32]

Another Polish ideologist, Mieczyslaw Michalik, argues that the state represents a "value" through which the entire people's fate, dignity and happiness can be realized.[33] This, according to Michalik, requires the existence of a "strong socialist state".[34]

Stanislaw Rainko goes even further in his apotheosis of the socialist state. In his view, the socialist state carries special political and economic responsibility which is difficult to compare with any other historical forms of state organization. Rainko believes that this special responsibility of the socialist state "cannot be transferred to any social bodies" because, as he puts it, "this would transform these social bodies into a sort of state within the state...".[35]

According to various other official or semi-official statements, it is the state rather than the Party or the society as a whole which expresses the "universal rationality".[36] In other words, the "general will" can be defined and executed only by the state. And the freedom of the individual is threatened by "self-governmental group collectivism" rather than by the omnipotence of the state.[37] The Polish state as such is therefore of the greatest value to Poland.[38].

In fact, man does not know any freedom other than "freedom within the state and freedom with the state".[39]

The above-mentioned opinions resemble the Hegelian philosophy of state. However, the intentions of their authors are much more limited and they are of a pragmatic nature. It may be an exaggeration to say that there exists in Poland a complete and officially recognized vision of the new statist system. Nevertheless, the theoretical and practical consequences of this new view on the nature and role of the communist state are remarkable.

First, they stress the all-national interest rather than the proletarian one. The industrial working class not only failed to recognize its "real interest" in August 1980 (especially by joining and supporting Solidarity), but also its historical social role as such should no longer be over-estimated.[40] Naturally, this implies a new approach to the whole problem of the dictatorship of the proletariat.[41] In consequence, a new corporate vision of Polish society is presented. A vision which promotes nationalism and facilitates the openness towards the Catholic Church among other things.

Second, the state rather than the Communist Party is destined to

including next page.

define general social interest. The state acts as the "super-arbiter" in resolving social conflicts rather than as a supplier of social goods.[42] It is the Army and the state authorities who should play a leading role in the country. The Party should inspire fulfilment of this role, but in reality plays a secondary role within this system.

Third, the state should be equipped with the tools it needs to play its new role. On the one hand, this implies the new role of law and the state's compulsory power. On the other hand, it implies the creation of new organs of the state and modification of the already existing ones. The newly created state institutions - the State Tribunal, and the Constitutional Tribunal - are supposed to strengthen the credibility of autonomous state judgements.

Moreover, the new system of law is supposed to create a new source of political legitimacy for the ruling elite.

I will try to elaborate these three major elements of Polish statism.

THE ARMY VERSUS THE PARTY

According to the 1982 declaration of the Polish Communist Party, the state embodies the highest political value, and the Army is the key political subject of the state.[43] The Party is still needed in order to overcome the crisis, but it first has to regain "a wide social acceptance". It needs to clean up, and renew itself.[44] Until it succeeds in this it should concentrate on secondary matters rather than on the direct execution of political power. According to General Jaruzelski, the first task of the Party is to promote good work and to condemn irregularities.[45]

Official Polish rhetoric continues to emphasize the leading role of the Party, but the inconsistency of its principal set of arguments makes it difficult to define precisely what the leading role of the Party actually means.

In 1986 Party leaders were still unable to say that their Party had fully recovered. Instead they continued to talk about the process of regaining the strength of the Party and overcoming its weaknesses.[46]

The Party's new position is a direct result of its practical failure rather than the effect of any theoretical reconsiderations The military take-over in December 1981 - only post factum accepted by the Party-was the most evident example of the inability of the Party to cope with the problems it faced. The Party had lost its position as the mass and disciplined organization which was able to mobilize its rank and file as well as the people as a whole. It had also lost its ability to administer the state and direct its institutions. The Party had lost its ideological influence and its leaders had become deeply demoralized and corrupted. It lost organizational discipline as well as its political identity. The ruling elites in Poland had to turn to political organizations other than the Party in order to preserve their power and, by the same token, Soviet domination. Ironically, this political shift also prevented the lasting collapse of the Party.

The huge crisis within the Party was elaborated extensively by the Party leaders themselves. General Wojciech Jaruzelski stated that the Party had "lost the support of the working class even before August 1980".[47] Later, Party organizations were "paralyzed because of the activity of the enemies", but also because of their own "weaknesses".[48]

Kazimierz Bracikowski, a Politbureau member, indicated that the Party lost 760,000 members during one year (1982).[49] The report of the Party's special commission, led by Hieronim Kubiak, pointed to the low moral principles of Party members.[50]

The criticism of independent observers was more bitter and more comprehensive.[51]

Under traditional doctrine the Party's functions can be grouped into five categories:

(a) the Party represents and expresses the socialist ideology underlying the entire political system. It determines the fundamental aims and values which constitute the basis for the functioning of the state and its institutions;

(b) through the activity of its members in the institutions of the state and social organizations, the Party "harmonizes the functioning of these institutions with the goals of the system";

(c) the Party determines the directives of policy-making by the state institutions;

(d) it "mobilizes citizens to participate in political decision-making at various levels of government";

(e) it recruits and educates cadres of political leaders operating within the Party as well as within the institutions of the state.[52]

It is a truism to say that after December 1981 the Party had ceased to fulfill most of these functions.[53] The implementation of these functions have had to be taken over by institutions other than the Party itself.

A public opinion poll carried out in late 1980 by sociologists from the Polish Academy of Sciences, indicated that only 32% of the respondents declared confidence in the Party.[54] Institutions enjoying the greatest confidence were: the Catholic Church (94%), Solidarity (90%), the Army (89%), the Sejm (82%), the Council of State (73%).[55] The high rating of the Army is very significant, and it is interesting to note that the two state institutions, namely the Sejm and the Council of State, maintain a relatively high level of confidence of the people, despite the fact that they are entirely controlled by the Party.

Another sociological survey from that time indicated some additional elements of Polish public opinion.[56] The survey studied models of the execution of political power - the monocentric and polycentric ones, and indicated that most Poles are against "the strengthening of the role of the Party", (32% in favour, and 55.4% against), but at the same time many of them accept the "growth of the authorities' control over society" (48.5% in favour, and 43.1% against).[57] According to the authors of this study, the results suggested that many Poles would welcome a strong authoritarian power on condition that it is disassociated from the Communist Party.[58]

The sociological inquiry presented above adds important elements to the well-known facts about political bargaining in the early 1980's evoked by the existence of the independent trade union Solidarity. In this context, the growing influence of the Army requires the greatest attention.

Lenin's original view of the role of a traditional Army in socialism was very sceptical. According to him: "a standing army is an army that is divorced from the people and trained to shoot down the people...a standing army is not in the least necessary to protect the country from an attack by an enemy: a people's militia is sufficient".[59]

Nevertheless, the Army was not replaced by a civil militia after the Revolution, but it was placed under strict control by the Party. Initially, it was necessary to keep a strict watch over the former Tsarist generals and officers who had remained in service; later, Stalin had to find the means to ensure that the military would not be able to step in and play a political role during times of pressure and crisis (such as 1931-32, or at the time of the Great Purge in 1937).

Generally speaking, the Party's domination over the Army was achieved by: (a) strong political assertion of control over military policies; (b) granting the military a well-defined professional status; and (c) a compromise on the status of Party organizations in the military structure.[60]

In consequence, the Army never played an independent political role in the Soviet system, although it was able to preserve some kind of original identity within this system.[61] The rise and fall of Marshal Tukhachevsky in 1935/37, as well as of Marshal Zhukov in 1956/57, indicated the very limited engagement of military men in politics. There appear to be no indications that the role of the Army has grown in the Soviet Union since the beginning of the 1980's.[62] In this respect the current situation in Poland is very exceptional.

Prior to 1981 the political position of the Polish Army was similar to the position of other armies within the Soviet block. Professional officers of the Polish Army enjoyed a relatively high standard of living and education, but they never played a key political role. Nearly 100% the senior officers were members of the Party and as a consequence the Army played the role of the "armed arm of the Party", rather than of an independent political factor within the state.[63]

The Army, however, tried to promote an image which differed from the Party's (patriotic rather than ideological rhetoric, and a generally indifferent approach towards the internal conflicts of the Party, traditional military symbols, different principles of internal organization and discipline, etc.). Nevertheless, the career structures of top military officers were closely linked to the development of the communist system, and military men were loyal to the Party.[64]

The role of the Army quickly grew during the political crisis of 1980-81. On the one hand, the Party was in trouble and failed to carry out its basic political functions. As a consequence of this the Polish ruling elites were forced to fill the resulting vacuum. The Army was one of the strongest candidates for this role. On the other hand, the Army was generally trusted by the Polish population which by then was looking for some sort of political stability and, at the same time, a reduction in the role of the Party.[65]

In the Autumn of 1981, General Jaruzelski was elected the First Secretary of the Party. He already held the position of Prime Minister

132

and Minister of Defence. It was at this time also that the first "military operational groups" began to supervise local administration, and by the same token they began to function in what had been the traditional roles played by local Party committees.[66]

The introduction of martial law was only post-factum accepted by the Polish United Workers' Party Central Committee. The Party fully identified itself with the military coup, but it was the Army which had the decisive political voice from then on.

According to General Szacilo, the Army carried out four functions during the period of martial law:

(a) the political-administrative function which was implemented by military commissaries at the shop and plant as well as the local administrative level;

(b) the political-educative function, directed towards the whole of society and not only towards soldiers;

(c) the security function directed against "violation of public orders";

(d) the traditional military-operational function.[67]

According to communist doctrine, at least the first two functions are supposed to be carried out by the Party.[68]

Martial law was lifted in the Summer of 1983 and since then the official Polish rhetoric has been suggesting that the situation, while still difficult, no longer requires that the military directly interfere with the conduct of affairs of the country.[69] The Military Council of National Salvation was formally dissolved and General Jaruzelski resigned from the post of Prime Minister and Minister of Defence.

However, it would be a mistake to believe that in 1983 the Army returned to its barracks. Despite the lifting of martial law the influence of the Army continued to be enormous. First, the key ministerial positions as well as many local administrative posts, are occupied by generals.[70] Second, the new laws give the Army special supervisory powers during the "period of overcoming the socio-political crisis".[71] Third, the so-called "military groups" continue their bi-annual activity at the local administrative level.[72] Fourth, Army officials declare the Army's leading position in "educating society" as well as "promoting ideology".[73] Fifth, the amendments to the Constitution gave the Committee for the Defence of the Country prerogatives similar to those of the Military Council of National Salvation.[74]

The above review of the Party-Army relationship in contemporary Poland should not lead to any simplistic conclusions. It is in some ways confusing to say that military men, rather than Party men, control the administration. The ruling generals are faithful Party members and are, therefore, in principle, supporters of Soviet communism. As Robin Alison Remington put it, the Army became "the vanguard not of the workers, but of the Party".[75] Moreover, careful studies on the Polish Army indicate that it was only the political elite within the Army which played a leading role in preparing and implementing the political take-over in 1981. According to George Malcher: "True active support in the Army was rather limited. It came mainly from the political apparatus of the Army, which consists of full-time professional officers. Together with activists of the Communist Party organization in the Army who are mostly regular Army officers they secured an essentially passive support from serving conscripts".[76]

The ideological position of the Army is also somewhat confusing, and despite some rhetorical zig-zags it does not differ greatly from the ideological position of the Party. After all, the Army has never denied Marxism-Leninism.

Division of the roles between the Army, the Party, and the local administration will also have to be defined. After lifting martial law it became increasingly clear that the military penetration of Party-state positions was far from wholesale. It was more significant in qualitative than in quantitative terms. We could also observe a progressing fused symbiosis marked by the interchangeability of cadres from the Army, the Party and the Administration. The Army indeed put greater emphasis on the state rather than Party institutions, but as George Sanford rightly argued: "The evidence is unclear whether there was any serious attempt by the Generals to use martial law conditions to transform Poland's Party-State permanently into an Army-State".[77]

Nevertheless, despite still existing question marks and problems of evidence, the above description of events after December 1981 indicates a significant evolution of the traditional roles of the Party and the Army. Therefore, although we are unable to describe fully the complex power relationships in Poland, we may agree with J.F. Brown that the martial law experience began a gradual shift in power relationships by revealing that "in the last analysis the system's salvation rests not with the Party, but with the forces of coercion and oppression".[78] Moreover, since 1981 it is no longer possible to understand the political decision-making process within the ruling elite in Poland by studying developments within the Party alone. The "nomenklatura" rule in Poland cannot be identified merely with the rule of the Party apparatus, etc.

Thus, the power relationships in Poland became much more complex, with the growth of importance of various state organs and especially of the Army as the most significant feature in the new situation. This should not necessarily lead to the conclusion that, as Remington put it, "Jaruzelski comes considerably closer to the military leaders, who play the role of iron surgeons in developing countries, than he does to the other leaders of communist parties in Eastern Europe".[79] The organizational, functional or doctrinal profile of the Polish Army differs from the profiles of most Third World armies.[80] The Polish Army also operates in a different socio-economic and geopolitical environment.[81] In this context, the Soviet penetration of the Polish Army should especially be mentioned.

Nevertheless, the growth of the political position of the Polish Army at the expense of the Party is evident and open conflicts which arise from time to time between some "Party men" and "military men" indicate that the interests of the Party and the Army are not always identical.[82]

TOWARDS CORPORATISM

If one defines corporatism as "state domination founded on the principle of organic societal unity, order and discipline, nationalist collectivism, and the elevation of goal attainment above due process", one observes its striking affiliation with communist systems.[83] Not surprisingly therefore, there already exist interesting studies indicating relations between the practice of a communist system and corporatism in such different countries as Hungary, the Soviet Union or Rumania.[84] These studies, however, can give rise to confusion, since the amount of autonomy of various social or institutional interests is very restricted in the communist system (especially as compared with West European countries). And these interests could hardly be aggregated as well as articulated.

The corporatist interpretation of the Soviet system is therefore limited in its application. Nevertheless, despite all constraints, such an interpretation could still be useful in order to indicate a certain pattern of dealing with the spontaneous development of quasi-pluralistic elements within the communist state.

In theory neither original Marxism nor its contemporary elaborations sound particularly corporatist. Whereas the communist ideal is to entirely eliminate class difference, corporatists propose the integration of classes into functional, vertical organizations. Communists want to realize their goals through the unitary or homogeneous party. Corporatists oppose this idea and opt for the corporatist assembly and a series of "concordats between corporations".[85]

The Communist Party harmonizes various group interests of a professional and functional nature. It does so through a number of institutions which are supposed to link the Party with society. For instance, the purpose of Soviets and their executives is to represent the general interests of all sectors of society, and specific interests based on territorial factors. Other such institutions are the trade unions, various economic ministries, youth and women's organizations, the collective farm councils, and others - the so-called "transmission belts".[86] The Party itself is not to be composed of formal representatives of this or that interest group. Party membership is based not on the group principle, but on the individual principle, and the Party is not the official representative of different social groups, but of "people who subscribe to the Marxist-Leninist doctrine".[87]

On the other hand, according to corporatist ideas, various corporate bodies (economic, religious, professional, cultural, etc.) should be semi-independent and should conclude voluntary agreements ("concordats") with each other and with the state to ensure mutual harmony. Corporations would select their own representatives who would combine at the top in a national corporatist parliament.[88]

But in spite of all the doctrinal differences, political practice within communist systems greatly resembles corporatism. In both communist and corporatist systems interests are vertically ranked by the political authorities. And both types of systems exercise a "dictatorship over needs".[89] They do so for the same reason: to prevent the crystallization of class interest, and the domination of politics by class conflict. To counter the articulation of social class interests, both communist and corporatist states emphasize "cross-cutting functional attachments and affiliations".[90] The different interests to which these give rise are considered to be of secondary importance since both

Communist Party and corporatist state creeds proclaim a belief in the organizational unity of society. [91]

Even the major difference between private and public ownership of the means of production fades considerably when stripped to the essentials of control. In corporatism and communism alike, the state "megabureaucracy" steers economic activity.[92]

In consequence, the only major obstacle to making a comparison between communism and corporatism arises from the role of the Communist Party. In Soviet communism the leading role of the Party is a question of practice and not merely of theory. This contradicts state corporatism which is defined as having a weak dominant party.[93]

However, in contemporary Poland this major obstacle has ceased to exist. Since the mid-1970's it has been interesting to observe how the erosion of the Party's strength was accompanied by the development of a corporatist approach by the authorities. The Polish version of corporatism was, from the very beginning, strongly associated with nationalism, development and statism.[94]

A Polish sociologist, Jacek Kurczewski, termed this trend of the 1970's "a patriotic organicism".[95] It was based on the assumption that the Polish people form a homogeneous social organism, interconnected by various functional relationships which could be easily transformed into the corporatist mode of interest representation. The Party is still the leading force in society, but this leadership is exercised through the "scientific management of society" rather than through ideological dictatorship. The goal of this state organicism consists of social and economic development rather than of the elimination of class enemies and dictatorship of the proletariat. A given citizen has in this model the same interest as other citizens, and his supreme interest is the good of the mother country, as the organism which organizes development within the framework of the state machine.

In practice this model implied that various professional or functional corporate social groups could organize themselves into institutions which no longer merely played the traditional role of a "transmission belt". Since all these institutions could contribute to the development of the state, their role grew steadily. Particular enterprises or professional associations even started to operate their own restaurants, shops, vacation rest-homes, medical services, and recreational facilities. And, as in the case of other typical corporate

137

organizations, the membership in these institutions was practically compulsory.[96]

At the same time the role of the leaders of these institutions grew. Professional politicians, Army and Police officers, top managers of state-owned enterprises, heads of cultural, educational and scientific institutions, etc.; all of these comprised the new ruling class.

Since the Communist Party had become the "party of the whole people", without any specific ideological aspirations, there was no significant conflict of interests between these corporate institutions and the Party itself. Their roles and functions in the development of "patriotic organicism" merged and converged.

In accordance with the doctrine, the Party still retained the leading role but in practice, particular corporate groups often dominated the Party (e.g., the coal and steel industrial circles). More importantly, the state rather than the Party proved to be a more appropriate institution to organize societal unity between different corporations and to play the role of arbiter between them. The state could also involve the one missing element of this corporate organization of society - the Catholic Church.

The corporatist mode of interest representation was, for a time, helpful to the authorities to segment social problems and to slow down the growth of social tensions by a sequence of decisions based on different (and often conflicting) standards and criteria. This in turn led to the semi-feudalization of society observed since the mid-seventies in Poland, with segments of society operating on the basis of different values, status arrangements and special privileges.[97] This unavoidable also accelerated a rapid increase in social stratification, with increasing differences between particular regions, branches of industry, and social groups, according to their relative bargaining power. The problem was that corporatist links between the state and society were realized outside the existing system of law and in contradiction to the official communist doctrine. In consequence, this semi-legal and unofficial corporatism led either to corrosion of the legal system or to further depolitization of the Party.[98]

Even more serious problems arose with the development of a democratic opposition, and especially of Solidarity. New institutions emerged - independent trade unions and associations - which could not easily be subjected to the arbitration of the state machine. From the

138

very beginning, Solidarity adopted the idea of political and industrial bargaining rather than the corporatist idea of "social contract", based exclusively on the conditions presented by the authorities.

As we have already pointed out, the crushing of Solidarity brought about the further strengthening of the state rather than a new dictatorship by the Party. The policy of "patriotic organicism" could then be continued under new circumstances. A severe crisis in the Party provided special impetus for the development of corporate ideas. Martial law was aimed at securing organic societal unity through strict order and military discipline. At first, all social and professional institutions were banned. But soon, the authorities began to encourage their re-emergence on the condition that they agreed to subject themselves to state arbitration.

This whole process was conducted under the cynical slogan "national agreement". On the one hand, this implied that all social organizations which attempted to be independent from the state and to attain their democratic aspirations through the process of political bargaining (e.g., Solidarity), should definitely be banned. On the other hand, it implied that all organizations which could agree to the conditions of the "national agreement" presented by the authorities, could continue to exist without any specific ideological discrimination.

As is usually the case with historical forms of corporate political models, the conditions of the "agreement" excluded any form of participatory democracy. Semi-compulsory membership in pro-governmental institutions (directly, or indirectly, through the system of penalties and rewards), and institutionalized arbitrariness of the state apparatus was introduced.

Nevertheless, this new semi-corporatist model differed from the original Leninist-Stalinist model. The privileged position of the Party was no longer a matter of fact.[99] Instead, all social and professional groups, atheists or catholics, craftsmen, peasants or blue-collar workers, etc. were welcomed to contribute to the development of the state organicism under the conditions of "national agreement".[100] The state rather than the Party was to harmonize their interests from then on. The state was to act as a super-arbiter basing its rulings on criteria of "national interest", as well as on criteria of economic and organizational efficiency when making its judgements.

This new attitude modified the whole concept of socialism.

According to the spokesman for the Government, Jerzy Urban, socialism is "not a method of realizing a completely new, splendid and all-embracing vision, but the most rational system of rules assuring the satisfaction of the basic interests of society". Socialism "has shrunk to a method of rule and of balancing various social aspirations".[101] According to Jerzy Urban, the Party should intellectually inspire this process, but it is the state which rules and balances social aspirations.[102]

In consequence, there was a steady growth in the role of institutions which loyally agreed to join the "national agreement" (especially as compared to the situation before August 1980). Among these were, for instance, the Peasant Party, the Communist Youth Organization, the Association of Consumers, pro-governmental Catholic political clubs, official trade unions, etc. Their position vis-à-vis the Party became significantly stronger than in the original communist model. The newly created Patriotic Movement for National Rebirth was supposed to act as an umbrella organization which united all various groups and political orientations in their work for the common good of the state.[103]

On the other hand, efforts were made to incorporate into the framework of the "national agreement" some remaining independent institutions, and especially the Church. Here, a concept of corporate agreement was promoted in order to bring together two big national corporations: the Church and the Army. The state again was supposed to play a role of mediator and arbiter. So far, however, the Church has resisted the state's definition of its proper role. For instance, the Church hierarchy neither joined the Patriotic Movement of National Rebirth nor supported the authorities during the 1985 elections to the Sejm.

LAW AS A NEW SOURCE OF LEGITIMACY

Before we begin our analysis of the political legitimacy in contemporary Poland we will pay some attention to the traditional Communist source of legitimacy.

The political legitimacy of the communist system is traditionally based on ideology. According to the doctrine, the Communist Party rules because it embodies society's interests and aspirations.[104] In other words, the Party is "the mind, honour, and conscience" of the Soviet people.[105]

Officially, the people's interests and aspirations are expressed by Marxism, and the Party is the only institution which interprets Marxist theory. However, because of political necessity, Marxism had to be-from the beginning of the Soviet state - so vague and general as to justify any particular policy in home or foreign affairs: NEP or collectivism, friendship with Hitler or war with Hitler, any toughening or relaxation of the internal regime, and so on.[106]

Marxism-Leninism as understood in this extremely confusing way was mixed with elements of autocracy, bureaucratic orthodoxy, and Russian nationalism. Due to the excessive ritualization of ideology, the significance of new myths produced by the regime, the traditionalism of "socialist" celebrations or rites, where the past reigns over the present, Marxism-Leninism became a "liturgical" element of the Soviet system; the element which legitimizes every policy of the Party rather than setting up any political principles and directions.[107]

The official communist ideology is both meaningless and powerful. Even today, the general scorn for this official ideology in no way diminishes its greatness. This is because "it suited almost everybody".[108] The Party is still "the carrier of the ideological truth" in the Soviet Union.

In Poland, however, the role of communist ideology differed from the very beginning. Communism came to Poland not as a result of any spontaneous revolution; it came on Soviet tanks. The predominantly Catholic society consistently resisted the atheistic elements of official Marxism-Leninism. Christianity cultivates spiritual idealism and opposes historical materialism. Religious rites and celebrations could hardly be replaced by communist liturgies. Polish nationalism had a long tradition of anti-Sovietism which did not allow the use of Soviet propaganda.

The Communist Party claimed its right to rule Poland not only because it had the blessing of the Soviet leadership: It claimed to be the Party of the working people, representing the historical mission of the proletariat. However, successive protests by the working class against the Party greatly undermined this kind of legitimacy. Communist rhetoric manifested its emptiness as compared to the arguments of the Catholic Church, and the democratic opposition. Three decades of communist rule brought neither welfare nor social justice. It corrupted its leaders and undermined Polish national independence. In consequence, the huge social protests of the Summer of 1980 united the majority of the working class under slogans of truth, solidarity, national sovereignty and social justice. The independent trade union Solidarity, rather than the Communist Party represented these values. Society turned its back on the Party.

The repressions under martial law could not return the Party to its former political legitimacy based on ideology. Moreover, it was now the Army and state bureaucracy rather than the Party which executed political power. There was an urgent need to discover new sources of legitimacy other than those based exclusively on repression. Any new legitimacy would need to be harmonized with the growing role of the state. Not surprisingly, therefore, the authorities have placed great emphasis on the system of law.[109]

The post-revolutionary theories of Yevgeny B. Pashukanis and Peter I. Stuchka, which state that the phenomenon of law as a whole is a product of fetishistic social relationships and that therefore in a communist society the law must wither away in the same manner as the state and other creations of commodity fetishism were never realized in the Soviet Union.[110] The law has not withered away, on the contrary it continues to exist according to Lenin's statement that "a will, if it is the will of the state must be expressed in the form of a law established by the state".[111] Moreover, Lenin had laid down that the law in the new society must have nothing to do with the law in the traditional sense, i.e., it must not be allowed to limit governmental power in any way.[112]

In consequence, the function of law has changed drastically. For instance, the constitutions in communist states are not constitutions in the usual sense, that is to say expressions of the constituent will of the people, but simple sets of rules laid down by the authorities, which also specify the organization and responsibilities of the public powers.

Soviet legal culture as such can be understood within what can be described only as a dual system of law and terror within society, between which the "evidence tends to show a surprising degree of official compartmentalization of the legal and the extra-legal".[113] This means that there is no distinction between law and force, but the question remains - what type of "force"? In this sense, the Soviet "dual state" controlled by the Communist Party could be divided into a "prerogative state" governed directly by the rule of force, and a "normative state" regulated through a system of legal norms prescribing the permissible boundaries of inter-personal relations and citizen-state relations. However, the distinction between normative and prerogative can be very misleading. The "normative state" does not exist independently of the "prerogative state" but is absorbed by it and is part of it.[114]

The jurisprudence of terror flourished especially during the Stalinist period. It took two forms. First, there was the tendency to posit loosely defined, as opposed to clearly defined, rules. Thus, vague or ambiguous legal norms denied the principle of predictability, leaving open a large area of discretionary space which, in turn, permitted arbitrariness.

The second form taken by the jurisprudence of terror was the tendency to make abrupt, undiscussed, or unannounced changes in legal rules (or in their application) which leaned in the direction of maximizing the power of the state at the expense of the individual.[115]

Paradoxically, the expansion of the normative state and the development of a legal culture in the Soviet Union received its major impetus under Stalin. For Stalin, in the mid-thirties, a viable legal culture was essential to help consolidate and legitimize systemic social changes and to overcome the years of violence and uncertainty by providing a framework for greater regularity and predictability in relations between the citizen and state.[116] This process was suspended during the war, but was resumed in the mid-fifties, encompassing not only the Soviet Union but also all other East European countries.

Although the new legislation still left unresolved the relationship between law and terror within the social regulation process, it did represent a legal expression and institutionalization of social quasi-stability of the communist system at that time. The new legislation encompassed nearly every branch and institution of law, but the above described process was especially visible with regard to constitutional law.

In Poland, as well as in other East European countries, a new constitution was adopted at the beginning of the 1950's, at the height of the Stalinist regime. In fact, the Polish Constitution of 1952 neither reflected political reality at that time, nor did it contain any real normative elements. On the contrary, the Constitution created, as Alexander Smolar expressed it, a "completely new reality, sui generis, which differed from the reality experienced by the people", but which was equally comprehensive and contained.[117] In this new super-reality created by the Constitution, Poland is a sovereign, independent, and democratic state; its Sejm diet rather than the Communist Party executes state powers. The judicial system is independent, members of the Sejm are democratically elected, they are responsible to their voters who could suspend their mandate; all Polish citizens are equal, and their freedom of opinion, religion, and assembly is guaranteed, etc.

This open constitutional lie could be formulated because the Constitution was not supposed to allow the authorities any political legitimacy. The legitimacy was based on factors other than law. The Party was strong and powerful, and therefore the Constitution could create a super-real legal order which had nothing to do with contemporary political phenomena. Besides, as far as penal and administrative law were concerned, restrictions remained which made individual resistance difficult. (Although at that time repressions against dissent could easily be conducted outside the system of law.)

However, during the 1970's the political situation was significantly different from that in the 1950's. On the one hand, the successive crises in Poland undermined the strength and relevance of legitimacy based on ideology. On the other hand, the political opposition began to use declarative legal norms in defence of civil freedom and basic human rights. The coexistence of political reality and legal super-reality started to weaken the prestige of the authorities. Changes in law were required and, traditionally, these came first in the area of constitutional law.

The Polish Constitution was amended in 1976.[118] The Polish People's Republic, which was formally described in the Constitution of 1952 as a "state of people's democracy" was now to be a "socialist state". The Communist Party was recognized as the "leading force" of society, and Poland was obliged to "strengthen its friendship and cooperation" with the Soviet Union and other communist states.[119] It was, however, first of all a symbolic step towards bridging the gap between political reality and legal super-reality. The Constitution was no longer an embarrassing decoration. It had become a means of defence, although it was a means of defence for the authorities against the citizens rather than a means of defence for citizens against the authorities as is the case in traditional constitutionalism.[120]

This new formula of the Constitution soon began to serve as an

144

important source of political legitimacy. For instance, striking workers during the Summer of 1980 were pressed to officially recognize constitutional provisions providing for the leading role of the Party and friendship with the Soviet Union. At the time of the mass strike movement in Poland, the Party did not (or could not) any longer support its right to rule with the argument that it "expresses the interests and aspirations of the working class". Since that time the Party has argued that it is designated to power by the system of law, and especially by the Constitution.

Paradoxically, Solidarity did press for observance of the rule of law rather than for basic constitutional changes. On the one hand, Solidarity advocated real implementation of constitutional provisions, as for instance, the execution of the constitutional principle of a free press, by abolishing censorship. On the other hand, it tried to set up institutional guarantees wich would constrain the authorities in their arbitariness, e.g., through free trade unions, industrial self-management, the National Economic and Social Council, etc.

The imposition of martial law was illegal in both a narrow and a broad sense. A wave of severe terror overran the whole country, and most of the legal norms which were supposed to protect citizens against the state were suspended.[121] However, following this wave of direct repression there was a need to stabilize the political situation in Poland and to find some institutional ways of dealing with existing problems. Dictatorship, although illegal - or because it is illegal - is careful to maintain the illusion of legality. In this respect General Jaruzelski followed the policy of Stalin in the 1930's. Extensive legislative activity became the first concern of the Polish authorities.[122]

As a consequence of this policy, more than one hundred legal acts were adopted by the Sejm during the following three years. On the one hand, they represented a new version of the "legislation of terror", institutionalizing repression by martial law, which was formally lifted in the Summer of 1983. These included, for instance, the amendment to the Constitution, which gives the Committee of the Defence of the Country the right to proclaim a state of emergency if it finds it appropriate; the new provisions in the Penal Code, which impose strict sanctions on all people who engage in any oppositional activities, even on participants in meetings in private homes; the law on the Ministry of the Interior which authorizes the use of armed forces and live ammunition under the same conditions as those provided under the martial law decree; the so-called anti-parasite law; and the work-referral law, which institutionalizes forced and compulsory labour as a means of labour discipline, political constraint, and economic development. This is true also of the juvenile delinquency law which allows the punishment of young people who exercise the right to free assembly; the censorship law, which places a variety of publications under strict governmental control; the law on trade unions, which eliminates workers' rights to free association and collective bargaining, etc. According to Kazimierz Barcikowski, a member of the Politbureau, "the state cannot resign its rights to use force when other means have failed to be effective, because the interest of the state requires the execution of the law".[123]

In this way the jurisprudence of terror achieved a further stage of development. The law became openly repressive and it widely justified the state's use of compulsory force against its citizens. The government no longer has to implement its iron fist policy outside the law, for it can now do so according to the letter of the law. The gap between political reality and legal super-reality has almost been bridged. By the same token, the Soviet traditional choice between "partiinost" and "zakonnost" is also no longer relevant.[124] Political terror can be realized directly through "zakonnost".

The new laws mention, with remarkable frequency, the words "in accordance with", "on the basis of", and "following from" the Constitution of the Polish People's Republic. The mandatory "socialist state" is always there too. These phrases occur all over the place. The state always comes before the citizen. The phraselogy of the civil servant's oath is characteristic: "I shall serve the state and its citizens" and in that order.[125]

In some way this new jurisprudence of terror opens doors to create a new source of legitmacy. People are persecuted not because they act against the Party or directly against communism, but because they violate the positive law. Dura lex sed lex (sic.). But there also exists something more.

The intensive development of a "jurisprudence of terror" is accompanied by new legislation which sets up new institutional infrastructures of the state.

Previous Polish crises gave rise to significant discussion about the role of the Sejm and other organs of "democratic representation" in the communist system. The Party was usually ready to increase to some extent the power of the Sejm and the Soviets, as well as to improve their representativeness by giving a hearing to the voices of various non-communist members among them. During the current crisis this has not been the case. It was said that the improvement of the role of the existing state organs of democratic representation (e.g., the Sejm) should be achieved by these organs "approaching the interests of society" rather than by "increasing representation of the society in them".[126] In other words, there should be a development of enlightened absolutism rather than development of participatory democracy.

In consequence, one observes the creation of new state organs which are aimed at strengthening the credibility of autonomous state "judgements". They are intended to equip the state with special institutional tools which help it to play the role of national super-arbiter.[127] In this way the State Tribunal and the Constitutional Tribunal were created.[128]

In this situation the law is intended to protect the rights of the state against the libertarian aspirations of its citizens rather than to protect the rights of its citizens against the dictatorial powers of the state. And the state institutions are intended to help the authorities to supervise and organize the life of citizens according to legal norms created by them, rather than to increase citizens' participation in decision-making and to carry out their sovereign will.

This system of law, no matter how repressive, and no matter how arbitrarily created, still serves as a source of political legitimacy. It serves this purpose because other sources of legitimacy are either weak, or no longer functioning. It serves this purpose because a normative approach is very relevant to all sorts of statism - the super-rational state is super-legislator. It serves this purpose because behind the legal norms of the state there are the basic forces of the state's compulsory power - the Army and the Police. It serves this purpose because the semi-abstract character of legal norms permits the authorities to escape from discredited, and therefore difficult, questions of an ideological nature.

CONCLUSIONS

It is too early to say whether the Polish experiment with statism and corporatism will have a long life. Various basic political questions remain unresolved. For instance, it remains an open question whether the Party will finally be able to re-emerge as a powerful political factor, and, if it does, what will be its new relationship with other political forces, and especially with the Army. It is also difficult to predict whether communist statism can secure power for the authorities without ideological legitimacy, or whether the corporatist model can be realized with the existence of an independent Church and a developed network of underground political opposition. No one can predict the long-term approach of the Soviet block towards the Polish development of statism. Despite the fact that many other communist countries experience problems similar to those of Poland, they continue to try to resolve them in an orthodox Marxist-Leninist manner.

Finally, one can always say, as Richard Crossman did, that statism makes the role of an autonomous and neutral state similar to the role of a car, which can be driven either to the right or to the left. The important question arising from this statement is - who is the driver?[129] In consequence, one can very well imagine a situation in which the state is deprived of its ideological legitimacy and domination by the Communist Party and is superseded by the democratic opposition. This option has not yet been sufficiently elaborated by both sides of the Polish conflict.

   However, we may certainly expect that the coming years will bring about some answers to these vital basic questions.

NOTES

1.   Joseph Stalin. Voprosy Leninisma, 11th ed., Gospolitizdat, Moscow 1953, p. 429.

2.   See especially: Maciej Kiersnowski. Dyktatura Rozsadku. Puls no. 18, London 1983, pp. 25-26.

3.   Daniel Passent in: Polityka no.7, Warsaw 1982.

4.   Maciej Kiersnowski. Op.cit...p. 36.

5. Krystyna Piotrowska-Hochweld in: Polityka no.15, Warsaw 1983.

6. Wojciech Lamentowicz in: Panstwo i Prawo no.2, Warsaw 1980.

7. This essay deals only with some political elements of the communist version of statism. Etatisation of the communist economy has already been elaborated by many writers. See especially: Wlodzimierz Brus. Socialist Ownership and Political Systems. Routledge and Kegan, London 1975, 222 pp., or A. Heydel. Etatyzm po polsku. Oficyna Liberalow, Warsaw 1981, 50 pp. A careful analysis of the functioning of the state bureaucracy in Poland is presented in: Maria Hirszowicz. Coercion and Control in Communist Society. The Visible Hand of Bureaucracy. Harvest Press, Oxford 1986, 221 pp.

8. Leszek Kolakowski. Main Currents of Marxism, vol. I. Clarendon Press, Oxford 1978, p. 123; My meaning of statism expresses the positivistic etatism of Thomas Hobbes rather than the political philosophy of the state in Hegel. (See, e.g., Thomas Hobbes. Leviathan. Dent/Dutton, London 1970, pp. 63-66, 90-96 and ff.) Nevertheless, I refer in my essay to the idea of Hegel who was directly discussed by Karl Marx.

9. J.L. Talmon. Political Messianism. Secker and Warburg, London 1960, p. 205.

10. J.L. Talmon. Op.cit...p. 207.

11. Karl Marx. Critique of the Gothe Programme. Foreign Languages Publishing House, Moscow 1954, p. 41.

12. Robert J. Osborn. The Evolution of Soviet Politics. The Dorsey Press, Homewood 1974, p. 244.

13. See, e.g., V.I. Lenin. The Fight for the Vanguard Party (especially, "What is to be Done?"), in: V.I. Lenin. Collected Works. Lawrence and Wishart, London/Moscow 1946, pp. 27-193.

14. Sidney and Beatrice Webb. Soviet Communism: A New Civilization, vol.I. Golancz, London 1937, especially pp. 1070-1073.

15. Robert J. Osborn. Op.cit...p. 245.

16. G.K. Bertsch. Power and Policy in Communist Systems. John Wiley and Sons, New York 1978, p. 115.

17. The classic description of totalitarian systems was presented by Carl J. Friedrich and Zbigniew K. Brzezinski in: Totalitarian Dictatorship and Autocracy. Harvard University Press, Cambridge 1956, especially pp. 9-10. Compare also the Soviet critique of this work in F. Burlatsky. The Modern State and Politics. Progress Publishers, Moscow 1978, p. 57.

18. J. Stalin. Op.cit....pp. 249 and ff. See also: A.Y. Vyshinsky, (ed.). The Law of the Soviet State. Greenwood Press, Westport 1948 (repr. in 1979), pp. 13 and ff.

19. In my opinion, any identification of Stalinism with Hegelianism has a rhetorical rather than scientific meaning. Compare, for instance, W.W. Rostow, (ed.). The Dynamics of Soviet Society. Mentor, Massachusetts 1954, p. 22. See also: Mariusz Gulczynski. Karol Marks o klasowym charakterze panstwa, in: Panstwo i Prawo no.3, Warsaw 1983, pp. 3 and ff.

20. Leszek Kolakowski. Marxist Roots of Stalinism, in: Robert C. Tucker, (ed.). Stalinism. W.W. Norton and Co., New York 1977, p. 294.

21. Leszek Kolakowski. Marxist Roots. Op.cit...p. 289.

22. See e.g., N.V. Khrushchev. Fundamentals of Marxism-Leninism. Foreign Languages Publishing House, Moscow, n.d., p. 843.

23. Khrushchev's interview for the London Times, quoted by Robert J. Osborn. Op.cit...p. 249.

24. For a comprehensive analysis of the concept of "developed socialism" see: Ronald J. Hill and Peter Frank. The Soviet Communist Party. George Allen & Unwin, London 1981, pp. 15-18.

25. See: On the 60th Anniversary of the Great October Socialist Revolution. Resolution of the CPSU Central Committee of January 31st, 1977. Novosti Press Agency, Moscow 1977, p. 13.

26. "After the complete and final victory of socialism when the state of the dictatorship of the proletariat grows into the state of the whole people in which the leading role is played by the working class, the communist party becomes the vanguard not only of the working class, but also of the whole people", - P.N. Fedoseyew et al. The Groundless Social Reformist Falsification of the Democratic Nature of Existing Socialism, in: What is Democratic Socialism. Progress Publishers, Moscow 1980, p. 125.
Hill and Frank observe that under the concept of developed socialism the role of the Party becomes somewhat more restricted in scope, but more concentrated: it becomes more one of adjudicator, assessing which demands and interests are compatible with communism. The Party is supposed to exercise the role of "leader", "guide", and "co-ordinator". See: Ronald J. Hill and Peter Frank. Op.cit...p. 18.

27. More about this problem in: Maria Hirszowicz. The Bureaucratic Leviathan. A Study in the Sociology of Communism. Martin Roberts, Oxford 1980, especially pp. 8 and 81.

28. Polish one-person authocracy was identified with Stalin himself rather than with his Polish partner, Boleslaw Bierut.

29. In this respect I will only refer to the relevant literature. See especially: Timothy G. Ash. The Polish Revolution. Solidarity 1980-82. Cape, London 1983. Neal Ascherson. Polish August. Penguin, Harmondsworth 1982. Jakub Karpinski. Count Down. The History of the Polish Upheavals. Karl-Cohl Publ., New York 1982.

30. Jerzy Smialowski. Zagadnienie przyslosci panstwa w historii mysli socjalistycznej. Wyd. Uniwersytetu Jagielonskiego, Cracow 1978, pp. 9, 32, 167, 180.

31. Kazimierz Kozniewski in: Polityka no.6, Warsaw 1982.

32. Ibidem.

33. Mieczyslaw Michalik. Panstwo i obywatel. Nowe Drogi no.3, Warsaw 1986, p. 11.

34. Ibidem, p. 97.

35. Stanislaw Rainko. O osobliwosciach socjalistycznego panstwa. Nowe Drogi no.2, Warsaw 1985, p. 43.

36. Maciej Kiersnowski. Op.cit...p. 26.

37. Jerzy Smialowski. Op.cit...p. 232, and Maciej Kiersnowski. Op.cit...p. 31.

38. O co walczymy, dokad zmierzamy. Programme declaration of the P.U.W.P. in: Nowe Drogi no.3, Warsaw 1982, p. 50.

39. Stanislaw Rainko. Op.cit...p. 47.

40. See, e.g., an interview with the member of Politbureau, Hieronim Kubiak in: Polityka no.17, Warsaw 1983. As well as Artur Bodnar. Porozumienie i co dalej. Zycie Warszawy, 5-6 May, Warsaw 1984.

41. The above observation is relevant despite governmental efforts to set opinions of the leaders of Solidarity against the opinions of the working class as such.

42. In the above quoted interview, Hieronim Kubiak openly criticized the latter approach: "We were always telling the working class that the state can do everything". According to Kubiak this should be changed. Kozniewski criticizes the concept of the welfare state - the state which provides citizens with various social goods.

43. The P.U.W.P. declaration O co walczymy, dokad zmierzamy, in: Nowe Drogi. Op.cit...pp. 45-48.

44. Ibidem, p. 48.

45. Wojciech Jaruzelski, Speech at the VII Plenary meeting of the aP.U.W.P. Central Committee in: Nowe Drogi no.3, Warsaw 1981, p. 15.

46. See e.g., Wlodzimierz Mokrzyszczak. PZPR-partia socjalistycznej odnowy. Nowe Drogi no.6, Warsaw 1986, pp. 18-19, or Wojciech Jaruzelski's interview, in: L'Humanité, Paris, 3-4 June 1985, published also in: Nowe Drogi no.7, Warsaw 1985, p. 7.

47. Wojciech Jaruzelski, in Nowe Drogi. Op.cit...p. 14.

48. Ibidem.

49. Kazimierz Barcikowski. Zagadniena i Materialy no.5, Warsaw 1983.

50. The Kubiak Report in: Survey, Summer 1982, p. 96. See also the interview with Kubiak in: Polityka no.17, Warsaw 1983.

51. See for instance: Waldemar Kuczynski. Solidarni i Niepokonani. Aneks no.29/30, London 1983, pp. 17-20.

52. Jerzy Wiatr. Hegemonic Party System, in: Studies in Polish Political System. Ossolineum, Wroclaw 1967, p. 113.

53. There are many official Party statements as well as articles which indicate a deep crisis of the P.U.W.P. See, for instance, W. Pawlowski in: Polityka no.46, Warsaw 1981; Stanistaw Bejger in: Sztandar Mlodych, 4-6 February, Warsaw 1983; Maciej Krajewski in: Nowe Drogi no.6, Warsaw 1982, and many others. All these publications indicate that the crisis within the Party had begun long before December 1981. In fact, since the late 1970's there had been intensive discussions both within and outside the Party about the failure of the political system and the need for "renewal" starting with the Party itself.

54. Anna Jasinska and Ryszarda Siemienska. The Socialist Personality: A Case Study of Poland. International Journal of Sociology no.1, London 1983, p. 64. See also: David S. Mason. Public Opinion and Political Change in Poland, 1980-1982. Cambridge University Press, Cambridge 1985, p. 205.

55. Ibidem.

56. Lena Kolarska and Andrzej Rychard. Polacy 80. Wizje ladu spolecznego. Aneks no.27, London 1982, pp. 101 and ff.

57. Lena Kolarska and Andrzej Rychard. Op.cit...p. 111.

58. Ibidem.

59. V.I. Lenin. To the Rural Poor, in: V.I. Lenin. Selected Works. vol.2. Lawrence and Wishart, London 1946, p. 281.

60. Robert J. Osborn. The Evolution of Soviet Politics. Op.cit...p. 290. According to Krasnaia Zvezda (October 22nd, 1946) "the party organizations of the armed forces are an organic part of the Bolshevik Party...they are enlightened, the Red Army men, cemented in their values, implanted strictest discipline among them, rallied them around the Bolshevik Party and educated them in the spirit of selfless devotion to the motherland and the cause of communism..."

61. See: Carl J. Friedrich and Zbigniew K. Brzezinski. Totalitarian Dictatorship and Autocracy. Op.cit...pp. 278 and ff.

62. See: Jerry F. Hough. Andropov's First Year. Problems of Communism no.6, Washington D.C. 1983, pp. 49 and ff. Compare also with Joseph Kraft. Letter from Moscow. The New Yorker, January 31st, 1983. Joseph Kraft presents opinions of Roy Medvedev which represents the opposite approach, namely that there is a growing role of military men in the Soviet Union.

63. See: Adam Krzeminski. Wojsko i Cywile. Polityka no.47, Warsaw 1981.

64. See: Michael Sadykiewicz. Jaruzelski's War. Survey, Summer 1982, p. 20.

65. Compare with above quoted sociological studies: Polacy 80.

66. See especially: Leszek Nowak. Wojskowe Grupy Opercyjne, in: Ani Rewolucja ani Ewolucja. Dialog, Frankfurt/Main 1984, pp. 71-73, and W. Pawlowski in Polityka no.46, Warsaw 1981.

67. General Tadeusz Szacilo quoted in: Zolnierz Wolnosci no.57, Warsaw 1983.

68. Compare with Jerzy Wiatr. Hegemonic Party System. Op.cit...pp. 113 and ff.

69. See e.g., Wojciech Jaruzelski's speech, in: Zycie Warszawy, 29 March 1985.

70. For instance, five generals have assumed ministerial posts (Kiszczak, Siwicki, Hupalowski, Piotrowski and Oliwa). Other generals assumed direct control of departments of the Central Committee of the Party, (e.g., Dziekan and Drega). General Janiszewski became the equivalent of Jaruzelski's Chef de Cabinet for the state apparatus.

71. See: The Law on Special Regulations, in: Analysis of the Legal Situation in Poland. After the Lifting of the State of War. Helsinki Committee in Poland. Co-ordinating Office Abroad of NSZZ Solidarnosc, Brussels 1983.

72. See: Polityka no.18, Warsaw 1983.

73. Jerzy Michalak, in: Zolnierz Wolnosci no.57, Warsaw 1983.

74. The Committee of the Defence of the Country has become the supreme authority in matters of defence and security and is, in practice, the supreme state authority. It has the power to propose the introduction of a state of emergency, a state of martial law, general mobilization, and a state of war. It becomes the "administrator" when such states are declared. The chairman of the Committee (General Jaruzelski) is the supreme authority of the Armed Forces in peacetime. Currently the Committee deals even with questions of communications in the country. See: the Communiqué concerning the meeting of the Council, in: Trybuna Ludu. Warsaw, 1 July 1985.

75. Robin Alison Remington. The Leading Role of the Polish Military: Implications, in: J.L. Black and J.W. Strong, (eds.). Sisyphus and Poland. Reflections on Martial Law. Ronald P. Frye & Co., Winnipeg 1986, p. 59.

76. George L. Malcher. Poland's Politicized Army. Communists in Uniform. Praeger, London 1984, p. 2.

77. George Sanford. Military Rule in Poland. The Rebuilding of Communist Power, 1981-1983. Croom Helm, London/Sydney 1986, p. 211.

78. J.F. Brown, in: David Holloway and Jane O. Sharp, (eds.). The Warsaw Pact. Alliance in Transition. Macmillan, London 1984, p. 209.

79. Robin Alison Remington. Op.cit...p. 59.

80. This is very well illustrated by George C. Malcher, in: Poland's Politicized Army. Op.cit...pp. 1-53.

81. This point is well presented by George Sanford, in: Military Rule in Poland. Op.cit...pp. 24-46.

82. See, for instance, the interview with Mieczyslaw Rakowski in the Italian magazine La Republica, quoted also in the NRC Handelsblad. Rotterdam, 29 March 1984.

83. See: J.T. Winkler. Corporatism. Archives Europeennes de Sociologie no.17, 1976, pp. 105-110.

84. Alex Pravda. Trade Unions in East European Communist Systems. Towards Corporatism? International Political Science Review no.2, 1983, pp. 241-260, and Daniel Chirot. Corporatism, Socialism and Development in Rumania. Amsterdams Sociologisch Tijdschrift no.3, 1978, pp. 389-409, and V. Bunce and J.M. Echols. Soviet Politics in the Brezhnev Era: "Pluralism" or "Corporatism"?, in: D.R. Kelly, (ed.). Soviet Politics in the Brezhnev Era. Praeger, New York 1980, pp. 1-21.

85. See, e.g., Emile Durkheim. The Divisions of Labour in Society. The Free Press, New York 1964, pp. 1-31.

86. G. Shaknazarov. Socialist Democracy. Aspects of Theory. Progress Publishers, Moscow 1974, p. 59.

87. G. Shaknazarov. Op.cit...p. 56.

88. Daniel Chirot. Op.cit...p. 391.

89. M. Vajda. The State and Socialism. Alison and Busby, London 1981, p. 135.

90. Alex Pravda. Op.cit...p. 243.

91. This problem is approached in different ways by different corporatist schools. See especially: Phillippe C. Schmitter. Still the Century of Corporatism?, in: P.C. Schmitter and Gerhard Lehmbruch, (eds.). Trends Towards Corporatist Intermediation. Sage, London 1979, pp. 7-53.

92. Alex Pravda. Op.cit...pp. 243.

93. Phillippe C. Schmitter. Op.cit...pp. 13-16.

94. See especially: Jadwiga Staniszkis. Op.cit...p. 6.

95. Jacek Kurczewski. The Old System and the Revolution. Sisyphus Sociological Studies vol.3. Warsaw 1982, p. 22. In doctrinal terms one may argue that "patriotic organicism" of the Gierek regime in Poland was a peculiar combination of the Brezhnev concept of "developed socialism" and the rhetoric of Polish nationalism.

96. Compare with W. Korpi. Political Democracy as a Threat to Capitalism: a Comparison Between Pluralism, Neo-Corporatism and a Power Resource Perspective, in: Krise der Arbeitsgesellschaftz. Campus Verlag, Frankfurt/New York 1983, p. 69.

97. Jadwiga Staniszkis. Evolution of Working-class Protest in Poland. Soviet Studies no.2, Nottingham 1981, p. 227.

98. Jadwiga Staniszkis. Op.cit...p. 230.

99. The recognition of the leading role of the Party meant in practice obedience to the state machine rather than to the Party one.

100. See, for instance, a speech of Stefan Olszowski reprinted in: Nowe Drogi no.4, Warsaw 1982, pp. 28-29.

101. Jerzy Urban quoted in: Survey, Summer 1982, p. 190.

102. NRC Handelsblad, 2 February 1984, p. 5.

103. See especially: Jerzy Jaskiernia. Istota, pozycja prawnoustrojowa i dylematy rozwojowe Patriotycznego Ruchu Odrodzenia Narodowego. Panstwo i Prawo no.7, Warsaw 1986, pp. 17-35. Most recently the authorities created a new institution to promote a corporatist mode the so-called Consultative Council.

104. See e.g., V.I. Lenin. The Fundamental Tasks of the Party After the Seizure of Power by the Proletariat, in: V.I. Lenin. Selected Works, vol.III. Op.cit...pp. 343-344.

105. D.E. Powell. The Soviet Union in the 1980s: A Crisis of Leadership and Legitimacy. Soviet Union, vol.9, part I, Tempe/Arizona 1982, pp. 82 and ff. See also an interesting analysis of legitimacy in the communist states by Adam Podgorecki, in: The Polish Burial of Marxist Ideology. Poets and Printers Press, London 1981, pp. 12 and ff.

106. Leszek Kolakowski. Main Currents of Marxism, vol. III. Op.cit...p. 104.

107. Ludomir Sochor. Contribution to an Analysis of the Conservative Features of the Ideology of "Real Socialism". Research project: Crises in Soviet-Type System. Directed by Zdenek Mlynar. Study no.4, Munich 1984, pp. 5 and 7. See also Ch. Lane. Legitimacy and Power in the Soviet Union Through Socialist Ritual. British Journal of Political Science, vol.14, part 2, Cambridge 1984, p. 207.

108. Alexander Zinoview. Totalitariansim from Below. Bodley Head, London 1974, p. 259.

109. As far as the legislative power is concerned see, for instance: Adam Podgorecki. Law and Society. Routledge and Kegan Paul, London/Boston 1974, p. 250.

110. Leszek Kolakowski. Main Currents of Marxism, vol.III, Op.cit...pp. 50-51.

111. L.S. Jawitsch. The Central Theory of Law. Progress Publishers, Moscow 1981, p. 47.

112. See, e.g., A.Y. Vyshinsky, (ed.). The Law of the Soviet State. Op.cit...pp. 13 and ff.

113. See: Barrington Moore. Terror and Progress. Harvard University Press, Cambridge, Mass. 1954, pp. 174-78.

114. Ferdinand Feldbrugge. Soviet Corrective Labor Law, in: D.Barry, G. Ginsburgs, P. Maggs, (eds.). Soviet Law After Stalin, Part I: The Citizen and the State in Contemporary Soviet Law. Sijthoff, Leiden 1977, pp. 46-48.

115. Robert Sharlet. Stalinism and Soviet Legal Culture, in: R.C. Tucker, (ed.). Stalinism. Op.cit...pp. 164-165.

116. Robert Sharlet. Op.cit...p. 179.

117. Aleksander Smolar. Przeciwko legalizacji bezprawia. Aneks no.11. London 1976, p. 4.

118. Similar constitutional changes took place not only in Poland but also in other communist countries.

119. See: Jakub Karpinski. Count Down. Op.cit...p. 186

120. Jan J. Lipski. KOR. Aneks, London 1983, pp. 24-28.

121. As far as legal analysis of martial law repressions is concerned see especially: Poland Under Martial Law. A Report on Human Rights by the Polish Helsinki Watch Committee. English Edition, New York 1983, 325 pp.

122. See General Jaruzelski's speech at the National Conference of the P.W.U.P. delegates, in: Zycie Warszawy, 17-18 March 1984.

123. Kazimierz Barcikowski, in: Polityka no.9, Warsaw 1984.

124. Robert Sharlet. Op.cit...p. 156.

125. See: Tygodnik Mazowszwe no.36, Warsaw 1982.

126. E. Sieminski, quoted in: Panstwo i Prawo no.3, Warsaw 1983, p. 125.

127. See especially: Lech Mazewski. O stanie polskiej doktryny jednolitosci wladzy. Panstwo i Prawo no.2, Warsaw 1984, pp. 55, 60-63.

128. See: Andrzej Sylwestrzak. Leninist Principles of State Control. Panstwo i Prawo no.11, Warsaw 1983, as well as Zbyslaw Rykowski and Wojciech Sokolewicz. Konstytucyjne Podstawy Systemu Naczelnych Organow Panstwowych. Panstwo i Prawo no.5, Warsaw 1983. In addition to the State Tribunal and the Constitutional Tribunal, one can also mention the Highest Administrative Court, which was created in 1979. On the one hand, the Highest Administrative Court indeed helps the state to play a role of national super-arbiter. On the other hand, however, the Court was established in order to secure a judicial review of state administration (especially, the local ones).

129. Richard Crossman, in: F. Bealy, (ed.). The Social and Political Thought of the Labour Party. Weidenfeld and Nicolson, London 1970, p. 182; Harold Wilson, quoted by David Coates, in: The Labour Party and the Struggle for Socialism. Cambridge University Press, Cambridge 1975, pp. 142-143. Compare also with: Carl J. Friedrich and Zbigniew K. Brzezinski. Totalitarian Dictatorship and Autocracy. Op.cit...pp. 278 and ff.

VI Poland between the superpowers

Solidarity never articulated an independent foreign policy stance, beyond the symbolic "Message to the Peoples of Eastern Europe" adopted during its first National Congress in 1981.[1] Solidarity was preoccupied with domestic problems and therefore international issues had to take second place.

There were also important tactical reasons which argued against the raising of international issues by the union. The communist authorities in Poland claimed an absolute monopoly on the country's foreign policy and there were good grounds to believe that this monopoly was of particular interest and importance to Moscow.

Moreover, public debate within Solidarity about international issues would certainly highlight the difficult question of Soviet domination in Eastern Europe, thus making Moscow even more uneasy in its attitude towards the Polish independent trade union movement.

The fact that international issues were hardly ever discussed within the union as such does not mean that there was no debate on these issues within Polish oppositional circles. On the contrary, many independent writers tried to initiate discussions on a broad range of international questions, and especially on those linked with the recent crisis in Poland.

This essay will try to analyse this debate. We begin by pointing to the most characteristic features of independent foreign policy thinking in Poland. These are: (a) the special concern about Poland's geopolitical position; (b) the preoccupation with the heritage of Yalta which confirmed Poland's place within the Soviet sphere of influence; (c) the Eurocentric perception of international politics; and (d) the promotion of the idea of the brotherhood of democratic nations.

One of the most characteristic features of Polish independent foreign policy thinking is its preoccupation with the geopolitical position of Poland. Preoccupation with geopolitical problems has a long tradition in this country. After all throughout the ages, Poland has been repeatedly confronted with the aspirations of its powerful German and Russian neighbours. In consequence, its domestic as well as its foreign policy had always to be accommodated to requirements which emerged from Poland's difficult geographical position.

Western students of international relations have pointed out that modern technology can alter the political and economic significance of geopolitical characteristics.[2] It seems, however, that the technological developments of recent decades such as those in the fields of nuclear defence or universal communication hardly reduced the importance of geographical factors for Poland. Poland's political, economic and even cultural fate is still very much dependent on its relations with the Soviet Union and both German states. Not surprisingly therefore, the foreign policy debate in Poland has often been dominated by geopolitical arguments.[3] And successive generations of Polish writers have tried to elaborate the optimal ways of dealing with Poland's powerful neighbours.

Of course, the geopolitical position of Poland has not resulted exclusively from geographical factors. It has also emerged from political developments in Europe after the Second World War which led to the division of Europe into two opposite blocks. The division of Europe is usually linked with the results of the Yalta Conference in February 1945. Since Yalta Poland has been generally considered as a country which belonged to the Soviet sphere of influence.[4] Political opposition in Poland has never accepted such a "legacy of Yalta" and debates about the ways to annihilate the heritage of Yalta have dominated all foreign policy considerations.

In the West the problem of Yalta has hardly ever been a key issue of political debate (certainly not before the Polish crisis of 1980).[5] Moreover, in the West the Yalta axiom has usually helped to form the outlook of the policy of detente with the Soviet Union.[6] The legacy of Yalta was identified with the desire to maintain peace and security in Europe. However, for the Poles Yalta symbolizes insecurity and injustice. A special preoccupation with the negative heritage of Yalta represents the second characteristic feature of independent foreign policy thinking in Poland.

The reluctance to accept the division of Europe is linked with the Eurocentrism of the Polish opposition. "Poland belongs to Europe" - is the repeated cry of independent writers.[7] In their view Europe possesses a special kind of identity. This European identity is based on certain cultural and legal traditions, on common principles of democracy and the common religious roots of Christianity.[8] Such a notion of Europe is not necessarily identical with a geographical Europe, and can reach over the Urals and the Atlantic. Certainly, such a notion of Europe can hardly be limited to countries West of the river Elbe. According to Polish writers, a notion of Europe must include all nations which cultivate the tradition of European identity regardless of 40 years of Soviet domination. In their view there is one Europe and the Poles are ready to work for its unity. As John Paul II has put it: "Europe, which during its history was many times divided; Europe, which toward the end of the first half of our country was tragically divided by the horrible world war; Europe, which despite its current still continuing divisions of regimes, ideologies and economic-political systems cannot cease to seek its fundamental unity...".[9]

The Eurocentrism of the Polish opposition does not imply that it ignores the Third World and its problems. For instance, Lech Walesa has repeatedly criticized the policy of apartheid in South Africa or repressions in Chile. Nevertheless, the Eurocentrism of the Polish opposition implies that in all political deliberations Europe and its problems always comes first, regardless of the technological, economic or political developments of recent decades. In this respect, again, the climate of political discussions in Poland is different than the climate in many Western European countries, such as Britain, Holland or Spain.

A study of independent literature in Poland makes it clear that the Poles do not count on any significant support from the West in their struggle for democracy and national independence.[10] At the same time, however, they seem to suggest a sort of alliance, if not a brotherhood, of free and democratic nations. Daniel Warszawski has expressed this idea in the following words: "Europe has a chance-maybe the last one - to show that it is ready to stop trading Eastern European slavery for Western freedom. However, there is only one way to achieve this goal - Western Europe has to take risks in helping Eastern European nations to achieve freedom and liberty."[11]

The idea of a brotherhood of free nations thus has both moral and pragmatic dimensions. In moral terms no country should be deprived of certain rights. The freedom of Western Europe cannot be bought by the slavery of Eastern European nations. As John Paul II has put it: "there can be no just Europe without an independent Poland".[12] However, there is also a pragmatic aspect to this call for a brotherhood of democratic nations. According to the Poles "a lasting peace will reign in Europe only when it becomes a continent of democratic states".[13] In order to achieve this state, however, one must "give up the policy of temporary gains for the sake of long-term advantages, making it easier for the people of Central and Eastern Europe to struggle for the implementation of the principles written in the Declaration of the Rights of Man".[14]

In fact, the idea of a brotherhood of free nations has a long tradition in Poland. The famous XIXth century Polish poet, Adam Mickiewicz, wrote: "Poland says to the people: abandon all your local interests and go after liberty".[15] Today, his call is echoed in contemporary Poland.

HOW TO LIVE WITH THE SOVIETS

The history of Polish-Russian relations is full of violent conflicts, mutual aggression, hatred and bitterness. The establishment of the Soviet state intensified rather than reduced Polish-Russian animosity. In 1920 the Poles had to resist a Soviet invasion which reached Warsaw before it was halted and driven back. In August 1939 the Soviet Foreign Minister Molotov concluded a secret pact with Hitler's Foreign Minister Ribbentrop to partition Poland for the fourth time in its history. In consequence, on September 17, 1939 Soviet troops began to occupy vast tracts of Poland. The rest of the country was occupied by the German

Army.

Since the end of World War II Poland has been under Soviet domination, which implies not only military command by the USSR but also the ideological rhetoric of Marxism-Leninism, an economic system of bureaucratic mismanagement, and the cultural sovietization of the Polish nation.

This difficult history of Polish-Russian/Soviet relations required the Polish opposition to address two basic questions: (a) what should be the Polish attitude toward the marxist leadership of the Kremlin; and (b) what should be the Polish attitude toward the Russian nation or more broadly, toward the people of the Soviet Union.

The latter question was especially important in the light of the historical tradition of Polish-Russian antagonism. Namely, long-lasting antagonism between the Polish and Russian nations stimulated the creation of national stereotypes cultivating mutual distrust if not hatred between the people of both countries. In the eyes of many Poles the Russian stereotype means "obscurantism, cultural underdevelopment, blind obedience to authority and civilizational backwardness".[16] The Russians on their part often used to characterize the Poles as "insolent rebels", "the Judas of Slavdom", a French "watchdog" in the East or as a "snake spouting its venom at us".[17]

Political opposition in Poland has had to cope with all these national stereotypes. And in fact, a remarkable number of Polish independent publications have been devoted to an analysis of Russian society and its attitude towards the Polish nation. Many of these publications tried to unmask the totalitarian nature of the Russian/Soviet state, denounced Russian imperial ambitions and described the crimes committed by the Russians against neighbouring nations. (All subjects strictly forbidden by the official censor in Poland.) Nevertheless, independent writers have made it clear that their denouncements of the dark aspects of the Russian/Soviet state are supposed to promote historical truth about Soviet domestic and international conduct rather that to cultivate hostility and hatred between the Poles and the Russians. In fact, most Polish independent writers have repeatedly called for efforts to bring the Russian and Polish nations together, to abandon historical animosities and to unite on the basis of mutual respect, independence and cooperation.[18] In their view, the major obstacle to development of friendly relations between the Polish and the Russian people is the existence of the Soviet totalitarian system rather than a difficult past or conflicting national aspirations. As Jozef Szrett has put it: "The evil is in Sovietism and not in Russophilism".[19]

In the same critical manner, the Poles have also reviewed their relations with the Ukrainians, Lithuanians and Byelorussians. Most independent writers insist that Poland should not have any territorial claims in the East and call for mutual understanding and cooperation between the Poles and all neighbouring Eastern nations in their struggle for national independence and democracy.[20]

However, to say that the opposition should work for a genuine understanding between the Poles and the Russians is one thing. To deal with the present Soviet regime is another. As already mentioned the opposition also had to elaborate a realistic program of dealing with the current policy of the leadership in the Kremlin. In this respect, the basic question which the opposition had to address was: how much freedom of manoeuvre is there within the Soviet bloc? And in particular, which changes would be realistically possible in Poland, taking into account its geopolitical situation?

Of course, the opposition has been unable to give any simple answer to this crucial question. Nevertheless, we can identify three sets of basic arguments presented to the public by Polish independent writers. First of all, they argue that, historically, Soviet policy towards Eastern Europe has been flexible to a remarkable extent. In the case of Poland, neither freedom of religion, nor private agriculture or various other freedoms were generously granted to the Poles by Moscow. The Poles succeeded in obtaining successive concessions from the Soviet Union through a hard and painful process of bargaining. This bargaining consisted of broad public pressure, but also of certain efforts on the side of the Polish communist rulers to negotiate some sort of a compromise with Moscow.[21]

Second, the opposition argue that the exact limits of Soviet tolerance and flexibility are not known. What was always essential in Poland was the art of bargaining which determined what could be obtained under certain circumstances and at what price. Here, we are in the domain of practice, the skills of balancing and trade-offs rather than in the domain of any codified communist decalogue.[22]

Three, the opposition expresses the opinion that the Soviet

authorities prefer to negotiate and bargain with contesting Eastern Europeans rather than to crush any sort of protest by tanks. In other words, in solving problems, the use of military force against dissent in Eastern Europe is for Moscow the last rather than the first resort. This has been shown not only by the Polish experience but also by that of Hungary in 1956 and Czechoslovakia in 1968. In all these cases, the Soviets tried to get what they wanted through political pressure (or even blackmail) before they used the Red Army.

Having said that a certain freedom of manoeuvre exists within the Soviet block, the opposition tries to suggest some concrete ways of negotiating and bargaining with the Soviets. In this respect, we can distinguish at least two schools of thought.

The first school argues that the Polish communist authorities have to be pressed by the domestic opposition to negotiate eventual concessions with the Soviet Union. Such concessions could meet at least some of the basic aspirations of the Poles for national independence and sovereignty. At the same time, they might allow for domestic reforms and by the same token, reduce the omnipotence of the Polish nomenklatura. In the view of this school of thought two former leaders of the Polish Communist Party, Wladyslaw Gomulka and Edward Gierek, manifested that it is possible to exploit a potential for flexibility and tolerance on the part of the Soviet Union with respect to Eastern Europe. Of course, this policy consolidated both Gomulka's and Gierek's power. However, it also brought some relief to the Polish people. If sufficiently pressed by the opposition, General Jaruzelski would also be able to exploit the potential for Soviet flexibility. So far, however, according to the first school, it seems that he has merely sought support and legitimacy from Moscow for his iron fist policy.[23]

The second school believes that the opposition should try to negotiate directly with Moscow and above the heads of communist leaders in Poland. In its view the national spirit is threatened more by communist rule in Poland than by Poland's international dependence on Moscow. Besides, in Poland's geopolitical position, a full national sovereignty is not possible. The Poles should therefore promise to be a faithful member of the Warsaw Pact but at the same time they should relieve themselves of the ideological grip of the communists. After all, Moscow would have a certain interest in dealing with a representative non-communist Polish government, provided that this government does not question the existing system of international security and alliances.[24]

According to the second school of thought, the domestic nomenklatura in Poland would always try to convince Moscow that its existence is the only means of protecting Soviet interests in Poland. If pressed by the opposition, Polish communists would sooner or later ask for direct Soviet military assistance, and therefore they cannot be considered as an eventual mediator between the libertarian aspirations of Polish people and the leadership in the Kremlin.

The first school opposes such a reasoning and insists that because of geopolitical constraints the power of Polish communists should be reduced rather than eliminated. In its view, the Kremlin's rule is to a great extent based on ideology. This implies that Moscow would always insist on a Polish government which is communist and not merely friendly.

Discussions about Polish-Soviet relations gained new momentum after 1985, in the light of the new course in Moscow initiated by Mikhail Gorbachev. The attitude to Gorbachev and his policies has been evolving in independent opposition circles in Poland from one of disillusioned pessimism to one of interest and cautious optimism. Pessimists argue that changes that have taken place in the Soviet Union are mostly in the sphere of culture and information. They are considerable and at times quite sensational, but they can be revoked very quickly, because the essential power structure has remained unchanged.[25] Gorbachev's aim is not that of genuinely changing the system but simply making it more efficient. All changes would be made within strictly defined limits, in particular, the present level of centralization would remain unchanged, as would the one-party system and ideological unity. According to pessimists that sort of change may prove to be a considerable threat to the West in general and to Poland in particular, since, as Karol Grodkowski put it, the present reforms "are aimed at increasing the efficiency and might of a totalitarian, one-party, and aggressive Soviet Union that remains essentially unchanged".[26] Cautious optimists within the Polish opposition argue that Gorbachev's new course might open up new possibilities for the Poles and bring more "openness" to Polish-Soviet relations. Jacek Kuron, for instance, expressed the hope that the effects of Soviet developments would be felt throughout the block: "If Gorbachev survives no one will be able to stop the process of reform".[27] Kuron also believes that Gorbachev has no intention of abolishing the existing power structure, but one should not assume that the politicians would indeed achieve what they have been aiming at. In Kuron's words: "Gorbachev wants to absorb all the criticism not in order to change the system but to strengthen it- except that a great revolution is taking place in people's minds in the USSR, and words are not without importance. They only take a long time to bear fruit; but national, religious, and economic resistance must then grow out of them. Social forces must be put into motion, and this is positive, this is our hope".[28]

Adam Michnik appeared to express even stronger support for taking advantage of Soviet restructuring. Michnik claimed that there were new grounds for hoping for political compromises with Moscow that would lessen international conflicts as well as the social conflicts prevailing in communist countries. In Michnik's view, the Soviet publication of an interview with Cardinal Glemp, the Primate of the Polish Catholic Church, represents a public recognition by the Kremlin of the fact that there is a powerful institution in Poland that is independent of the state and that is widely respected by Polish society. "It has been shown for the first time" -claimed Michnik - "that communist Russia has a partner in dialogue other than the communist nomenklatura".[29]

Bronislaw Geremek, another Solidarity activist also expressed a cautious optimism concerning the new policies of Mikhail Gorbachev. In his opinion, the events in the Soviet Union could not help but have a positive influence on developments in Poland; while the fact that the "Jaruzelski team fails to make use of it in any available way shows once again that the interest of the country, the interest of Poland, lies outside its scope".[30]

Nevertheless, a positive evaluation of Gorbachev's policies has not necessarily led to uncritical support for Gorbachev's regime. As Zbigniew Bujak put it: "The chance [for Poland - J.Z.] lay not in falling back on Gorbachev but in taking advantage of the situation and doing one's own thing. To act like a classic labour movement, the opposition should drop the attempts to be co-responsible for the running of a factory or the country and return instead to making demands and when they [i.e. the authorities - J.Z.] hit us cry - how about perestroika?"[31]

THE GERMAN QUESTION

The history of Polish-German relations is no less difficult than the history of Polish-Russian relations. Germany (or Prussia) participated in all the successive partitions of Poland and the Second World War which began with the Nazi invasion on Poland caused six million Polish deaths.

Nevertheless, a study of the contemporary independent literature in Poland indicates that a negative stereotype of the Germans appears less frequently than a negative stereotype of the Russians or the Soviet Union as such. A statistical study of general popular perceptions existing in Poland vis-á-vis its neighbours shows a similar trend. For instance, the opinion polls conducted by the Polish Academy of Sciences in 1980 indicated that only 4 per cent of the persons polled fear the Germans, while no less than 49.6 per cent of them fear the Soviets.[32]

The movement away from a deep-rooted negative perception of the Germans in Poland was inspired by the Polish bishops' letter to "German Brothers in Christian Pastoral Office" in 1966.[33] In this letter Polish bishops called for mutual foregiveness and the beginning of a dialogue between Polish and German Christians.

In 1966 the Polish government sharply criticized the bishops' conciliatory attitude towards the West Germans. However, some time later the authorities also began negotiations with the Brandt government which resulted in the Polish-German agreement of December 1970. In the 1970's various forms of economic, political and cultural cooperation between Poland and the FRG developed which further contributed to a gradual softening of the traditional negative stereotype of the German nation. As Jozef Szrett has put it: "the contemporary Pole did not began to love the Germans, but he did admire them for their high standard of civilization, and more importantly – he liberated himself from a fear of the Germans".[34]

However, it should be mentioned that this evolution of opinions concerns the Germans living in the Federal Republic rather than the Germans living in the Democratic Republic. The Polish opposition has repeatedly criticized the militarization of society in the GDR as well as the revival of Prussian traditions in that country.[35]

This new and more friendly perception of the German nation did not automatically eliminate basic concerns about the international consequences of the so-called "German question".[36] In this context especially, the issue of the unification of Germany became a subject of frequent debates within the Polish opposition.

In principle, most independent Polish writers considered German aspirations to unite their country as justifiable if not welcome. The division of Germany was viewed as a part of the legacy of Yalta which was always refuted by the Polish opposition. Moreover, the Poles apparently did not want to use double standards in defining the legitimate rights of all European nations to sovereignty and self-determination. As one author has put it: "the Germans, like any other nation, have the right to live in a united state".[37]

The opposition thus seemed to accept the moral and political right of the Germans to unite their country. Nevertheless, the question of how to proceed with the unification of the two German states time and again raised serious doubts and controversies. The discussion concentrated on two possible models of unification, the so-called "European" model and the so-called "Rapallo" model.

The European model assumes the incorporation of a united Germany into Western Europe. This would be combined with a remarkable but not complete reduction of American influence in Europe. Such a policy would not necessarily lead to the dismantling of NATO but it would deprive it of any political or military substance. The united Germany would be transformed into a quasi-neutral member of NATO, thus meeting the basic security requirements of the Soviet Union.[38]

The European model of German unification usually assumes a more neutral and independent position of Poland, and other Central European states, which could be welcomed by the Polish opposition. On the other hand, however, some authors have warned that the adoption of this model might imply a concentration of Soviet forces on the Polish-German border.[39]

Nevertheless, the European model of German unification came under fire within the Polish opposition for entirely different reasons. Namely, it was described by some authors as being totally unrealistic; that is as a model which enjoys neither Soviet nor Western European support. As Stefan Kisielewski has put it: "I do not consider any plan of German unification according to any Western [European - J.Z.] scheme because I do not see such an option – the West does not look for this option and it seeks nothing in this respect".[40]

In consequence, much more attention has been given to possible application of the second model of German unification. The Poles call it the "Rapallo" model.[41]

This second model assumes purely neutral status for a united Germany. Moscow's eventual consent to the creation of a confederation of the two German states is dependent upon West German withdrawal from NATO. A new German Confederation would be allowed to go ahead with economic and cultural integration of the two Germanies. At the same time, however, the privileged position of the East German nomenklatura could not be reduced nor put into question.[42]

Of course, the Rapallo model is much more attractive to Moscow than the European model of German unification. Moreover, Polish writers are of the view that the application of the Rapallo model would also be acceptable to many Germans.[43] In this context the Poles have pointed out to the three recent developments in West Germany.[44] First, it has been indicated that many German politicians seem to believe that the key to the German question lies in Moscow, and that the Rapallo model of unification could be achieved through a compromise rather than a process of bargaining with Moscow. (Such a compromise could hardly be expected if Germany were to insist on proceeding with the European model of unification).

Second, Polish writers have noticed that many Germans feel that the eventual compromise with Moscow would require merely military neutralization of Germany rather than any immediate reduction of the political and economic freedoms enjoyed by the FRG. (By the same token, the West German principle which says: "Die Freihart hat Vorfahrt vor der Einheit" - is not automatically challenged by the new Rapallo.)

And three, it has been pointed out that many Germans believe that neutralization of Germany and German withdrawal from NATO are desirable political goals as such, regardless of the unification dilemma.

The Rapallo model came under severe criticism within the Polish opposition. In its view any historical compromise between the FRG and the Soviet Union, eventually leading toward German unification, would create an enormous threat to Polish national sovereignty. As Jan Morawski has put it: "the Poles must hope that there will be no new Rapallo nor any new Ribbentrop-Molotov Pact, that there are no Soviet-German arrangements which would threaten the independence and sovereignty of Poland".[45] According to Morawski, German concessions which are supposed to gain Soviet consent to the unification of their country should not affect development opportunities for Poland.

Another Polish writer, Socjusz, explained that the Poles fear that Soviet-German cooperation or even a sort of alliance would dramatically reduce any Polish freedom of political and economic manoeuvre.[46]

One of the reasons why the opposition in Poland has criticized the Rapallo model was that it assumed a preservation, if not a strengthening of the power of the communist nomenklatura in East Germany as well as in the Soviet Union (and by the same token in Poland). For instance, the economic fruits of German unification, mainly due to an expected development of Soviet-German economic cooperation, could make it possible to sustain the repressive system of nomenklatura without introducing any democratic reforms in these countries.

The Poles also opposed the Rapallo model of unification because it would lead to a drastic reduction of the American influence in Germany and in Europe as such. This in turn would strengthen the strategic position of the Red Army on the whole European continent and facilitate the use of Soviet military blackmail vis-à-vis most European states, including Poland.

Thus, although many Polish writers have expressed a certain amount of sympathy with the West German desire to unite their country, they are, nevertheless, unable to support any theoretical model of German unification. The European model was considered as being unrealistic, while the Rapallo model was considered as being undesirable, taking into account Polish national interests.

Moreover, the question of the Polish-German boundary was potentially also a difficult question. All oppositional writers in Poland insisted on the inviolability of the Polish-German boundary on the Oder-Neisse. This position is not equally shared by all German supporters of German unification.[47]

POLISH PERCEPTIONS OF THE POLICY OF DETENTE

Polish controversies around West German foreign policy did not end with debating the abstract question of German unification. They re-emerged during debates about the policy of detente in East-West relations.[48]

There can be little doubt that in the 1970's the policy of detente was generally welcomed by the Polish opposition. This was especially manifested during the strikes of 1980 when the Helsinki Final Act was invoked by the striking workers during the negotiations of the Gdansk Agreements which gave rise to Solidarity. However, in the eyes of many Poles the military coup d'etat of December 1981 has challenged the basic principles of detente in Europe. Since that time, the opposition has adopted a much more critical view of those Western initiatives which recommended continuation of all sorts of cooperation with the Soviet block regardless of the repressions in Poland. This position implies neither a total abandonment of all hopes linked with detente nor an advocacy of a policy of East-West confrontation. Nevertheless, since December 1981 some specific currents of the policy of detente have come under fire within Polish oppositional circles.

The first criticized current was that which considered the policy of detente as the only alternative to the cold war between East and West. Accordingly, any confrontationist statements evoked by the suppression of Solidarity could only contribute to yet a greater tension in Western relations with Moscow, and by the same token stimulate the arms race and increase the danger of nuclear catastrophe. Besides, as, for instance, Enrico Jaccia has put it, eventual liberalization in Poland "would provoke further acceleration of the arms race and dash hopes for a lessening of international tension" as the Soviet Union would feel more vulnerable.[49]

Independent Polish writers fiercely opposed such a perception of East-West relations. Solidarity leaders repeatedly stated that it is not weapons which create threats, but the minds behind the weapons. They further argued that lasting peace in Europe cannot be secured unless certain basic rights and aspirations of Eastern European nations would be met.[50] (We shall return to this problem a bit later.)

The second pro-detente current which was criticized in Poland is much more pragmatic and sophisticated than the first one. Representatives of this current argue that despite a certain disillusionment with the policy of detente - caused by misbehaviour on the part of the Soviets or by Jaruzelski, it can still play an important role in East-West relations. In international politics, they argue, the real choice is not between all and nothing. Therefore, at present the real choice in policy with Moscow, East Berlin or Warsaw is between a greater or lesser evil. As Theo Sommer has put it: "However awful this basic truth may sound to us, we have no choice but to return to detente after each case of suppression [i.e., of Eastern Europeans - J.Z.] resuming the effort to limber up, to humanize, or as it were, to "Finlandize" Eastern Europe".[51]

Thus, as it is unable to achieve any comprehensive solution for security and justice in Europe, the West should try to extract at least some limited Soviet concessions concerning small but important issues such as family re-unification, military confidence-building measures, selected forms of economic cooperation, etc. This in practice implies giving up the more ambitious demands concerning, for example, freedom of trade unions or freedom of information. After all, it is hard to expect Moscow to make concessions in any field where there is a direct threat to the integrity of the communist system.

In principle, many Poles welcomed the endorsement of some sort of compromise with Moscow and the rejection of the reasoning according to the rule "all or nothing". Nevertheless, they raised important arguments against the specific model of compromise advocated by this second pro-detente orientation.

First of all, many Polish writers argued that there is a danger that the adoption of this policy would result in unwanted appeasement of the Soviet Union. Limited Soviet concessions in the field of family unification, however desirable, cannot compensate for the crushing of Solidarity or for the invasion of Afghanistan. Moreover, the obsession with good relations with Moscow, which could in turn produce some limited progress in the field of economic or diplomatic cooperation, makes it easy for the Soviet Union to mislead or even blackmail Western Europeans for concessions to achieve such progress. Finally, the small compromise advocated by the pragmatic model of detente is probably insufficient to deal with the deep political and economic crises in countries such as Poland, Romania or Yugoslavia. In other words, small compromises with communist regimes would tend to stimulate conflicts in some Eastern European countries rather than contribute to the peaceful settlement thereof. Western failure to exert strong pressure on governments in Warsaw, Bucharest or Belgrade to put their economies in order and to restrict their violations of human rights could have very negative consequences for developments in these countries and therefore for Europe as a whole. The West can hardly afford yet another crisis in Poland or a pro-Moscow military coup d'etat in Yugoslavia.[52]

It should also be mentioned that the fact that the second pro-detente orientation was especially popular in the Federal Republic of Germany caused additional problems for the Poles. Of course, the Polish writers had to acknowledge that a German model of detente would be governed by considerations that were different to Polish priorities in East-West relations. For instance, the question of trade union freedom within the communist block is not necessarily a priority of the German Ostpolitik. First, no one has so far tried to create a Solidarity in East Germany. Second, German insistence that Moscow accept free trade unions might jeopardize any progress in the field of family re-unification.

In the economic field there is no urgent need for the Germans to insist on economic reforms in Eastern Europe. Due to special tariff and credit arrangements between the two German states, the GDR is the wealthiest communist country although it has never even tried to introduce serious economic reforms.

The question of freedom of information is not necessarily a priority for the Federal Republic either. East Germans can easily watch West German television or listen to West German radio.

Many more examples could be given to illustrate the different priorities of the Poles and the Germans as far as the model of detente is concerned.

In principle, many Poles recognized the Germans' specific concerns as natural and justifiable. At the same time, however, the Polish opposition made it clear that it refused to accept the point of view which suggests that the policy which is good for both German states is also good for Poland or for the whole of Europe. In particular, the opposition criticized the development of special relations between certain leading German politicians and General Jaruzelski's regime. The opposition argued that these relations could serve neither peace nor human rights in Europe. Moreover, they could threaten the development of friendly relations between the German and Polish nations.[53]

SOLIDARITY AND THE POLICY OF SANCTIONS

The two models of detente criticized by the Polish opposition were usually promoted by socialist circles in Western Europe as well as by liberal circles in the United States. However, this criticism of certain principles of detente did not automatically imply overwhelming Polish support for the policy of East-West relations suggested by certain conservative circles in the West.

The Soviet adventurist policy of the late 1970's promoted serious concern, especially in the United States. The crackdown on Solidarity was yet another confirmation of the aggressive nature of Soviet conduct. In consequence, President Reagan himself described the Soviet Union as an "evil empire" and even the usually cautious George Shultz declared in August 1984 that the United States "will never accept the idea of a divided Europe" and that "the tide of history is with us".[54]

However, American (but also European) conservatives demanded that Western governments perform certain deeds against the Soviet block and not merely indulge in rhetoric. They especially supported: (a) the imposition of economic sanctions against Poland as well as against the Soviet Union; and (b) the denunciation of the CSCE Helsinki process.[55]

In principle, many Poles seemed to agree with the arguments of conservative circles against any hopes that "if the Soviet Union can be talked into talking, and into adopting the forms of orderly relations, then the substance of such relations will somehow follow".[56] (After all, the Poles knew something about the real nature of the Soviet system.) Nevertheless, most independent writers had difficulty in comprehending how the specific recommendations of the conservatives would indeed serve the interests of the people in Eastern Europe and especially in Poland.

As far as the CSCE process is concerned, the Poles knew that the Helsinki Accords could not liberate Eastern Europe from the communist yoke. However, they did provide the diplomatic means to assist Eastern European efforts to make the Soviet system more human and less repressive. Therefore, from the Polish perspective, the point was to use these diplomatic means with wisdom and determination rather than to abandon them. In particular, Polish writers insisted that the whole point of the Helsinki Accords was mutual monitoring, not mutual evasion of difficult problems. They also called for coordination of Western efforts as well as for consistency in pursuing a human rights policy in Eastern Europe.[57]

The attitude of the Polish opposition towards the policy of economic sanctions is much more difficult to explain. Initially the policy of sanctions was very popular within the opposition. Solidarity activists feared that further unconditional Western credits would allow General

Jaruzelski to motivate those in Poland who held bayonets, rather than provide help for Polish citizens. The Polish experience in the 1970's had shown that Western credits tended to corrupt communist leaders rather than improve the state of the Polish economy.[58]

Nevertheless, the popularity of sanctions gradually declined in Poland. As a result, in December 1983, Lech Walesa himself asked for a relaxation of the sanctions.[59] One can indicate three basic reasons for this development.

First, Western (or in fact American) sanctions provided the Polish regime with an excuse for its economic mismanagement and its unwillingness to introduce any comprehensive economic reform. General Jaruzelski was desperately seeking popular legitimization of his regime, and someone had to be blamed for the prolonged misery of the Polish people. In this way, American sanctions became the key element of official propaganda in Poland.

It is difficult to estimate the various repercussions of the policy of economic sanctions. Nevertheless, it was widely regarded in Poland that some of the sanctions affected the Polish authorities rather than the Polish people (i.e., the U.S. denial of the most-favoured-nation treatment with respect to Poland). However, certain other sanctions directly affected the Polish people and therefore could hardly be popular in Poland (as e.g., the suspension of fishing rights in U.S. waters for the Polish fishing fleet, or the withdrawal of the American export of feed for Polish chickens).

Second, the American policy of sanctions did not leave any freedom of political manoeuvre for Lech Walesa and Solidarity. Several remarkable arguments were raised, namely that the negative policy toward the Polish military government should be combined with some positive elements, which could motivate Jaruzelski to lift repressions and give ordinary Poles hope for a better future in the event that Solidarity would again be legalized. This was usually called the idea of "mini-Marshall aid" to Poland.[60] But President Reagan did not go beyond an ambiguous statement that "if the Polish government introduces meaningful liberalizing measures, we will take equally significant and concrete actions of our own".[61] By the same token, the idea of the "mini-Marshall aid" to Poland was never instituted, and the conditions under which the American sanctions would be lifted were changeable and often unrealistic.

Third, the Poles realized that the policy of sanctions could hardly be effective enough without the coordinated support of all Western states. In fact, however, the policy of sanctions was never as popular in Europe as it was in the United States. Western European governments failed to develop any solution for the Polish crisis, though by and large they opposed the American policy of sanctions. Even though several European governments officially endorsed sanctions, Europeans considered the American actions as unilateral and inconsistent (for example, Americans boycotted a gas pipeline deal between Europe and the USSR but promoted a grain deal with Moscow).

Of course, many Poles found it difficult to understand why European advocates of detente, who for a dozen years had supported the idea of economic aid to the East as a means of pacifying communist regimes, declined to reduce such aid in 1982, in spite of the evidence provided by the imposition of martial law – that the policy had failed. Nevertheless, the Poles also had to acknowledge that disagreements within the Western Alliance undermined the effectiveness of sanctions and by the same token made any further support for sanctions questionable.

WAYS OF PRESERVING PEACE IN EUROPE

Solidarity was born in Poland at a time when Western Europe was witnessing a remarkable development in anti-nuclear campaigns. At first, Solidarity activists were apparently indifferent towards the Western peace movement. However, in 1982 several peace organizations, such as the British END, the Dutch IKV or the Italian Coordinamento began a campaign of solidarity with Polish nonviolent resistance. This campaign was initiated in peace movement publications and was followed by efforts to establish direct contact with underground organizations in Poland.

In particular, Western anti-nuclear activists suggested that mass emancipatory movements in the East and in the West share basic principles concerning the right to live, the right to national self-determination, the right to peace, justice and freedom and therefore they should "support each other and recognize each others aims".[62]

Some peace campaigners went even further and stated that: "Soviet leaders must be made to understand the existence in the West of millions of people whom... they would regard as anti-Soviet... (who are) supporters of Solidarity and the Polish renewal... and who also support the peace movement".[63] For a grassroots initiative against nuclear missiles to be taken seriously by the rulers of any European country, it must become "pandemic, by spreading to every country in Europe".[64]

The peace movement's call for a dialogue and cooperation did not evoke any official reaction from Solidarity's leadership. Nevertheless, it was widely debated in several underground publications. Moreover, a number of underground groups issued separate statements directed to anti-nuclear activists in the West.[65]

Some groups insisted that Western anti-nuclear campaigns serve the ends of Soviet imperialism and are therefore not in the interest of peace.[66] By the same token, eventual cooperation with the peace movement could enhance totalitarianism in Europe rather than the course of peace and justice.

At the same time, however, some other independent groups in Poland responded to the initiatives of the peace movement in a positive way. In particular, they accepted the invitation to a dialogue and specified conditions which could make further cooperation between Solidarity and the Western peace movement possible. Tygodnik Mazowsze explained this decision by pointing to the common characteristics of Solidarity and the peace movement. In its words: "each of these movements has, in its own manner, totally changed our contemporary thinking about practical politics. Both the peace movement and Solidarity are democratic; both break national barriers. Both unite millions of people around a "negative" programme, that is, around a refusal to accept the inherited reality which is seen as a threat to fundamental values: those of freedom and human dignity. Both prefer to use moral rather than political terms; in both, the religious inspiration is strong."[67]

Nevertheless, all groups within the Polish opposition which expressed their willingness to continue a dialogue with Western anti-nuclear campaigners made it very clear that development of mutual cooperation could only take place if major political differences between them were bridged. And in fact these differences touched upon all the basic principles on which the anti-nuclear peace campaign was founded. Let us try to elaborate on these differences.

One may indicate three basic arguments (or concerns) which lie behind various peace campaigns in the West. First of all, there is the threat of nuclear confrontation which inspired the development of the peace movement. Usually those who promote peace campaigns consider the question of nuclear weapons as one of the most crucial domestic and international problems.[68]

Secondly, there is the concern about (or distrust of) American foreign policy as such, and U.S. nuclear policy in particular, which has encouraged people to organize peace actions, although only very few supporters of anti-nuclear campaigns take the Soviet line in explaining the current state of East-West relations.[69] Most of them, however, adopt an equally symmetrical perception of both Soviet and United States policy.[70]

Thirdly, anti-nuclear campaigners are deeply concerned about, what they call "the renewal of cold war" in East-West relations.[71] They advocate the "real detente policy", which should be encouraged by unilateral disarmament gestures on the part of the West and a development of economic as well as cultural cooperation between the two parts of Europe.

Careful study of Solidarity's publications indicates that all these three basic sets of beliefs held by Western anti-nuclear campaigners are not equally shared by independent groups in Poland, including the groups which engaged in a public dialogue with the peace movement.

There is no doubt that independent groups in Poland are concerned about nuclear issues. There is even evidence that after the Chernobyl accident this concern is deeper than ever before.[72] At the same time, however, it would be wrong to assume that they consider the question of nuclear weapons as one of the most crucial domestic and international problems. A study of the Polish literature indicates that Solidarity activists are basically concerned about questions of human rights, social justice and national independence rather than about questions concerning the nuclear arms race. According to most of them peace is a direct function of liberty and justice rather than a function of military arsenals. In other words, it is not weapons which create threats, but the minds behind the weapons. In this context, Komitet Oporu Spolecznego in its declaration entitled "Solidarity in Defence of Peace" stated that "a struggle for peace cannot be separated from a struggle against totalitarianism and for liberty and democracy".[73]

The statement of the Wroclaw-based group, Szeregi Pokoju i Solidarnosci, expressed this idea in similar words: "Until the nations of

179

Eastern Europe are liberated, until the ideals of democracy and freedom became reality in our countries, there can be no such thing as a genuine or lasting world peace. The struggle for peace is inextricably tied to the struggle for human rights for all people".[74] In these and other statements the issue of weapons has certainly been put in the shade.[75] Moreover, the question of militarization of society in Eastern Europe comes usually before the question of the nuclear arms race.

Western symmetrical perception of both superpowers represents the second major point of disagreement between the anti-nuclear peace campaigners in Western Europe and independent activists in Poland. The fact that the Poles perceive East-West relations in terms of Soviet totalitarian domination rather than merely in terms of nuclear confrontation implies that any symmetry between the United States and the Soviet Union is to them totally inappropriate. After all, the Polish authors argue, it was the Soviet Union who incorporated parts of Poland, Romania and the three Baltic states into the USSR. It was also the Soviet Union who installed by force puppet regimes in East Berlin, Budapest and other Eastern European capitals. It was and to acertain extent still is the Soviet Party which guards the communist system of economic mismanagement, legitimizes abuses of human rights and promotes cultural socialist realism.

Many more examples could be given to illustrate the point which suggests that there is nothing in American relations with Western Europe which could seriously be compared to Soviet relations with Poland, Hungary or the GDR. Most independent Polish writers would, therefore, have trouble in agreeing with, for instance, Edward P. Thompson's view that "the aims of the Soviet state are not by its nature aggressive and expansive".[76] They would rather tend to agree with the "Open Letter to the Western Peace Movement" in which the Komitet Oporu Spolecznego states that "Soviet policy of expansion is based on military blackmail and on aggressive propaganda".[77]

At the same time, it is difficult to find any independent Polish researcher who like Mary Kaldor identifies United States policy with a role of the world policeman.[78] Of course, this does not mean that there are no critics of American foreign policy among activists of the Polish opposition.[79] However, their criticism of the United States has hardly ever led to a symmetrical perception of both superpowers.

Finally, there is the question of perceiving East-West relations in terms of "cold war" and "detente". In fact peace activists have never come to any agreement concerning the exact meaning of "cold war" and "detente". Nevertheless, they have continued to praise all efforts towards "detente" in East-West relations and have condemned the "cold war" policy conducted by a number of Western governments.

Such a way of thinking is alien to independent activists in Poland.[80] A study of independent literature indicates that Solidarity activists tend to believe that political relations with Moscow cannot be perceived in any black-and-white bi-polar terms such as "detente" and "cold war". In other words, the world is not simply divided into ethically motivated pacifists and cold war militarists. Nor is it divided into the peace loving forces of progress and the forces of reaction, as peace activists used to describe it. For instance, does criticism of Soviet violations of the Helsinki Accords in the field of human rights represent a cold war policy or a step towards a real detente?[81] In the field of East-West economic relations the experience of the last two decades has indicated that economic sanctions, boycotts and embargoes stimulate divisions within the Western Alliance rather than constrain or humanize Eastern European regimes. However, those who claimed that large-scale economic assistance would automatically restrain communist adventures are today disappointed as well.[82] Many more examples could illustrate this point.

It has already been mentioned that Solidarity activists view their relations with Moscow in terms of political bargaining, which consists of broad political pressure, but also of certain efforts to negotiate and compromise with Moscow. Such bargaining cannot be practiced if one applies the simplistic reasoning according to the rules "all or nothing", "red or dead" or "cold war versus detente".[83]

The attitude of the Polish opposition towards the Western peace movement could be summarized by a statement made by Adam Michnik. In 1983 Michnik wrote from prison: "Solidarity, pushed underground, calumnied and persecuted, pays a high price to keep the chance of dialogue alive. I wish the peace campaigners in the West took this dimension of Solidarity's actions into account, for it is certainly not unthinkable that a spectacular peaceful solution in Poland will become the starting point for the resolution of international tensions; that it will become a source of strength and hope for all who prefer negotiations, however, difficult and protracted, to a dialogue by means of truncheons and tear gas, tanks and guns, and finally missiles of tactical, medium and strategic range".[84]

NOTES

1. The Message to the Peoples of Eastern Europe stated: "We support those of you who decided to begin the difficult struggle for free trade unions. We believe that our and your representatives will soon be able to meet and exchange common trade unionist experiences". Reportedly, the Message was opposed by Lech Walesa and leading advisers to Solidarity such as Kuron, Geremek and Mazowiecki. See: Jerzy Holzer. Solidarnosc. 1980-1981. Instytut Literacki, Paris 1984, pp. 271-272.

2. See e.g., K.J. Holsti. International Politics. A Framework of Analysis. Prentice Hall Inc., New Jersey 1977, p. 384.

3. See especially: Stefan Kisielewski. Czy geopolityka stracila znaczenie? Res Publica no.1, London 1979, pp. 56-76. Jozef Szrett. Dolina miedzy gorami. Kultura no.1-2, Paris 1984, pp. 3-17, or S.C. Geopolityka? Res Publica no.7-8, London 1980, pp. 67-75.

4. Although historical records of the Yalta Agreements hardly support such an interpretation. See e.g., Herman de Lange. De mythen over Jalta en de dynamiek van de Koude Oorlog, in: G. van Benthem van den Bergh, Duco Hellema and Herman de Lange. Europa Eenmaal Andermaal. Uitgeverij Jan Mets, Amsterdam 1985, pp. 13-15.

5. After 13 December 1981 a remarkable number of Western politicians and public commentators raised the issue of Yalta. For instance, much international attention was given to the public statement of President Ronald Reagan on 17 August 1984 in which he said that the United States reject any interpretation of the 1945 Yalta agreement "that suggests American consent for the division of Europe into spheres of influence". As quoted in the International Herald Tribune, 18 August 1984.

6. See e.g., Daniel Yergin. Shattered Peace. The Origins of the Cold War and the National Security State. Penguin, Harmondsworth 1977, p. 11.

7. See e.g., Marek Beylin, Konrad Bielinski and Adam Michnik. Polska Lezy w Europie. Krytyka no.5, London 1980, pp. 3-4.

8. See e.g., Jozef Szrett. Do panow Rosjan list niemal otwarty. Kultura no.11, Paris 1984, p. 6.

9. John Paul II in: The Pope in Poland. Radio Free Europe Research, Munich 1979, p. 70.

10. See e.g., Adam Michnik. Polska wojna. Solidarnosc. Biuletyn Informacyjny no.12, Paris 1982, p. 10, or Polska wobec stanu wojennego. IV Raport DiP in: Solidarnosc. Biuletyn Informacyjny no.24, Paris 1982, p. 8.

11. Daniel Warszawski. Przeklenstwo Jalty. KOS no.48, Warsaw 1983, p. 8.

12. John Paul II quoted in: Radio Free Europe Research, Munich, 6 June 1984, p. 5.

13. Wojtek Wojskowy. Niepodleglosc, no.26, Warsaw 1984, p. 3.

14. Ibidem.

15. Adam Mickiewicz quoted in: J.L. Talmon. Political Messianism. Secher & Warburg, London 1960, p. 269.

16. Foreign Policy Issues in the Underground Press. Attitude to the USSR, in: Uncensored Poland. News Bulletin no.13, London 1984, p. 25.

17. Piotr S. Wandycz. Soviet-Polish Relations, 1917-1921. Harvard University Press, Cambridge Mass. 1968, p. 15, or Adam Michnik. 1863: Polska w oczach Rosjan, in: Szanse polskiej demokracji, Aneks, London 1984, pp. 171 and ff, or Arthur R. Rachwald. Poland Between the Superpowers. Westview Press, Boulder, Colorado 1983, p. 1.

18. See e.g., Adam Michnik. Puszkin i Rosjanie. Krytyka no.16, London 1983, p. 299, or Jakub Czechrynski. Isc z Rosja. Polityka Polska no.2-3, Warsaw 1983, p. 6. The opposite attitude is presented by the Niepodleglosc group which sees "the various proposals to gain the Russians' favour and the disgusting Russophile sentiments rife in certain quarters as an outright obstacle on Poland's road to real independence". Niepodleglosc no.13-14, quoted in: Solidarnosc. Biuletyn Informacyjny no.89, Paris 1984, p. 4. However, according to Stefan Kisielewski the attitude of Niepodleglosc is exceptional within the Polish opposition. See: Stefan Kisielewski. Probuje podsumowac. Res Publika no.7, London 1980, p. 89.

19. Jozef Szrett. Do panow Rosjan list niemal otwarty. Op.cit...p. 5.

20. See e.g., an interview with Stefan Bratkowski. Tygodnik Mazowsze no.176, Warsaw 1986, p. 5, or Wojtek Wojskowy. Europa Przyszlosci. Niepodleglosc no.26, Warsaw 1984, p. 4, or Jozef Szrett. Dolina miedzy gorami. Op.cit...p. 17.

21. It is important to note the parallel between contemporary arguments saying that there is some room for manoeuvre for Poland in its relations with Moscow, and Kolakowski's arguments presented as early as in the beginning of the 1970's, (see the first essay).

22. For this argument see especially Adam Michnik, quoted in: Lech Walesa. De weg van de hoop. Autobiografie. Het Spectrum, Utrecht 1987, p. 165. First published in French by Fayard, Paris 1987.

23. The first school is represented by e.g., Socjusz. Polskie kwadratury kola. Kultura no.6, Paris 1980, pp. 113-115 or ZEY. O przyszlosci miedzynarodowo. Krytyka no.17, London 1984, pp. 212-253.

24. The second group is especially represented by Stefan Kisielewski, see: O podwojnym mysleniu i dzialaniu. Kultura no.3, Paris 1986, pp. 104 and ff, or Probuje podsumowac. Res Publica no.7-8, London 1980, pp. 75 and ff. See also: Jozef Kusmierek. O handlu z Rosja. Kultura no.3, Paris 1980, pp. 50 and ff.

25. See e.g., statements of Andrzej Celinski and Tadeusz Jedynak published in: Radio Free Europe Research. Press Review, Munich, 17 September 1987, p. 7.

26. Karol Grodkowski, in: Tygodnik Mazowsze, Warsaw, 11 March 1987.

27. Jacek Kuron quoted in: The Washington Post, 5 February 1987.

28. Jacek Kuron quoted in: Radio Free Europe Research. Press Review, Munich, 17 September 1987, p. 8.

29. Adam Michnik. Der Grosse Genereformator. Der Spiegel, 18 May 1987, p. 155. See also: Adam Michnik. Gorbatschow und die Polen. Der Spiegel, 26 October 1987, pp. 154-155, or Adam Michnik. De opstand der dingen dwingt Moskou perestrojka af. De Volkskrant, 6 January 1988, p. 4.

30. Bronislaw Geremek, quoted in: Radio Free Europe Research. Press Review, Munich, 17 September 1987, p. 7.

31. Zbigniew Bujak, quoted in Radio Free Europe Research. Op.cit...p. 8.

32. The results of these polls were published in: Krytyka no.13-14, London 1983, p. 59. The respondents were asked from where or from whom they might expect a threat to Polish national independence. 4 percent indicated the Germans, of which 5.1 percent indicated the GDR, and 10.7 percent indicated the FRG.

33. Oredzie biskupow polskich do ich niemieckich braci w chrystusowym urzedzie, in: Listy Pasterskie Episkopatu Polski. 1945-1974. Editions du Dialogue, Paris 1975, pp. 829-835.

34. Jozef Szrett. Dolina miedzy gorami. Op.cit...p. 9. See also Jan Jozef Lipski. Two Fatherlands. Two Patriotisms. Survey, Autumn 1982, pp. 162-165.

35. See e.g., Timur. Niemcy. Krytyka no.5, London 1980, pp. 100-103.

36. For a definition of the "German question" see e.g., Walter L. Kiep. The New Deutschland Politik. Foreign Affairs, Winter 1984/85, pp. 316 and ff.

37. Wojtek Wojskowy. Europa Przyszlosci. Op.cit...p. 5.

38. See especially: Timur. Niemcy. Op.cit...p. 7, or SC. Geopolityka. Res Publica no.7-8. Op.cit...p. 69. The American version of the European model of unification is presented e.g., by Zbigniew Brzezinski. The Future of Yalta. Foreign Affairs, Winter 1984/85, pp. 291-294.

39. MS. Polska, Niemcy i inni. Res Publica no.2, London 1980, p. 81.

40. Stefan Kisielewski. Czy geopolityka stracila znaczenie? Res Publica no.1, London 1979, p. 71.

41. The Rapallo model suggested certain patterns of Soviet-German reapproachement resembling the Rapallo secret agreement signed in 1922. According to E.H. Carr, the fact of signature was more important than the formal content of the treaty. Rapallo was a symbolic, but in that function, crucial event. It showed, first, that a defeated Germany and a weakened and beseiged Soviet Russia could reenter the heart of international politics as major forces to contend with, and second, that in a world of Maciavellian politics neither widely social structures nor equally diverging, even conflicting, ideologies were absolute barriers to strategic alliances. In particular, the treaty was clearly and consciously aimed against Poland. See: E.H. Carr. The Bolshevik Revolution, vol.3, Penguin, Harmondsworth 1933, pp. 375 and ff.

42. For more information about the Rapallo model see e.g., Ferenc Feher and Agnes Heller. Eastern Europe Under the Shadow of the New Rapallo, in: Zdenek Mlynar. Crises in Soviet-type Systems. Research Project no.6., Munich 1984, pp. 7-38.

43. See e.g., Socjusz. Tezy i wymiary polskich spraw. Kultura no.9, Paris 1982, p. 14, or Stefan Kisielewski. Czy geopolityka stracila znaczenie? Op.cit...p. 71, or Jan Morawski. Problem niemiecki i polskie nadzieje. Kontakt no.6, Paris 1986, p. 11.

44. The tendency toward a "Rapallo" solution could be observed within left-wing rather than right-wing political circles in West Germany. See especially: Peter Brandt and Herbert Ammon. Die Linke und die Nationale Frage. Rowohlt, Hamburg 1981, pp. 235-255 and ff; or Rudolf Bahro. Rapallo - Why Not? Telos, Spring 1982.

45. Jan Morawski. Op.cit...p. 11.

46. Socjusz. Tezy i wymiary polskich spraw. Op.cit...p. 14.

47. For an extensive elaboration on the Oder-Neisse boundary question in Polish-West German relations see e.g., Arthur R. Rachwald. Poland Between the Superpowers. Westview, Boulder, Colorado 1983, pp. 54-71.

48. For a more precise elaboration of the policy of detente see e.g., John Lewis Gaddis. The Rise, Fall and Future of Detente. Foreign Affairs, Winter 1983/84, pp. 354-377.

49. Enrico Jaccia, in: The International Herald Tribune, 10 September 1982.

50. See e.g., Lech Walesa's Nobel Prize Speech, in: Solidarnosc. Biuletyn Informacyjny, no.78, Paris 1983, pp. 3-5, or the TKK Statement on 30 January 1983 addressed to the CSCE Conference in Madrid, in Solidarnosc. Biuletyn Informacyjny no.58, Paris 1983, p. 64.

51. Theo Sommer. The Challenge to the West: Problems, Objectives and Policy Options. Adelphi Papers no.189, London 1983, p. 37.

52. See e.g., Adam Michnik. Analiza i Perspektywy. Kultura no.7-8, Paris 1983, pp. 77-79, or Stefan Kisielewski. Wschod i Zachod-swiaty nienormalne. Kultura no.1-2, Paris 1979, pp. 157-159.

53. See especially: List otwarty regionalnej Komisji Wykonawczej Solidarnosci Regionu Mazowsze do Willy Brandta, in: Solidarnosc. Biuletyn Informacyjny no.131, Paris 1986, pp. 12-14, or The Poles and the Germans: Jan Jozef Lipski. Unpublished Letter to the Editor of Der Spiegel, in: Uncensored Poland. News Bulletin no.6, London 1984, pp. 34-36, or Adam Michnik. Appeal to Leading German Writers and to Willy Brandt, in: Uncensored Poland. News Bulletin no.6, London 1984, p. 36.

54. Quoted in: The International Herald Tribune, 18 August 1984.

55. See e.g., Jean-Fran ois Revel. How Democracies Perish. Doubleday, New York 1984, pp.33-54 or Norman Podhoretz. The Reagan Road to Detente. Foreign Affairs no.3, 1985, pp. 447-464.

56. George F. Will in: The International Herald Tribune, 6 January 1985.

57. See e.g., the TKK letter to the CSCE Conference in Madrid, in: Solidarnosc. Biuletyn Informacyjny no.58, Paris 1983, p. 3, or the Statement on the Concluding Document of the Madrid Conference by Solidarity Coordinating Office Abroad, in: Uncensored Poland. News Bulletin no.18, London 1983, pp. 11-12 or successive reports of the Polish Helsinki Watch Committee, since 1983 published by the U.S. Helsinki Watch Committee and the Solidarity Coordinating Office Abroad.

58. See e.g., List Otwarty Regionalnej Komisji Wykonawczej Solidarnosci Regionu Mazowsze do Willy Brandta, in: Solidarnosc. Biuletyn Informacyjny, no.131, Paris 1986, p. 13.

59. See: Lech Walesa's press conference on Western sanctions on 5 December 1983, reported in: Uncensored Poland. News Bulletin no.23, London 1983, p. 14.

60. See especially: Stefan Kurowski. Co Zachod moze zrobic dla Polski? Kultura no.1-2, Paris 1981, pp. 6-12.

61. Quoted in: Current Policy no.621, 11 October 1984, Washington, D.C.: U.S. Department of State, Bureau of Public Affairs.

62. See e.g., Ben Ter Veer. The New International Peace Movement. Some Challenging Questions. A paper presented at the 32nd PUGWASH Conference, Warsaw, 26-31 August 1982, p. 4.

63. Edward P. Thompson. Normalizacja Europy. Aneks no.33, London 1984, p. 26.

64. Ibidem.

65. See especially: List do uczestnikow ruchow pokojowych. Komitet Oporu Spolecznego w Polsce. Warsaw, 9 May 1983, published e.g., in: Kontakt no.9, Paris 1983, p. 64, or Oswiadczenie grupy zalozycielskiej Szeregi Pokoju i Solidarnosci, Wroclaw, 4 March 1984, published e.g., in: Poland Watch no.6, Washington, D.C. 1984, pp. 30-31, or Deklaracja Zalozycielska Ruchu Wolnosc i Pokoj, published e.g., in: Solidarnosc. Biuletyn Informacyjny no.117-119, Paris 1985, p. 3.

66. See e.g., Antoni Wiechrzyciel. 11 listopada 1918 - 11 listopada 1983. Wola no.35 (77), Warsaw 1983, p. 1, or Oszustwo Pacyfizmu. Niepodleglosc no.23, Warsaw 1983, pp. 2-3, or Kassandra. Rakiety czy maslo. Tygodnik Mazowsze no.39, Warsaw 1983, pp. 2 and ff., or Stanislaw Pilka. Wojna i Pokoj. Mysl Niezalezna no.14, Warsaw 1982, pp. 1 and ff.

67. Tygodnik Mazowsze no.97, quoted in: Uncensored Poland. News Bulletin no.28, London 1984, p. 37.

68. See e.g., Hylke Tromp. Alternatives to Current Security Policy and the Peace Movements, in: P. van den Dungen, (ed.). West European Pacifism and the Strategy for Peace. MacMillan, London 1985, pp. 68-97.

69. One might interpret the Soviet line in various ways. W.Schütze has described Western European concerns in the following words: "Europe's young generation seems, to a very significant extent, more afraid of Reagan's tough stand on the need to upgrade U.S. military power than of the current Soviet military might. While NATO officials have not, for 30 years, been able to really agree on whether to address primarily Soviet intentions or Soviet capabilities, we now find ourselves in a situation where in the opinion of many people, including members of the governing parties in Western Europe, the intentions of the Kremlin leadership are more peaceful than those proclaimed by the White House". See: W. Schütze. European Security Policy in the 1980's: Rethinking Western Strategy, in: Sverre Loodgaard and Marek Thee. Nuclear Disengagement in Europe. Taylor & Francis, London/New York 1983, p. 83.

70. For instance, the Report of the British Alternative Defence Commission stated that: "The Commission considers that the main threats to Britain stem from the two great powers, directly or indirectly". See: Defence Without the Bomb. Taylor & Francis, London/New York 1983, p. 3.

71. See e.g., M. Saeter. Nuclear Disengagement Efforts. 1955–1980. Politics of Status Quo or Political Change?, in: Nuclear Disengagement in Europe. Op.cit...pp. 61–66, or Per Berg and Sverre Loodgaard. Disengagement Zones: A Step Towards Meaningful Defence. Journal of Peace Research no.1, Oslo 1983, p. 8.

72. In Poland various protest actions were organized in connection with the official Soviet and Polish management of the Chernobyl crisis. See e.g., Solidarnosc. Biuletyn Informacyjny no.139, Paris 1986, p. 6.

73. KOS. Solidarnosc w Obronie Pokoju, published e.g., in: Kontakt no.9, Paris 1983, p. 65.

74. Oswiadczenie grupy zalozycielskiej Szeregi Pokoju i Solidarnosci. Op.cit...pp. 30–31.

75. See also: Deklaracja Zalozycielska Ruchu Wolnosc i Pokoj. Op.cit...pp. 3.

76. Edward P. Thompson. Normalizacja Europy. Op.cit...p. 29.

77. KOS. List otwarty do uczestnikow ruchow pokojowych. Op.cit...p. 64.

78. Mary Kaldor. The Disintegrating West. Penguin, Harmondsworth 1978, p. 85.

79. In this respect one should especially refer to some above quoted works of Stefan Kisielewski, Zygmunt Kusmierek or Zbigniew Bienkowski.

80. One can trace Polish opposition to any simplistic application of various political terms in Leszek Kolakowski's open letter to E.P. Thompson. See: Leszak Kolakowski. Moje sluszne poglady na wszystko. Aneks no.18, London 1978, especially pp. 10–25.

81. See e.g., List do Kongresu Intelektualistow w obronie pokoju. Tygodnik Mazowsze no.153, Warsaw 1986, p. 1.

82. See e.g., Stefan Kurowski. Op.cit...pp. 6 and ff., or List Regionalnej Komisji Wykonawczej Solidarnosci Regionu Mazowsze do Willy Brandta. Op.cit...pp. 2–14.

83. See e.g., an interview with KOS, in: Poland Watch no.5, Washington, D.C. 1984, pp. 138–139.

84. Adam Michnik. Letter from Prison. Uncensored Poland. News Bulletin no.15, London 1983, p. 28.

Bibliography

Abramowski, E. Pisma popularno-naukowe i propagandowe. Ksiazka i Wiedza. Warsaw 1979.

Adelman, J. (ed.). Communist Armies in Politics. Westview Press. Boulder Col. 1982.

Analysis of the Legal Situation in Poland After the Lifting of the State of War. Helsinki Committee in Poland. Co-ordinating Office Abroad of NSZZ Solidarnosc. Brussels 1983.

Andelman, D. "Contempt and crisis in Poland". International Security. no.3. Cambridge Mass. 1981/82.

Anderson, R. "Soviet Decision-Making in Poland". Problems of Communism. March-April 1982.

Anderson, T. Russian Political Thought. Cornell University Press. Ithaca and New York 1967.

Arato, A. "Civil Society Against the State: Poland 1980-81". Telos. Spring 1981.

Ascherson, N. The Polish August. The Self-limiting Revolution. Penguin. Harmondsworth 1981.

Ash, T.G. The Polish Revolution. Solidarity 1980-1981. Jonathan Cape. London 1983.

Ash, T.G. "Poland: The Uses of Adversity". The New York Review of Books. 27 June 1985.

Backer, R. The Modern British Politics. Methuen Co. London 1979.

Bahro, R. "Rapallo - Why Not?" Telos. Spring 1982.

Barbash, J. Labor Unions in Action: A Study of the Mainsprings of Unionism. Harper & Row. New York 1948.

Bauman, Z. "On the Maturation of Socialism". Telos. Spring 1981.

Bealy, F. (ed.). The Social and Political Thought of the Labour Party. Weidenfeld & Nicolson. London 1970.

Bergh, B. van Benthem van den., Hellema, D. and de Lange, H. (eds.). Europa Eenmaal Andermaal. Jan Mets. Amsterdam 1985.

Bernhard, M. The Rebirth of Public Politics in Poland: Workers and Intellectuals in the Democratic Opposition. 1976-1980. Ph.D. thesis at Columbia University. New York 1988.

Bertsch, G.K. Power and Policy in Communist Systems. John Wiley and Sons. New York 1978.

Beylin, M., Bielinski, K. and Michnik, A. "Polska lezy w Europie". Krytyka. no.5. London 1980.

Bialer, S. "Poland and the Soviet Imperium". Foreign Affairs. Spring 1981.

Bielecki, J. Co wydarzylo sie w Polsce od sierpnia 1980 roku? Ksiazka i Wiedza. Wydzial Informacji KC PZPR. Warsaw 1982.

Bielesiak, J. and Simon, M. (eds.). Contemporary Polish Politics. Praeger. London 1984.

Black, J.L. and Strong, J.W. (eds.). Sisyphus and Poland. Reflections on Martial Law. Ronald P. Frye & Co. Winnipeg 1986.

Blazyca, G. "The Polish Economy Under Martial Law". Soviet Studies. July 1985.

Blazynski, G. Flashpoint Poland. Pergamon Press. New York 1979.

Blazynski, G. Pope John Paul II. Dell Publ. New York 1979.

Blumsztajn, S. Je rentre au Pays. Calmann-Lévy. Paris 1984.

Blumsztajn, S. "Reconcer à la violence". Alternatives. Non-violence. Hiver 1984.

Bornstein, M., Gitelman, Z. and Zimmerman, W. (eds). East-West Relations and the Future of Eastern Europe. Allen & Unwin. London 1981.

Brandt, P. and Ammon, H. Die Linke und die Nationale Frage. Rowohlt. Hamburg 1981.

Bromke, A. Poland. The Protracted Crisis. Mosaic Press. Oakville 1983.

Brown, A. and Gray, J. (eds.). Political Culture and Political Change in Communist States. Macmillan. London 1977.

Brumberg, A. (ed.). Poland. Genesis of a Revolution. Random House. New York 1983.

Brumberg, A. "Poland: The New Opposition" The New York Review of Books. 18 February 1988.

Brus, W. The Economics and Political Socialism. Routledge & Kegan. London 1973.

Brus, W. Socialist Ownership and Political Systems. Routledge & Kegan. London 1975.

Bruyn, S. and Rayman, P.M. (eds.). Nonviolent Action and Social Change. Irvington. New York 1979.

Brzezinski, Z. and Friedrich, C.J. Totalitarian Dictatorship and Autocracy. Harvard University Press. Cambridge Mass. 1956.

Brzezinski, Z. "The Future of Yalta". Foreign Affairs. Winter 1984/85.

Brzezinski, Z. "White House Diary". Orbis. Winter 1988.

Bujak, Z. "Positional Warfare". Survey. Summer 1982.

Checinski, M. Poland: Communism, Nationalism, Anti-Semitism. Karz-Cohl. New York 1982.

Chirot, D. "Corporatism, Socialism and Development in Rumania". Amsterdams Sociologisch Tijdschrift. no.3. Amsterdam 1978.

Clegg, H. The Changing System of Industrial Relations in Great Britain. Blackwell. Oxford 1979.

Cole, G.D.H. Guild Socialism. L. Parson. London 1920.

Cole, G.D.H. Guild Socialism Restated. Friedrich A. Stokes. New York 1921.

Colton, T.J. The Dilemma of Reform in the Soviet Union. Council of Foreign Relations. New York 1984.

Cywinski, B. "Mysl polityczna Edwarda Abramowskiego", in: Tworcy polskiej mysli politycznej. Ossolineum. Wroclaw 1978.

Cywinski, B. Doswiadczenie Polskie. Spotkania. Paris 1984.

Cywinski, B. Rodowody Niepokornych. Spotkania. Paris 1985.

Davis, N. God's Playground. A History of Poland. vol. 2. 1795 to the Present. Clarendon Press. Oxford 1982.

Davisha, K. and Hanson, P. (eds.). Soviet-East European Dilemmas: Coercion, Competition, and Consent. Heinemann. London 1981.

Demus, R. "The 1980 Polish Strike and the Strike Cycles in the 1970's". Telos. Spring 1981.

Drachkovitch, M. (ed.). East Central Europe. Yesterday-Today-Tommorrow. Hoover Institution Press. Stanford 1982.

Dunn, T. (ed). Alternatives to War and Violence: a Search. James Clark. London 1963.

Durkheim, E. The Divisions of Labour in Socialism. The Free Press. New York 1964.

Eidlin, F.H. "Capitulation, Resistance and the Framework of Normalization: the August 1968 Invasion of Czechoslovakia and the Czechoslovak Response". Journal of Peace Research. no.4. Oslo 1981.

Eisenstadt, S.N. (ed.). Socialism and Tradition. Humanities Press. Atlantic Highlands N.J. 1975.

Ellul, J. "Lech Walesa et le role du Christianisme". Esprit. March 1982.

Fallenbuchl, Z. "Poland's Economic Crisis". Problems of Communism. March-April 1982.

Feher, F. and Heller, A. Eastern Europe Under the Shadow of the New Rapallo. Research Project: Crises in Soviet-Type Systems. Dir. Z. Mlynar. Study no.6. Munich 1984.

Fetjo, F. Behind the Rape of Hungary. David Mcllay. New York 1957.

Fikus, D. Foksal 1981. Aneks. London 1984.

Friedrich, C.J. Tradition and Authority. The Pall Mall Press/Macmillan. London 1972.

Gaddis, J.L. "The Rise, Fall and Future of Detente". Foreign Affairs. Winter 1983/84.

Galtung, J. Peace, War and Defence. vols. I-II. Christian Ejlers. Copenhagen 1976.

Gandhi, M.K. Selected Works. vols. I-VI. Navajiran Trust. Ahmedabad 1968.

Garnisz, C. "Polish Stalemate". Problems of Communism. May-June 1984.

Gati, Ch. "Polish Futures, Western Options". Foreign Affairs. Winter 1982/83.

Gati, Ch. "Gorbachev and Eastern Europe". Foreign Affairs. Fall 1987.

Geeraerts, G. (ed.). Possibilities of Civilian Defence in Western Europe. Polemological Center of the Free University. Brussels 1977.

Gerner, K. The Soviet Union and Central Europe in the Post-War Era. Gower. Aldershot 1985.

Glucksman, A. "Miedzy czerwienia a biela". Aneks. no.32. London 1983.

Golan, G. The Czechoslovak Reform Movement. Cambridge University Press. Cambridge Mass. 1971.

Gouldner, A.V. The Future of Intellectuals and the Rise of the New Class. The Seaburey Press. New York 1979.

Gross, J.T. Polish Society Under German Occupation: The General Gouvernement 1939-1944. Princeton University Press. Princeton 1979.

Gulczynski, M. "Karol Marks o klasowym charakterze panstwa." Panstwo i Prawo. no.3. Warsaw 1983.

Heller, M. Sous le regard de Moscou. Pologne 1980-1982. Calmann-Lévy. Paris 1982.

Herspring, D.R. and Volgyes, I. (eds.). Civil-Military Relations in Communist States. Westview Press. Boulder Col. 1978.

Hettne, B. "The Vitality of Gandhian Tradition". Journal of Peace Research. no.3. Oslo 1976.

Heydel, A. Etatyzm po polsku. Oficyna Liberalow. Warsaw 1981.

Hill, R.J. and Frank, P. The Soviet Communist Party. George Allen & Unwin. London 1981.

Hill, R.J. Soviet Union. Politics, Economics and Society. Frances Pinter. London 1985.

Hiller, E.T. The Strike: A Study in Collective Action. University of Chicago Press. Chicago 1928.

Hirszowicz, M. The Bureaucratic Leviathan. A Study in the Sociology of Communism. Martin Roberts. Oxford 1980.

Hirszowicz, M. Coercion and Control in Communist Society. The Visible Hand of Bureaucracy. Harvest Press. Oxford 1986.

Hobbs, T. Leviathan. Dent/Dutton. London 1970.

Holloway, D. and Sharp, J.O. (eds.).The Warsaw Pact. Alliance in Transition. Macmillan. London 1984.

Holsti, K.J. International Politics. A Framework of Analysis. Prentice Hall. New Jersey 1977.

Holzer, J. Solidarnosc. 1980-1981. Geneza i Historia. Instytut Literacki. Paris 1984.

Hough, J.F. The Soviet Union and Social Science Theory. Harvard University Press. Cambridge Mass. 1977.

Johnson, C. (ed.). Change in Communist Systems. Stanford University Press. Stanford 1970.

Jasinska, A. and Siemienska, R. "The Socialist Personality: a Case Study of Poland". International Journal of Sociology. no.1. London 1983.

Jaskiernia, J. "Istota, pozycja prawnoustrojowa i dylematy rozwojowe Patriotycznego Ruchu Odrodzenia Narodowego". Panstwo i Prawo. no.7. Warsaw 1986.

Jarocki, S. Katolicka Nauka Spoleczna. Societé d'Editions Internationales. Paris 1966.

Jaruzelski, W. Przemowienia 1981-1982. Ksiazka i Wiedza. Warsaw 1983.

Jaruzelski, W. Przemowienia 1983. Ksiazka i Wiedza. Warsaw 1984.

Jones, C.D. Soviet Influence in Eastern Europe: Political Autonomy and the Warsaw Pact. Praeger. London 1981.

Kampelman, M. Three Years at the East-West Divide. Freedom House. New York 1983.

Kaplan, K. The Communist Party in Power. A Profile of Party Politics in Czechoslovakia. Westview Press. Boulder Col. 1987.

Karpinski, J. Count-Down. The Polish Upheavals of 1956, 1968, 1970, 1976, 1980... Karz-Cohl. New York 1982.

Karpinski, J. Slownik. Polska. Komunizm. Opozycja. Polonia. London 1985.

Karpinski, J. "Polish Intellectuals in Opposition". Problems of Communism. July-August 1987.

Kassandra. "Rakiety czy maslo". Tygodnik Mazowsze. no.39. Warsaw 1983.

Kelly, D.R. (ed.). Soviet Politics in the Brezhnev Era. Praeger. New York 1980.

Kemp-Welch, A. The Birth of Solidarity. The Gdansk Negotiations 1980. Macmillan. London 1983.

Khrushchev, N.V. Fundamentals of Marxism-Leninism. Foreign Language Publishing House. Moscow. n.d.

Kiep, W.L. "The New Deutschland Politik". Foreign Affairs. Winter 1984/85.

Kiersnowski, M. "Dyktatura rozsadku". Puls. no.18. London 1983.

Kijowski, A. "Literatura i kryzys". Kultura. no.6. Paris 1982.

Kirk, R. The Conservative Mind. From Burke to Elliot. Gateway Editions. South Bend 1978.

Kisielewski, S. "Czy geopolityka stracila znaczenie?" Res Publica. no.1. London 1979.

Kisielewski, S. "Probuje podsumowac". Res Publica. no.7. London 1980.

Kisielewski, S. "O podwojnym mysleniu i dzialaniu". Kultura. no.3. Paris 1986.

Kiszczak, C. "Realism w ocenie pozwala byc optymista". Polityka. 17 July 1982.

Kolakowski, L. "Thesis on Hope and Hopelessness". Survey. Summer 1971.

Kolakowski, L. The Main Currents of Marxism. vols. I-III. Clarendon Press. Oxford 1978.

Kolakowski, L. Czy diabel moze byc zbawiony i 27 innych kazan. Aneks. London 1983.

Kolankiewicz, G. "Renewal, Reform or Retreat. The Polish Communist Party After the Extraordinary Ninth Congress". World Today. October 1981.

Kolarska, L. and Rychard, A. "Polacy 80. Wizje ladu spolecznego". Aneks. no.27. London 1982.

Kolkowicz, R. and Korbonski, A. (eds.). Soldiers, Peasants and Bureaucrats. George Allen & Unwin. London 1982.

Kolodziej, M. "Podziemne Struktury NSZZ Solidarnosc". Zeszyty Historyczne. no.72. Paris 1985.

Korzec, M. "Oost-Europa, pacifisme en het satans denken". Transaktie. no.3. Groningen 1983.

Kowalik, T. "Proba kompromisu". Zeszyty Literackie. no.2. Paris 1983.

Kropotkin, P.A. Modern Science and Anarchism. Freedom Press. London 1912.

Kropotkin, P.A. Mutual Aid. A Factor of Evolution. Pelican Books. Harmondsworth 1939.

Krzeminski, I. "Solidarnosc - sens ludzkiego doswiadczenia". Aneks. no.40. London 1985.

Kuczynski, W. Oboz. Aneks. London 1983.

Kuklinski, R. "The Crushing of Solidarity". Orbis. Winter 1988.

Kulerski, W. "The Third Possibility". Survey. Summer 1982.

Kundera, M. "The Tragedy of Central Europe". The New York Review of Books. vol. 31, no.7, 1984.

Kurczewski, J. "The Old System and the Revolution". Sisyphus Sociological Studies. vol. 3. Warsaw 1982.

Kuron, J. and Modzelewski, K. An Open Letter to the Party. International Socialist Publications. London 1969.

Kuron, J. Zasady Ideowe. Instytut Literacki. Paris 1978.

Kuron, J. Polityka i Odpowiedzialnosc. Aneks. London 1985

Kurowski, S. "Co Zachod moze zrobic dla Polski?" Kultura. no.1-2. Paris 1981.

Kusmierek, J. Stan Polski. Instytut Literacki. Paris 1983.
Lakey, G. Strategy for a Living Revolution. W.H. Freeman and Co. San Francisco 1973.
Lamentowicz, W. "Adaptation through Political Crisis in Poland". Journal of Peace Research. no.2, Oslo 1982.
Lange, H. de "Gebruik en misbruik van historische case studies", in: Met/Zonder Geweld. Schotanus. Utrecht 1972.
Lenin, V.I. Collected Works. Lawrence and Wishart. London and Moscow 1946.
Lewis, P. Legitimation in Eastern Europe. Croom Helm. London 1985.
Lewis, P. "The PZPR Leadership and Political Developments in Poland". Soviet Studies. July 1985.
Lipski, J.J. KOR. A History of the Workers' Defense Committee in Poland. 1976-1981. University of California. Berkeley, Los Angeles and London 1985.
Lis, B. Trade Union in 1984. Co-ordinating Office Abroad of NSZZ Solidarnosc. Brussels 1984.
Listy Pasterskie Episkopatu Polski. 1945-1974. Editions du Dialogue. Paris 1975.
Litynski, M. "The Church: Between State and Society". Poland Watch. no.5. Washington D.C. 1984.
Lopinski, M., Moskit, M. and Wilk, M. Konspira - rzecz o podziemnej Solidarnosci. Spotkania. Paris 1984.
Luers, W.H. "The United States and Eastern Europe". Foreign Affairs. Fall 1987.
Majkowski, W. People's Poland: Patterns of Social Inequality and Conflict. Praeger. London 1985.
Malcher, G.C. Poland's Politicized Army. Communists in Uniform. Praeger. London 1984.
Markiewicz, S. Ewolucja spolecznej doktryny Kosciola. Ksiazka i Wiedza. Warsaw 1983.
Marx, K. Critique of the Gothe Programme. Foreign Languages Publishing House. Moscow 1954.
Mason, D.S. "Solidarity, the Regime and the Public". Soviet Studies. October 1983.
Mason, D.S. "The Polish Party in Crisis". Slavic Review. May 1984.
Mason, D.S. Public Opinion and Political Change in Poland. 1980-1982. Cambridge University Press. Cambridge 1985.
Mastny, V. Russia's Road to the Cold War. Diplomacy, Warfare, and the Politics of Communism. 1941-1945. Columbia University Press. New York 1979.
Mastny, V. (ed.). Helsinki, Human Rights and European Security: Analysis and Documentation. Duke University Press. Durham N.C. 1986.
Mastny, V. (ed). Soviet/East European Survey. Duke University Press. Durham N.C. 1986.
Mazewski, L. "O stanie polskiej doktryny jednolitosci wladzy". Panstwo i Prawo. no.2. Warsaw 1984.
Mazowiecki, T. Internowanie. Aneks. London 1982.
Mianowicz, T. "Konspiracja, podziemie, opor spoleczny". Kultura. April 1983.
Micewski, A. Wspolrzadzic czy nie klamac? PAX i Znak w Polsce. 1945-1976. Libella. Paris 1978.
Micewski, A. "Tradycje historyczne a nasladownictwo". Res Publica. no.3. London 1979.
Michalik, M. "Panstwo i obywatel". Nowe Drogi. no.3. Warsaw 1986.

Michnik, A. "We are all Hostages". Telos. Spring 1982.
Michnik, A. Letters from Prison and Other Essays. University of California Press. Berkeley, Los Angeles and London 1985.
Michnik, A. "Gorbatschow und die Polen". Der Spiegel. 26 October 1986.
Milewski, J., Pomian, K. and Zielonka, J. "Poland: Four Years After". Foreign Affairs. Winter 1985/86.
Milosz, Cz. The Captive Mind. Vintage Books. New York 1953.
Milosz, Cz. "O podboju". Aneks. no.29-30, London 1983.
Mink, G. (ed.). Pologne. L'Etat de Guerre. Le Documentation Francaise. March 1982.
Misztal, B. (ed.) Poland After Solidarity. Transaction Books. New Brunswick 1985.
Mlynar, Z. Krisen und Krisenbewaltigung im Sovjet-System. Braumuller. Cologne and Vienna 1983.
Modzelewski, W. "Nonviolence and the Strike Movements in Poland". Journal of Peace Research. no.2. Oslo 1982.
Mokrzyszczak, W. "PZPR-partia socjalistycznej odnowy". Nowe Drogi. no.6. Warsaw 1986.
Moore, B. Terror and Progress. Harvard University Press. Cambridge Mass. 1954.
Moore, B. Injustice. The Social Bases of Obiedence and Revolt. Macmillan. London 1979.
Morawski, J. "Problem niemiecki i polskie nadzieje". Kontakt. no. 6. Paris 1986.
Muller, J.M. Strategia politycznego dzialania bez stosowania przemocy. Wydawnictwo Krag. Warsaw 1984.
Mushkat, M. "The Evolution of the Situation in Poland in 1980". Berichte des Bundesinstituts fur Ostwissenschaftliche und Internationale Studien. no.15. Cologne 1981.
Muszynski, J. Dyktatura Proletariatu. Polskie Wydawnictwo Naukowe. Warsaw 1981.
Narkiewicz, O. Eastern Europe. 1968-1984. Croom Helm. London 1986.
Nelson, D.N. (ed.). Local Politics in Communist Countries. Kentucky University Press. Lexington 1980.
Newsom, D. (ed.). The Diplomacy of Human Rights. University of America Press. New York 1986.
Novak, M. Will it Liberate? Questions About Liberation Theology. Paulist Press. New York 1986.
Novak, M. Human Rights and the New Realism. Freedom House. New York 1987.
Nowak, J. "The Church in Poland". Problems of Communism. January-February 1982.
Nowak, L. Ani Rewolucja ani Ewolucja. Dialog. Frankfurt/Main 1984.
Nowakowski, M. The Canary and Other Tales of Martial Law. Hamill Press. London 1983.
Nozick, R. Anarchy, State and Utopia. Oxford University Press. Oxford 1974.
Orton, L. "The Western Press and Jaruzelski's War". East European Quarterly. Autumn 1984.
Orzechowski, M. Spor o marksistowska teorie rewolucji. Ksiazka i Wiedza. Warsaw 1984.
Osborn, R.J. The Evolution of Soviet Politics. Dorsey Press. Homewood 1974.
Pilka, S. "Wojna i Pokoj". Mysl Niezalezna. no.14. Warsaw 1982.
Ploss, S.I. Moscow and the Polish Crisis. An Interpretation of Soviet Policies and Intentions. Westview Press. Boulder Col. 1986.

Podgorecki, A. Law and Society. Routledge & Kegan. London 1974.
Podgorecki, A. The Polish Burial of Marxist Ideology. Poets and Printers Press. London 1981.
Pomian, G. (ed.). Polska Solidarnosc. Instytut Literacki. Paris 1982.
Pomian, G. (ed.). Protokoly tzw. Komisji Grabskiego. Instytut Literacki. Paris 1986.
Pomian, K. Pologne. Defi a l'impossible. Editions Ouvrieres. Paris 1982.
Pomian, K. "L'espoir s'effrite". Alternatives. Non-violence. Hiver 1984.
Pomian, K. Religion et Politique en Pologne. 1945-1984. Vingtiēme Siecle. Avril-Juin 1986.
Pomian-Srednicki, M. Religious Change in Contemporary Poland. Routledge & Kegan. London 1982.
Pontara, G. "The Rejection of Violence in Gandhian Ethics of Conflict Resolution". Journal of Peace Research. no.2. Oslo 1965.
Popieluszko, J. Kazania patriotyczne. Libella. Paris 1984.
Potel J.Y. The Promise of Solidarity. Praeger. London 1982.
Pravda, A. "Trade Unions in East European Communist Systems. Towards Corporatism?". International Political Science Review. no.2. 1983.
Rachwald, A.R. Poland Between the Superpowers. Westview Press. Boulder Col. 1983.
Raina, P. Independent Social Movements in Poland. Orbis. London 1981.
Raina, P. Poland 1981. Towards Social Renewal. George Allen & Unwin. London 1985.
Rainko, S. "O osobliwosciach socjalistycznego panstwa". Nowe Drogi. no.2. Warsaw 1985.
Rakowski, M.F. Czas nadziei i rozczarowan. Czytelnik. Warsaw 1985.
Revel, J.F. How Democracies Perish. Doubleday. New York 1984.
Rigby, T.H. and Feher, F. (eds.). Political Legitimation in Communist States. Macmillan. London 1982.
Ritter, A. The Political Thought of Pierre-Joseph Proudhon. Princeton University Press. Princeton N.J. 1969.
Roberts, A. and Windsor, P. Czechoslovakia 1968. Repression and Resistance. Chatto and Windus. London 1969.
Rousseau, J.J. The Social Contract and Discourses. E.P. Dutton. New York 1920.
Rupnik, J. "The Polish Army and the Crisis of the Party-State". Communist Affairs. July 1982.
Russett, B. "Ethical Dilemmas of Nuclear Deterrence". International Security. no.4. Cambridge Mass. 1984.
Rykowski, Z. and Sokolewicz, W. "Konstytucyjne Podstawy Naczelnych Organow Panstwowych". Panstwo i Prawo. no.5. Warsaw 1983.
Sadykiewicz, M. "Jaruzelski's War". Survey. Summer 1982.
Sanford, G. Polish Communism in Crisis. Croom Helm. London 1983.
Sanford, G. Military Rule in Poland. The Rebuilding of Communist Power. 1981-1983. Croom Helm. London 1986.
Schell, J. "Introduction", in: A. Michnik. Letters from Prison and Other Essays. California University Press. Berkeley, Los Angeles and London 1985.
Schmid, A. (ed.). Social Defence and Soviet Military Power: an Inquiry into Relevance of an Alternative Defence Concept. COMT. Leiden 1985.
Schmitter, P.C. and Lambruch, G. (eds.). Trends Towards Corporatist Intermediation. Sage. London 1979.
Schöpflin, G. "Introduction", in: Censorship and Political Communication in Eastern Europe. A Collection of Documents. Frances Pinter. London 1983.

Shapiro, J.P. and Potichnyj, P.J. (eds.). Change and Adaptation in Soviet and East European Politics. Praeger. London 1976.
Sharp, G. The Politics of Non-Violent Action. Porter Sargent. Boston 1973.
Sibley, M.Q. Political Ideas and Ideologies. Harper & Row. New York 1970.
Silnitsky, F. Communism in Eastern Europe. Karz-Cohl. New York 1979.
Simes, D.K. "Clash over Poland". Foreign Policy. no.46. Washington D.C. 1982.
Simon, M. and Kanet, R. (eds.). Background to Crisis: Policy and Politics in Gierek's Poland. Westview Press. Boulder Col. 1981.
Singer, D. The Road to Gdansk. Monthly Review Press. London 1981.
Skjelsbaek, K. "The Challenge before Churches". Bulletin of Peace Proposals. no.3. Oslo 1984.
S.M. "Geopolityka?" Res Publica. no.7-8. London 1980.
Smialowski, J. Zagadnienie przyszlosci panstwa w historii mysli socjalistycznej. Wydawnictwo Uniwersytetu Jagielonskiego. Cracow 1978.
Smolar, A. "Przeciwko legalizacji bezprawia". Aneks. no.11. London 1976.
Smolar, A. "Miedzy ugoda a powstaniem". Aneks. no.28. London 1982.
Skilling, H.G. Czechoslovakia's Interrupted Revolution. Princeton University Press. Princeton N.J. 1976.
Sochor, L. Contribution to an Analysis of the Conservative Features of the Ideology of "Real Socialism". Research project: Crises in Soviet-Type System. Dir. Z.Mlynar. Study no.4. Munich 1984.
Socjusz. "Teorie, Wytyczne i Spory". Kultura. no.11. Paris 1979.
Socjusz. "Polskie kwadratury kola". Kultura. no.6. Paris 1980.
Sommer, T. "The Challenge to the West: Problems, Objectives and Policy Options". Adelphi Papers. no.189. London 1983.
Spasowski, R. The Liberation of One. Harcourt Brace Jovanovich. San Diego, New York and London 1986.
Spielman, R. "Crisis in Poland". Foreign Policy. Winter 1982-83.
Spiski, P. (ed.). Od trzynastego do trzynastego. Polonia. London 1983.
Stalin, J. Voprosy Leninisma. Gospolitizdat. Moscow 1953.
Staniszkis, J. "On some Contradictions of Socialist Society: the Case of Poland". Soviet Studies. April 1979.
Staniszkis, J. "Martial Law in Poland". Telos. Winter 1982-1983.
Staniszkis, J. Poland's Self-Limiting Revolution. Princeton University Press. Princeton 1984.
Switak, I. "Lessons from Poland". Telos. Summer 1982.
Sylwestrzak, A. "Leninist Principles of State Control". Panstwo i Prawo. no.11. Warsaw 1983.
Szajkowski, B. Next to God...Poland. Frances Pinter. London 1983.
Szczypiorski, A. Z notatnika stanu wojennego. Polonia. London 1983.
Szrett, J. "Dolina miedzy gorami". Kultura. no.1-2. Paris 1984.
Szrett, J. "Do panow Rosjan list niemal otwarty". Kultura. no.11. Paris 1984.
Szymanski, A. Class Stuggle in a Socialist Poland. Praeger. London 1984.
Talmon, J.L. Political Messianism. The Romantic Phase. Secker & Warburg. London 1960.
Taras, R. Ideology in Socialist Poland. 1956-1983. Macmillan. London 1984.
Taras, R. "Official Etiologies of Polish Crises: Changing Historiographies and Factional Struggles". Soviet Studies. January 1986.
Terry, S.M. Soviet Policy in Eastern Europe. Yale University Press. New Haven and London 1984.

The Pope in Poland. Radio free Europe Research. Munich 1979.
Thompson, E.P. "Normalizacja Europy". Aneks. no.33. London 1984.
Tiersky, R. Ordinary Stalinism. George Allen & Unwin. Boston 1985.
Timur. "Niemcy". Krytyka. no.5. London 1980.
Tischner, J. Polski ksztalt dialogu. Spotkania. Paris 1981.
Tischner, J. The Spirit of Solidarity. Harper & Row. New York 1982.
Tischner, J. Polska jest ojczyzna. Dialog. Paris 1985.
Tolstoy, L. The Slavery of Our Times. Maldon. Essex 1900.
Tökēs, R.L. (ed.). Dissent in the USSR: Politics, Ideology and People.
    Johns Hopkins University Press. Baltimore 1975.
Tökēs, R.L. (ed.). Opposition in Eastern Europe. Johns Hopkins
    University Press. Baltimore 1979.
Toranska, T. "Them". Stalin's Polish Puppets. Harper & Row. New York
    1987.
Touraine, A., et al. Solidarity. Analysis of a Social Movement.
    Cambridge University Press. Cambridge 1983.
Tromp, H. "The Dutch Research Project on Civilian Defence, 1974-1978:
    An Inquiry Into Alternative Security and Nonviolent Conflict
    Resolution". Bulletin of Peace Proposals. no.4. Oslo 1978.
Tucker, R.C. (ed.). Stalinism. Essays in Historical Interpretation.
    W.W. Norton. New York 1977.
Turbacz, M. "Kosciol a komunizm w Polsce". Kultura. April 1985.
Uschakow, A. (ed.). Polen - das Ende der Erneuerung ? C.H. Beck.
    Munich 1982.
Vajda, M. The State and Socialism. Allison and Busby. London 1981.
Valenta, J. "Soviet Options in Poland". Survival. no.2. London 1981.
Vāli, F.A. Rift and Revolt in Hungary. Harvard University Press.
    Cambridge Mass. 1961.
Voslensky, M. Nomenklatura: Autonomy of the Soviet Ruling Class.
    Bodley Head. London 1984.
Walesa, L. Nobel Peace Price Speech. Solidarnosc. Biuletyn
    Informacyjny. no.78. Paris 1983.
Walesa, L. Un chemin d'espoir. Fayard. Paris 1987.
Walicki, A. Filozofia a Mesjanizm. PIW. Warsaw 1970.
Walicki, A. Philosophy and Romantic Nationalism: the Case of Poland.
    Clarendon Press. Oxford 1982.
Wandycz, P.S. Soviet Polish Relations. 1917-1921. Harvard University
    Press. Cambridge Mass. 1968.
Warszawski, D. "Przeklenstwo Jalty". KOS. no.48. Warsaw 1983.
Warszawski, D. "Cena koncesji". KOS. no.50. Warsaw 1984.
Webb, S. and B. Soviet Communism: A New Civilization. Longman. London
    1944.
Weydenthal, J., Porter, B. and Devlin, K. The Polish Drama. 1980-1982.
    D.C. Heath. Lexington 1983.
White, S. Political Culture and Soviet Politics. Macmillan. London 1979.
Wiatr, J. "Hegemonic Party System", in: Studies in Polish Political
    System. Ossolineum. Wroclaw 1967.
Wiechrzyciel, A. "11 listopada 1918 - 11 listopada 1983". Wola. no.
    35. Warsaw 1983.
Wierzbicki, P. Mysli staroswieckiego Polaka. Puls. London 1985.
Wildstein, B. "Jakiej prawicy Polacy nie potrzebuja". Kontakt. no. 2.
    Paris 1986.
Williamson, G.H. "John Paul II's Concept of Church, State and Society".
    Journal of Church and State. Autumn 1982.
Wojskowy, W. "Europa Przyszlosci". Niepodleglosc. no.26. Warsaw 1984.

Woodall, J. (ed.). Policy and Politics in Contemporary Poland. Frances
    Pinter. London 1981.
Woodcock, G. Anarchism. A History of Libertarian Ideas and Movements.
    Penguin. Harmondsworth 1979.
Wyszynski, S. The Deeds of Faith. Harper & Row. New York 1966.
Wyszynski, S. Zapiski Wiezienne. Editions du Dialogue. Paris 1982.
Zaslavsky, V. The Neo-Stalinist State. Class, Ethnicity and Consensus
    in Soviet sSciety. Harvest Press. Brighton 1982.
Zawiejski, J. Droga Katechumena. Biblioteka Wiezi. Warsaw 1975.
ZEY. "O przszlosci miedzynarodowo". Krytyka. no.17. London 1984.
Zielonka, J. Pools Experiment. Eisma. Leeuwarden 1982.
Zielonka, J. "Let Poland be Hungary?". SAIS Review. Summer/Fall 1984.
Zielonka, J. "East-West Trade: Is There a Way out of the Circle?" The
    Washington Quarterly. Winter 1988.
Zinoviev, A. Totalitarianism from Below. Bodley Head. London 1974.

Index

Abramowski, E.   79-81
anarchism   4, 14, 37, 80, 81
Anderson, T.   78
Andropov, Y.   126
Andrzejewski, J.   16, 17
anti-nuclear campaign   177-179
anti-semitism   5, 11
anti-statism   4, 71, 72, 74, 77-82, 120, 124
Appeal to Society   17
Arato, A.   19
Arendt, H.   1
Army
    generals   131, 133, 134
    Military Council of National Salvation   133
    military operational groups   133
    political apparatus of   134
    special supervisory powers   133
Aron, R.   1

Augustine	37
Baranczak, S.	17
Barcikowski, K.	146
Bernhard, M.	19
Bierut, B.	120
Borusewicz, B.	17, 20
Brezhnev, L.	126
Brown, J.F.	134
Bruyn, S.	14, 96
catholics	10, 96, 139
Celinski, A.	22
censorship	41, 107, 110, 145, 146
Charter of Workers' Rights	20
Chesterton, G.K.	79
Church	2-4, 10-12, 35-53, 71, 81, 126-128, 131, 138, 140, 141, 148, 167
Bishop's Episcopate	36
hierarchy	3, 36
liberation theology	37
Pastoral Letters	36
religious practices	52
social doctrine	35, 36
Cieszkowski, A.	49
class	
antagonism	52
rule	122
cold war	172, 179, 181
Cole, G.D.H.	78
collective bargaining	81, 146
collectivism	4, 77, 80, 81, 120, 121, 128, 135, 141
Committee of the Defence of the Country	145
Committees for Help to Internees	51
Congress of Polish Culture	74
conservatism	36, 37
Constitution	73, 124, 133, 143-146
Constitutional Tribunal	129, 147
cooperatives	73, 80
corporatism	3, 6, 81, 119, 135-138, 147

corruption 15

Crossman, R. 148

Czechoslovakia 11, 95, 101, 165

Daszynski, J. 79

decentralization 4, 96

Declaration of the Rights of Man 162

democracy 3, 4, 37, 38, 51, 72, 73, 75, 81, 94, 122, 124, 126, 139, 144, 147, 161, 162, 164, 179, 180

   parliamentary 73, 81

   participatory 51, 139, 147

detente 3, 161, 171-174, 177, 179, 181

dialogue (political) 12, 37-39, 47, 48, 167, 168, 178, 179, 181

dictatorship of the proletariat 2, 4, 74, 79, 120, 123, 126-128, 137

dignity 3, 12, 15, 37, 38, 40, 41, 43-47, 71, 75, 121, 128, 178

DiP 21, 71

Dmowski, R. 5, 47, 79, 80

East-West relations 171, 172, 174, 175, 179-181

Ebert, T. 97

END 14, 15, 76, 101, 121, 127, 161, 163, 171, 177

Endecja 47, 80

equality 15, 37, 79, 103

Erasmus 1

Eurocentrism 161

Euro-communists 2

evolution 1, 4, 6, 15, 35, 36, 76, 122, 127, 134, 168

exploitation 45, 78, 99

Fourier, Ch. 77

Frasyniuk, W. 98

Free Trade Unions of the Coast 20, 22

Friedman, M. 5, 79

Galtung, J. 97, 99

Gandhi, M. 37, 78, 94-96, 102, 103

Gdansk Agreements 172

Geremek, B. 167

Gierek, E. 120, 165

Glemp, J. 40, 52, 53, 167

Glucksman, A. 102

Gomulka, W. 120, 165
Gorbachev, M. 166, 167
grassroots initiatives 17
Grodkowski, K. 166
guild socialism 78
Gwiazda, A. 20, 22
Hayek, F. von 79
Hegel, H.W.F. 122, 125
Helsinki Final Act 23, 172
Hitler, A. 141, 162
Hlond, A. 52
hope (political) 3, 10, 12, 37-40, 44, 50-52, 75, 76, 166,
167, 170, 176, 181
human rights 4, 9, 15, 23, 38, 40-44, 46, 51, 53, 71,
75, 99, 144, 173-175, 179, 180, 181
Hungary 135, 165, 180
IKV 177
Ilowiecki, M. 73
individualism 2, 4, 78
Jaccia, E. 172
Jahn, E. 97, 99
Jan XXIII 37
Jaruzelski, W. 108, 109, 121, 129, 130, 132, 133,
135, 145, 165, 167, 172, 174, 176
John Paul II 36, 39, 42-44, 48-50, 96, 161, 162
jurisprudence 143, 146
justice 3, 12, 36, 38-42, 44-46, 48, 53, 75, 96,
103, 141, 142, 173, 177-179
Kaldor, M. 180
Khrushchev, N. 125, 126
Kijowski, A. 74
KIK 21
King, M.L. 94, 95
Kisielewski, S. 52, 169
Kolakowski, L. 11-13, 15, 76, 125
Komitet Oporu Spolecznego 179, 180
KOR 4, 9, 10, 13-23, 42, 71, 73-76, 79, 80, 95
Korwin, H. 47

Kowalik, T.	10
Kozniewski, K.	127
KPN	9
Kropotkin, P.	4, 77-79, 96
Krzeminski, I.	37, 38
Kubiak, H.	130
Kulerski, W.	73
Kurczewski, J.	137
Kuron, J.	11-18, 20, 22, 23, 72, 74, 75, 80, 99, 166, 167
Lakey, G.	14, 96, 97
Lamentowicz, W.	122
Lasch, Ch.	19
law	4, 5, 36-38, 42, 43, 48, 71, 72, 75, 98, 100, 101, 105, 120, 126, 127, 129, 133, 134, 138-140, 142-147, 177
Lawrence, D.H.	79
legal culture	142, 143
legitimacy	3, 4, 38, 119, 120, 129, 140-142, 144, 147, 148, 165
Lenin, V.I.	10, 80, 99, 100, 123, 131, 142
Leninism	51, 52, 134, 141, 163
Leo XIII	37
liberals	2, 79
liberty	36, 37, 40, 162, 179
Lipinski, E.	17, 23
Lipski, J.J.	75, 76
Lis, B.	20, 22
Locke, J.	1
Luxemburg, R.	80
Maciarewicz, A.	16, 80
Malcher, G.	134
Maritain, J.	37
martial law	42, 43, 71, 72, 98, 100, 101, 105, 133, 134, 139, 142, 145, 177
Marx, K.	4, 79, 122, 123
marxism	1, 2, 6, 10, 12, 37, 44, 51, 52, 80, 134, 136, 141, 163
messianism	49
Michalik, A.	128
Michnik, A.	12-15, 47, 72, 75, 76, 78, 80, 81, 103, 167, 181
Mickiewicz, A.	49, 162

mini-Marschall aid	176
Minister of Defence	133
Mises, L. von	79
MKS	22
Modzelewski, K.	11, 99
Molotov, V.	162, 170
moral order	3, 38, 44
Morawski, J.	170
Moscow	159, 164-167, 170, 172-174, 177, 181
Muller, J.M.	95
mutual aid	17, 77, 79
national	
agreement	101, 139, 140
interest	4, 120, 122, 128, 139
tradition	10, 36, 52
National Economic and Social Council	145
nationalism	3, 4, 47-52, 120, 128, 137, 141
NATO	169, 170
neoliberals	79
NEP	141
NKVD	125
nomenklatura	135, 165-167, 170, 171
nonviolence	4, 5, 6, 71, 76, 78, 93-97, 100, 103, 107, 108, 110
normative state	142, 143
Nowak, L.	76
Nozick, R.	77
Onyszkiewicz, J.	17
opposition	1, 4, 5, 9-15, 18, 20, 21, 35, 51, 53, 72, 76, 81, 95, 99, 108, 126, 127, 138, 141, 144, 148, 160, 161, 163-172, 174, 175, 178, 180, 181
Orwell, G.	1
Ostpolitik	174
Owen, D.	77
Party	2-4, 10, 11, 14, 16, 21, 41, 52, 73-77, 79-81, 99, 101, 104, 109, 119, 120, 121-142, 144-146, 148, 165, 166, 180
Pashukanis, Y.B.	142
Passent, D.	121
Patriotic Movement of National Rebirth	140

patriotic organicism 137-139

patriotism 47, 49, 50

Paul, St. 36, 37, 39, 42-44, 48-50, 96, 161, 162

peace 5, 39-42, 48, 53, 161, 162, 172, 174, 177-181

Pilsudski, J. 79, 80

Polish Academy of Sciences 131, 168

Polish conscience 49

Polish Helsinki Watch Committee 23

Polish nation 37, 48-50, 71, 163

Polish state 51, 128

Polish-Russian relations 2, 162, 163, 168

Pomian, K. 11

Popieluszko, J. 36, 39, 43, 50, 100

Popper, K. 1

positivistic tradition 48, 49

PPN 15, 16

PPP 73

PPS 79

Primate's Committee on Trade Unions 51

Primate's Social Council 51

Proudhon, J. 4, 77

Przemyk, G. 43

public opinion 131

Pyjas, S. 21, 42

Rainko, S. 128

Rapallo 169-171

Reagan, R. 175, 176

Red Army 165, 171

reformism 12, 13

Remington, R.A. 134, 135

resistance 2, 5, 10, 12, 13, 15, 35, 71, 73, 74, 76, 94-97, 100-102, 107-110, 123, 144, 167, 177

revolution 2, 11, 12, 14, 23, 52, 75, 76, 78, 99, 123, 131, 141, 167

Ribbentrop, J. 162, 170

Roberts, A. 97

Robotnik 20, 21

Robotnik Wybrzeza 20

Romania   173, 180
romantic tradition   48-51
Romaszewski, Z.   16
ROPCiO   71
Rousseau, J.J.   79, 108
Ruskin, J.   96
Sadurski, W.   74
Sanctions
    economic   175, 176, 181
    nonviolent   103
Schell, J.   19
Second World War   11, 15, 51, 160, 168
secular left   10-12
Sejm   36, 73, 106, 131, 140, 144-147
self-defence   10,13-15,18,20,21,96,99
self-education   21,73
self-government   5,14,21,71-75,77,79,81,93,96,101,121,124,128
self management   4,14,71-75,77,78,81,101,121,145
self-organization   9,15,18,20,23,71-73,75,80
Sharp, G.   95-97, 107
Shultz, G.   175
SKS   21
Slonimski, A.   11
Slowacki, J.   49
Smialowski, J.   127
Smolar, A.   82, 143
social movement   3, 13, 15
socialist democracy   126
socialist state   124, 126, 128, 144, 146
Socjusz   14, 171
Solidarity   1-6, 9, 10, 15-18, 21-23, 35, 37-40, 43, 45-47,
                    50, 53, 71-82, 93, 94, 96, 98-110, 120, 121, 127,
                    128, 131, 138, 139, 142, 145, 159, 167, 172-179, 181
    First National Congress   10, 23, 40, 74, 159
    National Coordinating Committee   22
    News Agency   22
    trade union   1, 9, 20, 22, 71, 73, 78, 81, 94, 106, 107,
                                              131, 142, 159, 174

Sommer, T.   172
sovereignty   13, 48, 50, 101, 120, 142, 165, 169, 170
Soviet Union   1, 3, 5, 109, 132, 135, 141–145, 160, 161,
163–173, 175, 180
Stalin, J.   12, 120, 124, 125, 127, 131, 143, 145
Stalinism   125, 126
Staniszkis, J.   75
state   3–5, 13–15, 18–20, 23, 41–44, 46, 48, 50–52, 71–75,
77–82, 99, 101, 103, 106, 107, 109, 119–132, 134–148,
162, 163, 167, 169, 176, 179, 180
   bureaucracy   3, 78, 142
   Council of   18, 131, 133
   of the whole people   126, 127
   prerogative state   142, 143
   Russian/Soviet   163
   withering away of   120, 125, 127
state tribunal   129, 147
statism   3, 4, 6, 37, 71, 72, 74, 80, 81, 119–123, 125,
126, 129, 137, 147, 148
Stirner, M.   77
strategy   4, 6, 52, 53, 76, 81, 93, 97, 102, 103, 109
strike   9, 10, 16, 20–22, 45, 46, 53, 76, 78, 82, 95,
99, 100, 103–107, 145
Switon, K.   20
syndicalists   78
Szacilo, T.   133
Szeregi Pokoju i Solidarnosci   179
SZSP   22
tactics   4, 6, 80, 93
Thomas Aquino, St.   37
Thompson, E.P.   180
Thoreau, H.D.   78, 94, 95
Tischner, J.   36, 37, 39, 40, 44–49
TKN   21
Tocqueville, A. de   1
Tolstoy, L.   77, 78, 96
totalitarianism   12, 72, 75, 124, 178, 179
trust (political)   19, 39, 77

209

truth	3, 12, 19, 37–42, 44, 45, 47, 53, 75, 121, 141, 142, 163, 172
Tukhachevsky, M.	132
United States	3, 6, 174, 175, 177, 179, 180
Urban, J.	140
utopia	13, 15, 40, 77
Vatican	36, 37
violence	2, 4, 12–14, 18, 42, 76–78, 93–97, 104, 106–108, 143
Vyshinsky, A.	127
Walentynowicz, A.	99
Walesa, L.	20, 22, 46, 47, 76, 78, 95, 103, 161, 176
Warsaw Pact	11, 165
Warszawski, D.	53, 162
Western Europe	3, 6, 82, 162, 169, 174, 177, 180
Wierny, J.	47
Wierzbicki, P.	47
Wiez	21, 95
Witos, W.	79
Wojtyla, K.	36, 39, 41, 42, 44
Wyszynski, S.	36, 38, 39, 41, 42, 44, 49, 52, 75
Yalta	5, 160, 161, 169
Young Poland	71
Yugoslavia	173
Zapis	21
Zhukov, G.	132
Zieja, J.	17
ZOMO	105